BLACK THEN

McGILL-QUEEN'S UNIVERSITY PRESS

MONTREAL & KINGSTON • LONDON • ITHACA

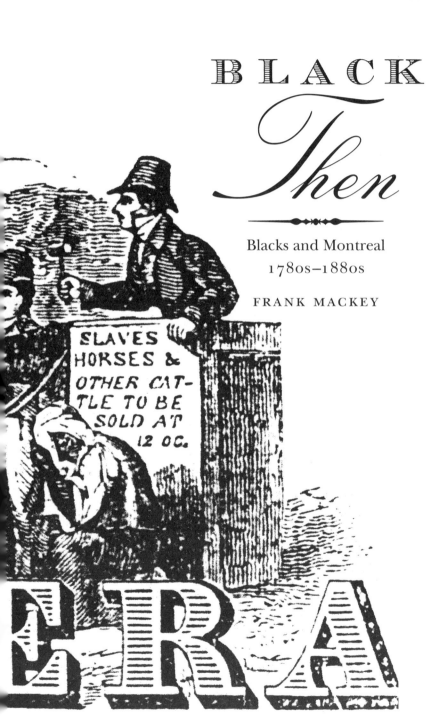

BLACK

Then

Blacks and Montreal
1780s–1880s

FRANK MACKEY

ERA

© McGill-Queen's University Press 2004

ISBN 0-7735-2735-4 (cloth)
ISBN 0-7735-2736-2 (paper)

Legal deposit second quarter 2004
Bibliothèque nationale du Québec

Printed in Canada on acid-free paper.

McGill-Queen's University Press acknowledges the support of the
Canada Council for the Arts for our publishing program. We also
acknowledge the financial support of the Government of Canada
through the Book Publishing Industry Development Program (BPIDP)
for our publishing activities.

National Library of Canada Cataloguing in Publication Data

Mackey, Frank
Black then : Blacks and Montreal,
1780s–1880s / Frank Mackey.

Includes bibliographical references.
ISBN 0-7735-2735-4 (bound)
ISBN 0-7735-2736-2 (pbk.)

1. Black Canadians – Québec (Province) – Montreal – History.
I. Title.

FC2947.9.B6M32 2004   971.4'2800496   C2004-900019-5

This book was designed and typeset by David LeBlanc.
Typeface is New Baskerville 10.5/13

*For Roselaine, who has adopted me,
and for Lia and Daniel, who had no choice –
I was theirs from the start.*

CONTENTS

BEACHCOMBING:
BY WAY OF INTRODUCTION

WE ARE ALL OF US WALKING BY the ocean of time. The waves cast up the past in pieces at our feet. Our eye is drawn to one piece by its colour, to another by its shape. On closer inspection, we see a whale or a heart in a worn stone, a wild horse in the driftwood, a bird's wing in a bit of shell. An archaeologist sees dinner – soup, salad, and dessert included, and one free drink! – in a few shards of crockery and a bottleneck. Another person sees something else – or nothing. We see what the objects themselves reveal and what our eyes, our imagining, and our understanding let us see. We see what we are open to seeing. We miss a lot.

This is what these stories are – bits and pieces, some of which needed only a little scraping away of sand and seaweed, a little rubbing and polishing or fitting back together to bring out their shape and to highlight those flashes of colour that caught my eye when they were wet and gleaming. They were lying scattered on a beach few people visit. All of them contain glimmers of the lives of black men, women, and children over a period of about one hundred years, from the last gasps of slavery in Montreal to the era of Canada's first transcontinental trains.

Some well-known signposts are there to help put you in the picture: the end of the American Revolutionary War in 1783, the abolition of slavery in the British West Indies in 1834, the passage of the Fugitive Slave Law in the United States in 1850, Canadian Confederation in 1867, and so on. You will also come across less widely known local reference points, such as the beginning of street lighting in Montreal in 1815 and the official opening of the Victoria Bridge in 1860.

Some of the people you will meet were born here, while others came from Africa, the Caribbean, the United States, and even England, Ireland, and Malta. Some washed up here and went away; others came and stayed. If you are looking for the famous Angélique, the slave executed in Montreal for arson in 1734, you will not find her here because the pieces of her life lie scattered farther down the beach, on a stretch that others have combed for relics. The people in these stories are for the most part unknown. So in a way this is an exercise in name dropping: not to dwell on the famous, but to draw attention to some people, ordinary and not so ordinary, who had their roles to play in the life of the city. You may think, "What's so special about a Charity or an Isaac Wily? Many white people had it as hard as they did, even harder." True. But the very fact that we can say this means that it is common knowledge. Nothing about black Montrealers of that day is common knowledge. Yet there they were.

And there they are still, lodged as firmly in our past as any other element of our history. We may not have the eyes to see them, but in the right light they are everywhere. The spirit of Charlotte Trim, African born, haunts McGill Street, where she lived after breaking free of slavery. When you walk out of Place d'Armes metro station on St Urbain Street, it might hit you that close by stood the boarding house where Thomas and Anna Cook sheltered people, some broken in body, some broken-hearted, some making do. And in every lamp that lights the streets, you may see a memorial to Warren Glossen.

Slavery is the backdrop to our walk by the shore – slavery in Montreal and, after it ended here, slavery in the West Indies and, for the longest time in the United States. In North America, it was the killer cloud parked low over the ocean of time until 1865. We haven't yet finished flushing its poisons out of our system. Some people never even knew they were there: you still run into grown men and women who have never heard that slavery had its day in Canada.

If all this talk of slavery and hardship makes it sound that this will be a walk through a century of deep gloom, you may be suprised. You may always have thought that racism picked up where slavery left off, limiting blacks to the worst, lowest-paid jobs. But how does Caesar Johonnot fit into that picture – a free black man, hired at the height of slavery to manage a white-owned industry? Or John Trim, who had amassed a small fortune in real estate by the time he died in 1833? Or Osborne Morton, a fugitive slave from Kentucky who operated a livery stable through the 1860s with his Scottish wife, then made his name as a jockey and horse trainer?

The picture, you see, was far from simple. It was not perfect either. Montreal was no promised land, free of prejudice. There was racism, certainly, but there was ... something else. It would be a big mistake to see all these people as no more than helpless victims who could do nothing for themselves. They had, like all of us, their strengths and weaknesses, their triumphs and defeats. You will see both survivors and goners, heroes and con artists and entrepreneurs; white masters of black slaves, yes, but black masters of white apprentices too. "It takes all kinds to make a world," and they were all kinds.

If you ask, "Are these stories true?" I would answer yes. If you need reassurance, you will find of some of the sources mentioned in the stories themselves. As well, a handful of documents are reproduced in the appendix, and the main references for each story are given at the back of the book. Which is not to say that, stumbling on these bits and pieces, you would see the same shape in them or polish them up in the same way that I have done. Your eye might fall on other fragments (there are many more where these came from) and give a different story. The fact is, these stories have waited a hundred and fifty or even two hundred years and more to be told. More important than who does the telling is that the telling begin.

Now, I might turn the tables on you and ask whether you think these stories are true. I mean, is their aim true? Only you can tell. If the words hit home, you will carry a scar where they hit you and not feel sore – feel better, in fact.

If you ask why we should bother about these long-gone people, I would say because they have been dying to tell us things for years – what life was like for them and how much things have changed, or how little. Only by rubbing shoulders with them will we know whether we have made any progress in our walk. Ask yourself: Are the lives of black Montrealers today, relatively speaking, (a) better than in Alexander Grant's day, (b) about the same, or (c) worse? To answer this, you have to know something about Grant and what he went through in his time and place.

So what is your answer?

Take your time.

BLACK THEN

1

The Truth about Rose

HERE'S A RIDDLE FOR YOU.

Rose was born a slave in Montreal in 1768, a few years after the British took Canada from France. In the summer or fall of 1791, when she was about 23, her master, a fur trader, took her to the Michigan Territory, then to his trading post at Prairie du Chien in what later became the state of Wisconsin. When he died, another trader took her to upper Louisiana, to St Louis in what is now Missouri. And finally, in 1798, she wound up as the slave of Auguste Chouteau, one of the founders of St Louis. And there she stayed, far from where she was born and grew up.

It's not as if she'd been aching to move to St Louis, halfway across North America from Montreal; she had no choice – it's what her masters wanted. That's all that counted. That's how it was in the days of slavery.

She had two children who lived to be adults, a son, Pierre, and a daughter, Charlotte. Since she was the slave of Chouteau, her children also were his from the get-go. That's how it was. And when

3

Rose died and her master died, her children became the property of her master's son.

Then in the 1840s, Pierre and Charlotte got it into their heads that they ought to be free. They went to court in Missouri to claim their freedom. Why were they slaves? Only because their mother had been considered a slave, that's all. But that was all a big mistake, they said: No, no, Rose was no slave – because there had been no slavery in Canada when she was born.

Now what kind of crazy argument was that? Of course, there was slavery in Canada, specifically in Montreal, when Rose was born – and for about forty years afterwards, right into the early 1800s. There were black slaves like Rose and also Indian slaves, called *panis* (French for Pawnee).

The *Montreal Gazette*, the only game in town in those days, advertised slaves for sale, and there were court cases as late as 1800 over slaves who had run away from their masters. The slave owners were so upset at the judges who let runaways go free that they petitioned the Assembly in Quebec City in 1799, and again in 1800, to spell out the rules regarding slavery. We know this for a fact – it's all down in black and white. You would have to be out of your mind to deny that slavery existed in Montreal when Rose was born.

Rose's children did not have much of a legal leg to stand on. And, sure enough, Pierre lost his case in 1845. Charlotte's dragged on from 1847 to 1862 – fifteen years!

What happened is that the judges of the Circuit Court in St Louis, instead of interpreting the laws of Canada, left it up to the juries to decide whether there had in fact been slavery in Canada. To help them make up their minds, the court asked for the opinion of two top Montreal judges who had been around when slavery was still practised here. The two judges, James Reid and Samuel Gale, both gave statements that, like it or not, slavery had existed in Canada even if there had been no single law that said flat out, "Hear ye, slavery exists in Canada." Other evidence was presented about treaties and laws and proclamations that spoke of slavery in Canada.

So you've got an all-white, all-male jury in the slave state of Missouri. You've got all the evidence proving that slavery existed in Canada when Rose, Charlotte's mother, was born. The deck is stacked against Charlotte. But, lo and behold, the jurors, all white,

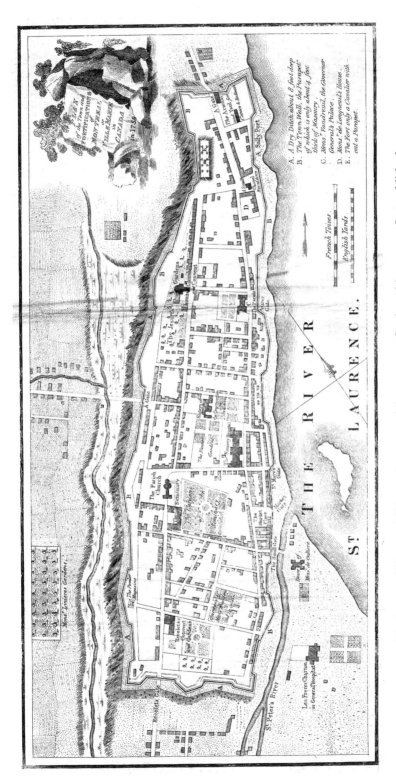

A PLAN of the Town and FORTIFICATIONS of MONTREAL or VILLE MARIE in CANADA Ao 1758.

A. A Dry Ditch about 8 foot deep
B. The Town Wall, the Parapet of which is only about 4 feet thick of Masonry
C. Mons.ˢ Vandreuil, the Governor General's Palace.
D. Mons.ᵈᵉ Longueuil's House.
E. The Fort only a Cavalier without a Parapet.

French Toises.

English Yards.

THE RIVER

Sᵀ. LAURENCE.

The layout of Montreal did not change much between 1758, when this map was first published, and 1768, when Rose was born, though Canada went from being a French colony to a British one.

all male, don't buy it. Despite all the evidence, to their way of thinking there had been no slavery in Canada. End of story.

Well, not quite. Charlotte's master appealed the verdict, and the Supreme Court of Missouri ordered a new trial, saying that it was up to the judge, not the jury, to decide whether slavery had existed in Canada. But the new trial ended with the same result, so there was yet another trial, with the same result.

Someone who was there near the tail end of it wrote up this game of legal ping-pong in a letter:

St Louis, March 13, 1859.
Last week, I was in the Circuit Court when the closing arguments were made in the case of Charlotte vs. Chouteau. Charlotte sues for her freedom. This case has been sixteen years [*sic*] in court. Charlotte beat him at first, but the case went to the Supreme Court, which reversed and remanded the cause, because the Court decided that the law of Canada on the slave question was matter for the consideration of the Court, and not for the jury. On the second trial, Charlotte beat him, and the Supreme Court reversed the decision, because the Circuit Court decided that the law of Canada on the slave question

The Chouteau mansion in St Louis in 1840, home
of Charlotte's master, Gabriel S. Chouteau

6

was matter for the consideration of the jury, and not of the Court, and the case was remanded for a new trial. She beat him again, and the case was reversed and remanded, because the law of Canada on the slave question was matter for the consideration of the Court, and not of the jury. It was submitted again, last week, and Charlotte has succeeded. It will go up to the Supreme Court again.

Chouteau is worth one or two millions; is seventy years old, has only one child, a daughter by a slave, whom he has educated. He has a lawyer who fully sympathizes with him, and whose eyes sparkled with holy indignation as he commented upon the testimony of Chief Justice Reed [*sic*] of Canada, who testified to the wicked character of slavery, as he considered it.

The judges on the Missouri Supreme Court knew that the jurors of Charlotte's case were out to lunch. But they also knew that while they could keep ordering new trials till the cows came home, if all of them were going to end the same way, well ... In the end, they recognized that so long as the existence of slavery in Canada was treated as a question of fact for a jury to decide, the jury had the final word. In effect, they said, "The juries have decided that there was no slavery in Canada when Rose was born; we know that's not so, but we can't do anything about it. Our hands are tied and Charlotte is free."

Yes! Yes! Free at last!

And all because some mule-headed men denied that Canada had ever known slavery. Go figure. If you'd been picked for the jury, knowing what you know, would you have set those other jurors straight?

The truth shall set you free, they say. Is that so? The truth – or as we like to call it, the facts – would have crushed Charlotte. Or is the truth sometimes something beyond the facts? You decide.

Missourians have a reputation for taking nothing at face value. You've got to show them proof. That's why Missouri is called the "Show-Me state." It says so on their licence plates. Quebec plates say "Je me souviens" – I remember. So if you spot a Missouri plate, remember Charlotte, who went free. And when you see a Quebec plate, remember Rose, the slave. She used to live here.

2

TOUJOURS
L'Amour

☞

HILAIRE PAID £100 FOR HIS WIFE. That was a heap of cash in 1787. Slave women generally sold for half that or less. How much would that be today? Hard to say. But you could get at least three eggs for a penny then; and since there were 12 pennies in a shilling and 20 shillings in a pound, that would make, let's see – 720 eggs, or 60 dozen, for a pound. And he paid a hundred times that, meaning he could have bought 6,000 dozen. Now if you figure that one dozen eggs today will cost you about $2, you would have to pay $12,000 for 6,000 dozen. That's one way of looking at it: on December 3, 1787, Hilaire bought Catherine, his wife, for what today might be about $12,000.

Wouldn't he rather have blown all that money on himself, maybe on a trip back to the island where he'd been born? You have to think that he could have done it if he'd cared to. Instead, he bought his wife and was happy about that – so happy he could have died and gone to heaven, as they say. He didn't, of course.

But supposing he had …

Hilaire has just died and gone to heaven, but he can't just barge in. He has to go through Immigration – wouldn't you know it? There used to be St Peter at the gates, screening the new arrivals, and that's who Hilaire is expecting to meet. But before he can catch his breath (dying takes a lot out of you) he is whisked into an office where this black lady is sitting at a big desk. The sign on the door says "Inquisitor." The plaque on the wall says "We've seen it all" (but Hilaire doesn't know that, because he can't read).

She is wearing a grey business suit and a black tie. Hilaire doesn't know it's a business suit – how could he? That's a twentieth-century invention and he is still back in the eighteenth century. But heaven is way ahead of him in the clothing department, as in everything else. All he knows is that this lady may not be God, but she's darn close, and she looks as if she means business. There is a clerk to do her bidding and a stenographer to take down every word.

"Case no. 6,000 dozen," the clerk barks, in French, because that's the language Hilaire speaks best (this is a translation). "Hilaire, dit L'Amour, slave owner from Montreal."

The inquisitor sizes him up slowly, with a frown growing more frowny as she goes.

"Name?" she asks, finally.

"Hilaire," he answers, a bit dazed, a bit dead, a little shocked at hearing himself called a slave owner. ("Me, a slave owner?" his mind sputters to itself.)

"Hilaire what?" she asks with a touch of impatience.

"Whaa?" he asks back.

"Mr Hilaire, your file identifies you as Hilaire, dit L'Amour. Now, is that your full name? Is L'Amour your family name or isn't it?"

"My family name? I don't know, your honour. My name is Hilaire. People call me that or they call me L'Amour. Sometimes they say Hilaire Lamour. Sometimes they say Hilaire, dit L'Amour."

"Right, then. Place of birth?"

"I was born in Saint-Domingue."

"Put down Haiti," she tells the clerk. The clerk nods. Turning back to him, the inquisitor asks, "Date of birth?"

"I don't know, your honour."

"How old are you? And please don't call me 'your honour.'"

"I don't remember, your honour. Some people say I'm about 50. I feel about that. Sometimes I feel 41, sometimes 56. I don't know." Silence. Finally he asks, "Is that right?"

9

"Mr L'Amour, this is not a skill-testing question. I asked you your age."

He says nothing. She turns to the clerk and says, "Make it 53."

See, she knew. She didn't have to ask, because she'd criss-crossed time often, beginning to end, and knew all birthdays. And she knew that he didn't know his own. As Frederick Douglass had shouted at her once when she was sailing by 1845: "I do not remember to have ever met a slave who could tell of his birthday." So when she asked Hilaire his age, it wasn't a test of skill. But it was a test. He aced it.

"Occupation?"

Silence.

"Mr Hilaire, what did you do for a living?"

"I worked."

"What kind of work?"

"I was servant to Captain Robertson for a long time. Then I did jobs here and there, this and that."

"Servant and labourer, then?"

"Yes, I was that."

Pause as the inquisitor writes something on the paper before her.

"Now, it says in your file that on 3 December in the year of Our Lord 1787, you bought a 34-year-old slave woman called Catherine. Is that correct?

"Yes, your honour."

"And you paid $12,000?"

"No, I paid £100 for her."

"I see. Mr Hilaire, were you not a slave yourself – not a servant, but a slave – until shortly before your death, to wit until November 16, 1787?"

"Yes, your honour. Until Captain Robertson freed me."

She glares and says, "And you no sooner were freed after – what was it, 25 years? – than you could think of nothing better to do than turn round and buy yourself a slave?" Pause. "Now, I really have seen everything!" Pause again. "And where on earth did you get $12,000 to buy yourself a slave woman? Did you steal that money? Were you dealing?"

"No, I didn't steal ... I can explain."

"I am all ears," she says.

"I was intending to do right by ..."

"The road to hell is paved with 'intending to's,' Mr L'Amour. We are here to judge what you have done with your life, not what you intended to do. Is that clear?"

"Yes, your honour."

"Do not call me 'your honour.' Now, let's look at your record. You were bought by Captain Daniel Robertson in 1762, is that correct?"

"That's so long ago. I don't know the name of the year. When the English army took Martinique from the French in the war, that's when he bought me, at Fort Royal. He was not a captain then. A lieutenant, I think. I was not feeling 50 then."

"Did you object?"

"Sorry?"

"Did you put up any resistance? Did you fight?"

"No, I …"

"Have you never heard of civil rights, civil disobedience, Mr L'Amour?"

Puzzled silence.

"Did you try to escape, to run off?"

"No, I never. He bought me. He paid."

"And then he took you to Canada?"

"Yes. After Cuba. There was fighting there. Then we sailed to Canada. He had a young wife in Montreal. She spoke French. I could understand her. She died some time ago."

"Yes, we are aware of that. And in Canada, did you try to get away, to go free? Were there not times when your Captain Robertson was away from home for months, years even, when you could have escaped?"

"No. I am not a white man …"

"I can tell you are not a white man, Mr L'Amour," she snapped. "Do you mean to tell me that only a white man would have the courage to claim his freedom? Is that what you are saying?"

"No, your honour. I mean, in Montreal, in Canada, there are many white men. Not many black men. There are hundreds of white people to every black. A black man can't change his skin to hide among whites. He's not a chameleon. And he's not a spider who can change his shape. Where would a black man hide?"

This seems to mollify her. "From your answer, am I to infer that you at least thought of escaping but banished the thought as chimerical?"

Puzzled silence again.

"You thought it was impossible to get away?"

"Oh yes."

"Mr L'Amour, did you enjoy being a slave? Were you content to be Captain Robertson's thing?"

"You mean, did I like it? I don't say that I liked it; but, like it or not, that's what I was until Captain Robertson found it in his heart to free me."

"Why did Captain Robertson free you?"

"He freed me because I stood by him a long, long time and did good at his house with him and his children. That's what he said when he freed me."

"You were happy to be free?"

"Yes, your honour. But it's hard. Sometimes I feel like I'm 54 or more, and work is hard when I am feeling I have to pay for a place to live and buy clothes and buy food and ..."

She cuts him off. "If you were happy to be free, Mr L'Amour, explain to me how it is that you denied that freedom to Catherine, the woman you bought for ..." (she pronounces the words very slowly as if every sound was underlined) "too-elve-thou-zz-and dollars?"

"£100," he corrects her. "And she's free. Catherine is my wife. She was a slave with me of Captain Robertson's. He set me free but not my Catherine. He wanted £100 for her. So I bought her. Then she was nobody's slave."

"She was your slave."

"Nooo, your honour! Not a slave."

"In my book, Mr L'Amour, if a man buys a woman, the way he buys eggs or a mousetrap or a horse, he owns that woman, just as he would the eggs, the mousetrap, or the horse. She is his slave, his property. That, to me, is as plain as A, B, and C."

"Yes, but ..."

"But what?"

"But she was not my slave. I bought her so she would be no slave, just my Catherine. I loved her and she loved me."

"Mr L'Amour, your sentiments do not make her free. Whether you love her or you don't, she is still your slave. God knows, we have people turning up here every day, high and low, even presidents, with fine sentiments, wringing their hands and saying they 'feel' for their slaves and 'what a curse slavery is.' But the truth is, they worked their slaves and did squat to end slavery while they lived."

The woman's eyes remain fixed on him. Hilaire is at a loss for words. Heaven is slipping away from him – he just knows it is. A gust of silence blows through the room. She scratches on the paper in front of her.

"Mr L'Amour," she says at last, "I cannot admit you as you are. You say you bought your wife from another man so that she would no longer be a slave. But the very fact that you bought her makes her *your* slave. That is the reality of it. I'm afraid that, where slavery is concerned, it's not the thought that counts, it's the deed.

"In view of the circumstances, I have no choice but to reject your application. I am sentencing you to life in Montreal. On probation. The terms of your probation are that you must free your wife at the first opportunity – and I mean the first opportunity, not when she is too old and worn to be of use to you or to enjoy her freedom. If you abide by these terms, I will be prepared to lift the probation and grant you immunity from death for – let me see – 35 years.

"If you do not abide by these terms, you will appear again before me and suffer the consequences. And that would be hell. Do you understand?" She doesn't wait for his answer. "Adjourned!"

Bang! The whack of the gavel wakes Hilaire from his dream. She never did press him on where he found the £100 to buy Catherine. It would have been interesting to know.

What rattles him, though, is that it's true – he has become a slave owner. This is not what he had in mind when he bought Catherine. Sure, she is his, but not "his property." Ooh, slavery has a way of turning the world upside down.

Well, if heaven needs proof, he'll get it. In writing, signed and sealed, the same as when Captain Robertson freed him.

The day after Christmas, Hilaire goes to Beek, the notary – the man before whom Captain Robertson had signed his freedom papers – a little man of law who had auctioned more than one black man, woman, and child in his time. (And isn't the inquisitor going to have a field day when he comes knocking!) For a fee, Beek turns Hilaire's thoughts into a deed that anyone could understand. In French, of course, because that's the language Hilaire speaks best (this is a translation again). See for yourself:

Be it known that I Hilaire, dit Lamour, free Negro residing in the city of Montreal in the Province of Quebec, having by deed of sale dated 3 December instant ... purchased from Daniel Robertson, Esquire, a Negress named Catharine, my wife; and being desirous of proving the friendship and affection which I bear her, have granted unto her and do by these presents grant her her Freedom, willing and desiring that the said Catharine be regarded and recognized as such now and forever; and to that end I do hereby renounce all right of property which I had, or might have had or might have claimed to have by virtue of the said purchase from Daniel Robertson, Declaring her from this moment Free and released from all servitude as a slave by these presents.

In testimony whereof I, Hilaire dit Lamour, not knowing how to sign my name, have made my ordinary mark.

At that, Hilaire was happy. He could have died and gone to heaven.

3

Mister Whisky Himself

YOU KNOW HOW CONTRARY PEOPLE CAN BE. You could say, "Don't read this if you're under 18, or even 21; it's about booze and you're too young." But it wouldn't help. Tell them not to look, they look. It wouldn't do any good, even if you wrote "Poison xxx" on top and lectured them about liquor's evil spell, as the Reverend Joseph Christmas did:

All manufacture and traffic in ardent spirits, except so far as the apothecary may need them, is criminal ... Good men have, doubtless, unthinkingly been engaged in this traffic ... Good men have even commanded slave-ships, but he who should now barter in the persons and liberties of his fellow man, would be branded with infamy – indelible as that of Cain. Yet intemperance has seized on more victims, inflicted more suffering, instigated to more crime, occasioned a greater waste of life, and entailed a more deplorable bondage, than the slave trade, with all the horrors of its burning villages, its heart-rending separations – its middle passages, its irons, and its bloody scourge – the barbarism of its shambles, and the hopelessness of its servitude. I trust in God the time is not far distant, when public sentiment ... shall deem it no less an outrage on humanity to land upon our shore a cargo of brandy, than to disgorge upon it a shipload of famished and manacled Africans.

Powerful stuff. That's what the Rev. Christmas, the first minister of the American Presbyterian Church in Montreal, told his congregation in 1828. He's long gone, of course, but liquor's still with us. Tell them not to taste, they taste.

The point is that like the Rev. Christmas, many white antislavery types were moral crusaders, as down on drink as on slavery. Evil was evil, whatever form it took. So when they wanted to point to a shining example of black success to counter the racist lie that free blacks didn't know which side of freedom was up, they weren't about to pick a man who drank, no matter how succesful he was. Much less would they have picked Caesar Johonnot, Mister Whisky himself, even if they'd remembered him. He didn't import the stuff – he made it from scratch.

When Johonnot turned up in Montreal in the 1780s, the powers that be were all for making liquor. There were no industries to speak of. Like liquor, most things – buttons, bottles, hairpins, cloth for a fine dress or suit, paper, you name it – had to be imported. That cost money and there wasn't much of that in Canada. But there was plenty of grain and plenty more land to grow it on. Plenty of thirst too. So liquor making sounded like a sure bet. Instead of importing all your booze, you buy the farmers' grain, add water (which is free), cook it, distill it, sell it at a good price – bingo! The money stays home instead of taking the first ship out.

Some businessmen twigged to this in 1785. They set up the Montreal Distillery Company, on St Sacrement Street, between St Nicolas and St Pierre. Fur traders, merchants, and the like, they knew how to drink. But what did they know about making good whisky and gin? They needed a distiller.

Caesar Johonnot? No. First it seems they picked John Lagord who, besides distilling, also bought and sold slaves left and right. It's hard to say whether Johonnot was even in Montreal yet. It's not clear when exactly he came, but we might take a stab at it.

First, look at his name. It's not a name he wears well – he changes the spelling every time he writes it: Cesar Johonnot, Ceaser Johnot, Casear Johonnott. (When others write it, it turns into Casar

Johanot, Cesar Johannote, Caesar Johnet, Cesar Janotte, Cesar Jahomet, Siserre Jennon ...) So it's his name and not his name. In fact, Caesar has slavemaster written all over it; it was a common name given to slaves in North America. Johonnot, not so common, had Boston written all over it. The Johonnots were a French Protestant family who had fled France for Boston in the late 1600s. Distilling was their trade. Zacharie Johonnot may have been old – in his mid-seventies – when the American Revolution broke out, but not too old to join the secret Sons of Liberty. He lived to see the Sons' dream of an independent United States come true, but barely. In his will, made out on March 1, 1784, days before he died, he left to Cesar, "formerly my negro man-servant, now a freeman ... £50 lawful money, to be paid him by my executor, within twelve months after my death."

So there was Cesar – Caesar Johonnot to us – in Boston in 1784, recently freed, with a knowledge of distilling picked up from his master and a £50 grub stake. Within the next two years, he left for Montreal. What made him do that, we'll probably never know. But a wave of black Americans – some free, some not – swept up to Canada at the time of the American Revolution.

Some were escaped slaves, others were slaves who had joined the British side on a promise of freedom; some were Loyalists, others slaves of white Loyalists or of military officers. That's when black slavery reached its peak in Canada – after the end of the revolutionary war in 1783. But Caesar Johonnot was free, his own man, with a valuable skill. And see how he signs that name: he's about the only black man in Montreal in the 1780s who could write. Most whites couldn't do so either.

Cæsar Johonnott

It's the spring of 1786, and Johonnot is in Montreal, standing on the mountain beside a clear stream. He's wandering or he's daydreaming, or maybe he's checking how pure the water is, as a distiller might. Maybe he has spotted the two soldiers at the fountain a little below him. One thing's sure: when the stick comes flying through the air and hits him, he knows where that came from. He marches down to the soldiers and gives them hell and tells them he's ready to take them on and the whole British army. At that, one of the brave fighting men knocks him down.

What's a black man to do? Johonnot takes on the army, or at least a regiment, but not with his fists. He lays a charge of assault against soldier Campbell. In court on June 2, Campbell claims he never struck the negro Cesar Jahomet – all he did was fling a stick at a dog and it accidentally hit a negro, and this negro got all upset. Campbell's pal Fairly backs him and says it was he, not Campbell, who punched out the negro. You get the feeling that the whole 34th Regiment is ready to step up and swear Campbell never raised a finger.

So Campbell walks and Johonnot loses his case. His only consolation may have been that at least he got a hearing – and maybe, in future, brave stick-flingers, in uniform or out, who aim at dogs but hit black people will think twice before messing with him.

Back to work. Lagord, the slave-trading distiller, fades from the scene, and the Montreal Distillery Company is dissolved early in 1789. Right away, the company is re-formed under new owners. Todd, McGill & Co., Forsyth Richardson & Co., and King & McCord, all top merchant houses in Montreal, each own one-quarter of the business; a couple of Quebec City men split the rest. On May 5, Johonnot signs a two-year contract with them "as a Distiller to Manage the Distillery in this Town as heretofore."

So he had been Mr Manager "heretofore." But for how long? Possibly only since May 1, the official beginning of his contract, or it might have been a little longer – maybe since the reorganization. After all, they had to know for sure not only that he could make decent liquor but also that he could run a business. On top of his salary of five shillings a day, Johonnot got a company house, rent-free. In fact, he was already living in it when he signed his contract. And they even supplied the firewood for his home. Not bad, considering that most blacks in town were slaves or servants or day labourers.

Think of Rose. Think of Hilaire. Think of Henry Moore, hired in November 1785 for one month, with three other men, to sweep every chimney in town – whew! – for about one shilling and four-pence a day, which was pretty good money, even if the job lasted only a month. Or think of Charity, ten years later, working as a tavern servant out at Coteau-du-Lac for five shillings a year, plus room and board. And here's Johonnot making five shillings a day, with a house thrown in.

His contract contained a clause saying it would be renewed at the end of the two years unless he wanted out or they wanted him out, in which case they had to give one another three months' notice. Looks as if Johonnot stayed about five years, until the company went bankrupt. He and his wife Margaret Campbell had a daughter, Ruth, who died as a baby in 1789; but their son Gabriel, born in 1793, was still kicking. They were living in the company house in the spring of 1794, but with the company up the creek, they had to move.

On April 14 they bought their own place, a small clapboarded log house in St Antoine Suburb, a little northwest of the city, beyond the western wall that stood roughly where McGill Sreet is now. The Little River ran by the property. It cost them £33, which they paid off in four years. The first year, Johonnot hired a carpenter to make about £20 worth of improvements. And in 1797, with £65 borrowed from Dr Jones and a £25 loan from notary Lukin, plus another £21, he bought a still so that he could make his own liquor, and he built an addition to his house to serve as his distillery.

So he was all set to go. By this time, there were four in the family: his daughter Catherine was born that fall. But maybe the money wasn't coming in fast enough. On January 23, 1798, for ten Spanish silver dollars a month, plus room and board, Johonnot was hired by Levy Solomon & Co. of Montreal and Cornwall for three years to work at Cornwall (where they had a distillery) "or at any other port within the Provinces of Upper and Lower Canada." In February, while he was out of town, Margaret Campbell leased the distillery and a room in their house to a distiller from Quebec for £20 a year (no point in letting all that equipment sit idle).

Johonnot's job with Levy Solomon & Co. seems to have ended well before his three years were up. Not to worry. On October 9, 1798, he signed up to work for two years for William Fortune, an Irish-born Loyalist from South Carolina who had a still at Point Fortune on the Ottawa River. The pay was good – £50 a year, plus room and board. And his boss threw in a perk: "William Fortune for the good esteem which he hath doth by these Presents grant and bequeath unto the sd. Caesar, Half an Acre Superficial Measure of Land near and next his own Building in the Township of Hawkesbury."

But, before his two years with Fortune were up, Johonnot died at Sorel, at the mouth of the Richelieu River, on June 8, 1800. He is buried there, under the name Caesar Johnet. He never got to see his youngest son, Alexander, born in Montreal six months later.

It's hard to say how he got on with other blacks. For instance, we know next to nothing about his wife Margaret Campbell. On February 6, 1797, he was a witness at the funeral of a Mary Campbell. Was she an in-law? They gave her age as 51 when she died and said she was "a black woman ... living at his Excellency General Christie." That didn't mean she was shacked up with Christie. "Living at" or "living with" was white-speak for "slave of," sometimes "servant of" (what Haitians call a *restavèk*, a lives-with, a slave in all but name).

General Gabriel Christie, 74 years old then, colonel commandant of the 1st Battalion, 60th (Royal American) Regiment of Foot, seigneur of Bleury, Lachenaie, Lacolle, Léry, Repentigny, and Noyan, had several slaves. He had shared the seigneury of Noyan, by Lake Champlain, with one of the biggest slave owners, Colonel John Campbell, until Campbell's death in 1795. Maybe it was from that Campbell that Margaret Campbell and Mary Campbell took the name. Slaves sometimes borrowed their master's family name, or it was given to them, whether they liked it or not.

A couple of weeks after Mary Campbell's funeral, on March 5, Johonnot was a sponsor at the baptism of Phillis Murray. The church record said she was a 42-year-old black woman "living with" Alexander Henry on Notre Dame Street. The co-sponsors with Johonnot were Mandaville Turner (one of the many names for Manuel Allen, sold that summer to tavernkeeper Thomas John Sullivan) and Margaret Plauvier, a free black woman, wife of Henry Moore, the chimney sweep.

Of Johonnot's children, all we know of Catherine is that she was born November 24, 1797, and that in 1832 she married the labourer Anthony Hinksman. Gabriel was apprenticed to a butcher in March 1807 at the age of 14. His name was written Gabriel Jonneau then. He was supposed to stay seven years, until he turned 21, but in June 1809 his mother placed him as a servant with the merchant Moses Northrop. This time he was called Gabriel Johnno. By then, Margaret Campbell was married again, to François Houle, a voyageur and small-time crook.

When war broke out with the United States in 1812, Gabriel was working as an orderly on the men's ward at the Hôtel-Dieu. In 1814 he joined the militia and served here and there through the last year of the war. Then he returned to Montreal, where he worked as a gardener on the old Simon McTavish estate on the mountain.

Funny thing about the Johonnots and the mountain. Caesar had been assaulted there by a soldier way back when, and on June 8, 1815 Gabriel was assaulted there by a soldier – Drum Major William Griffin of the Nova Scotia Fencible Regiment. This time the Johonnots won. A judge made Griffin promise to "keep the peace with all His Majesty's Subjects but in particular in regard to Gabriel Johannet," or he'd have to pay a £20 penalty.

Alexander, the baby of the family, went the way of his stepfather, into thieving, till it got him banished for seven years, in 1827.

That's about as much as we know of Caesar Johonnot and his family. At the height of slavery, he was black and he was free. He managed one of Montreal's first industries. You'd think there'd be a monument, a plaque somewhere, a street name, a brand of whisky, a word slipped in a book, something, anything. But you know how contrary people can be.

4

If You *Say* So

HENRI MCEVOY, WHAT DID HE KNOW? He never got to go to school, being a slave kid out in the country at Rivière-des-Hurons. So in January 1802, when he's telling people he's about 16, he's just guessing or parroting what he's been told.

He probably doesn't even know his mother. If you dropped in on him from the twenty-first century and told him "Henri, we think your mother may be Rose," he'd probably just blink, think hard, and hit a wall.

You might tell him, "Henri, it's as simple as A, B and C. We don't know where Rose wound up, but we think she belonged to Martin McEvoy of Saint-Jean, just up the river here, who put her up for sale in Montreal before you were born. Beek, the notary, auctioned her off on April 6, 1785, to Pierre Mézière, another notary and a lawyer too and commissioner of police. Then in August 1790, Mézière and his wife sold your mother and you to Louis Moquin. You had a sister called Jeanne, and at first Mézière kept her for himself. But in July 1794, after deciding he'd call her Marianne, he sold her to his son-in-law Adrien Berthelot. How do you like them apples, Henri?"

But Henri he still wouldn't get it, because he doesn't know A, B, and C, and if that's as simple as A, B, C gets, he'll never get it. Simple is being the first to know who's your mother, who's your dad. You could have said it was as simple as 1-2-3 – it would have made no difference. He can't count.

All that matters is the buzz, what he hears, what he sees out there on the flat sea of snow south of Mont-St-Hilaire. He's like Christopher Columbus out on the ocean; without the stars at night, he wouldn't have a clue where he stands. So you ask him his age and that's a tough one. He knows young, he knows old, and he's somewhere in between. You tell him he's about 16. Fair enough, if you say so, he's about 16 today.

This winter, out there on the big snow-covered space between the stars and Vermont, he picks up this buzz from Montreal. The buzz is that slavery is dead. England has passed a law that wiped out slavery all round the world.

Of course, England did no such thing. But what does a slave kid at Rivière-des-Hurons know about England and laws? It wasn't until five years later that England passed a law against the international trade in slaves. No more shipping slaves from Africa to the Caribbean, at least not when the navy's looking. Didn't mean slaves in Jamaica or Barbados or St Vincent or Trinidad or St Lucia or anywhere went free. If Henri had been to school, he might have written a letter "To Whom it May Concern" in any of the islands every year for thirty-two years asking Whom, "Are you free?" And Whom could have told him, "Dear Henry, No. Why do you keep asking?" How should he know?

But he knows the buzz and he believes it because he wants to. So he follows the river road to its end, where the Rivière-des-Hurons spills its heart out into the Richelieu, and he makes his way across that frozen river to Chambly. And he lets people know he's up for work.

On January 10, with William and Philip Byrne, he walks in on Pétrimoulx, the notary. Henri says yes, he's a slave, but he wants to take advantage of the English law freeing all slaves and he wants to go work for the Byrnes as a free man. And yes, you could say he's about 16 and maybe that's not old enough to be signing a contract; but he's alone in the world, got no mother, no father, nobody but the stars, so he has to sign for himself. But it will have to be an X because no star ever taught him to write.

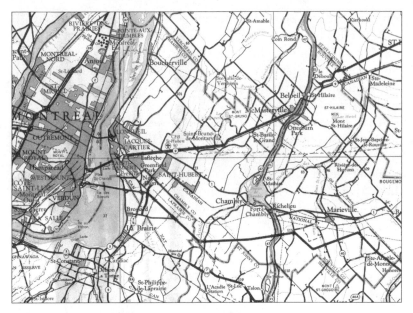

Rivière-des-Hurons, the hamlet east of Montreal where Henri McEvoy lived, does not figure on many maps nowadays.

Pétrimoulx knows the law, at least he ought to. It's his job. And the Byrnes know all about slavery and slave boys of about 16, because William gave one to Philip, his adopted son, as a wedding present; gave him a slave woman too. That was back in the summer of 1793. Besides, Philip Byrne is no dummy. He's the land agent of Sir John Johnson, big-time Loyalist, commander of the King's Royal Regiment of New York in the Revolution, in charge of Indian affairs, big landowner. They certainly know better than a country slave kid who's about 16.

So you might expect that one of them would say to Henri, "Hold it right there," and ask a few questions: Like, are you nuts? Like, what law? Like, your master, he know about this? They don't because, like Henry, they've picked up this buzz from town.

And Henri, who walked in there a slave, walks out a free man under that non-existent English law abolishing slavery. It's written in his contract with the Byrnes. It's like a genuine fake ID saying you are who you aren't and the law is a fact even if it's fiction. Worked for Henri.

5

Charlotte, She Got the Ball Rolling

FARMER EDEN JOHNSON FROM PLATTSBURGH, New York, crossed into Canada on September 23, 1794, to hunt down young Diah. Ten days earlier, Diah had run away from his master, Nathaniel Platt. As a bloodhound in human form, Johnson carried a power of attorney from Platt. He picked up Diah's scent in Montreal and learned he was living up at Rivière-du-Chêne (Saint-Eustache) on the Lake of Two Mountains. But he hit a snag. He was advised that to claim the runaway, he had to do better than a power of attorney. He had to show proof of ownership, either Platt's or his own.

So Johnson went all the way back to Plattsburgh, a good hike in those days, bought Diah from Platt for £80, and returned to Montreal, figuring there'd be no argument now about his being entitled to claim the black man. On October 8, he swore out an affidavit before Justice of the Peace Thomas McCord that Diah, his slave, was a runaway, and he got McCord to issue a warrant then and there for Diah's arrest. A constable picked Diah up at Rivière-du-Chêne on Saturday, October 11, and took him to jail in Montreal.

The case came up in the Court of Quarter Sessions the following Tuesday. An antislavery man may have hyped things a bit when he sent news of it to a paper in Quebec City, which published his account of the case on October 20. "The Court heard the argument on both sides," he wrote, "and made (much to their Honour, and the Honour of humanity) the following decree. That slavery was not known by the Laws of England and therefore discharged the negro man."

Wow, did slavery take a hit!

You might think that. A lot of good it did – slavery went on as before.

Until Charlotte came along.

She was African, in her mid-thirties. Came from Guinea. She'd been a slave of the Cook family since she was 12, first in the Caribbean, then in Canada. George Cook had been a soldier of the 60th (Royal American) Regiment. He'd been stationed in the West Indies during the American Revolution, when France was helping the American colonies fight the British. In the will he made out on St Vincent in 1777, shortly before he died, George Cook left "the Negro wench by name Charlotte" to his wife. And in her will, made out at Antigua two years later, his wife left "unto my best beloved daughter Jane Cooke the daughter of George Cooke by his desire before his death … a Negro wench named Charlotte." After her mother died, Jane Cook moved to Montreal, taking Charlotte, her hand-me-down.

It was from Jane Cook that Charlotte escaped on February 1, 1798. She didn't run fast and didn't run far. She hung around Montreal. Of course, they caught her and told her she had to go back to Jane Cook. But Charlotte played by her own rules. She said no.

What did she say?

"No."

Well, we'll just see about that.

So they hauled her off to jail.

Chief Justice Monk of the Court of King's Bench in Montreal was an independent cuss. Not a likable man, Monk – full of himself, a grasping man. He played by his own rules too. When Charlotte came up before him to be slapped back into slavery, he said no.

What did he say?

"You're free to go."

The slave owners of Montreal couldn't believe their ears. "Upon this enlargement," they complained to the Legislative Assembly in

Quebec, "the Negroes in the city and district of *Montreal* threatened a general revolt."

There they go with their BS. What revolt? There was no panic in the streets, no slave going for his master's gun or his master's throat, no lockdown, no martial law declared.

But it's true, Charlotte started the ball rolling. A couple of weeks later Judith Gray "revolted," running away from Elias Smith. He'd bought her for £80 in Albany, New York, three years before. Charlotte was a single woman, but Judith had a husband, John Gray, a slave of merchant John Shuter. She was a nursing mother too, her daughter not two months old. She couldn't run fast and she couldn't run far.

When the law caught up with her, she did what Charlotte had done and refused to go back to her master. They hustled her off to jail. That's where she was when her baby Emelia was baptised March 4. And when she came up before Judge Monk on March 8, he let her go, like Charlotte. And he said that he would "discharge every Negro, indented Apprentice, and Servant, who should be committed to Gaol under the Magistrates Warrant in the like cases."

Did you catch that, the way he said Negro to mean slave? Negro, slave – all the same. That's a puzzling thing about Monk. He kept throwing up roadblocks before the slave owners, but he didn't seem to be acting out of concern for the slave. Not openly, anyway.

In Judith Gray's case, Monk didn't declare slavery illegal. He said that by law, runaway slaves, like misbehaving servants, were supposed to be put to work in a "house of correction," not left to stew in jail. Problem: there was no house of correction. A Simon Legree might have shrugged that off and figured all you needed to keep slaves in line was a good fast horse, a whip and chains. But the slave owners of Montreal were a law-abiding bunch, and they were hung up because they didn't have the right kind of lockup.

And the "revolt" was not over. After Charlotte and Judith, it was Manuel Allen's turn to "revolt," on March 1, even before Judith Gray's fate was decided. Three slave escapes in a month … But Manuel's case was different from theirs, the heart of it being, Was he a slave at all?

He'd been sold as a slave on August 25, 1797, at the age of 33, under the name of Manuel, just Manuel. Thomas John Sullivan, owner of the Montreal Coffee House, had bought him for £36 from soldier Jervis George Turner and his wife. But at the time of the sale, Manuel had also signed a promise to work for Sullivan as a "covenant servant," with freedom in it for him after five years if he served his master well. So was he a slave, a servant, half-and-half, or what?

On October 29, Allen had married Sarah Jackson – John Gray was his best man – and barely four months after that he bolted. But Sullivan didn't set the law on him. So far he had paid only half of the £36 price for Allen, and he refused to pay the rest. Turner and his wife sued him for the balance. Sullivan countered by demanding his £18 back, pleading "that the sale was null and void in law, in as much as the said Negro-man was not at the period of the said sale and transfer a slave of the Plaintiffs to authorize or empower them to dispose of the term of his natural life and deceive the Defendant."

To make their case, Turner and his wife had to prove they owned Manuel Allen. They claimed they had got him from Turner's father, John Turner Sr, and said he had bought him from a man named Allen. It was a bit fuzzy. In the end, the court found that Turner and his wife had "no title or right to transfer and sell the property claimed in Manuel, a Negro-man, to the Defendant." Sullivan got his money back. Allen got his freedom.

Manuel Allen's case was still hanging fire that August when Robin and Lydia, with a four-year-old mulatto girl called Jane, ran away from farmer James Frazer of St Mary's Current (around where the Jacques Cartier Bridge is today). Robin was described as a negro, about five foot six inches tall, Lydia as "partly of the mulatto colour … she is thick and well set." Frazer posted a reward of $9 for their return and warned: "All masters of vessels and all others are hereby forbid to harbour, employ, carry off, or conceal, said negroes, as they will be prosecuted in the highest manner, the said James Frazer hath the Protection of Government for said negroes."

Frazer seems to have got his slaves back, because on March 19, 1799, Robin ran off again. It wasn't until almost a year later, at the end of January 1800, that Frazer informed the magistrates that he suspected Robin was camped out at Richard Dillon's tavern in Place d'Armes. The magistrates had Robin arrested, and since there was now a house of correction, that's where they put him.

Then along to his aid came 21-year-old Alexander Perry, who was just starting out as a lawyer and whose folks were friends of Dillon. Perry applied for a writ of habeas corpus to get Robin released. Meanwhile, Frazer filed papers in court to show that he

FOR SALE.

A Young healthy Negro Wen h between 12 and 13 years of age, lately from Upper Canada, where she was brought up.—Enquire of Gibb & Prior.

Montreal 24 *December* 1795.

A VENDRE.

Dix années de Service d'une Jeune Négreffe agée d'environ dix-fept ans——s'addrefler à l'Imprimeur.

FOR SALE.

Ten years Service of a Negro Girl aged about feventeen years——Enquire of the Printer.

FOR SALE.

AN excellent Negro Wench aged, about 30 years, can do all kind of work belonging to a houfe particularly wafhing and ironing. She has no fault, and is very honeft, fober and induftrious. Enquire at the Printing Office.

Montréal 18 *January* 1798.

Nine Dollars Reward.

RAN away from the Subfcriber, on the 12th inftant, a Negro Man named Robin or, Bob he is abo t five feet fix inches high, had on when he went away, a foarfe fhirt and trowfers, a light coloured cloth waitcoat, felt hat, and old fhoes, alfo a Negro Woman named Lydia or Lii, partly of the mulatto colour, about five feet high had on a blue and white ftriped fhort gown, a blue druggit pettcoat and black filk bonnet, fhe is thick and well fet, they may poffibly change their cloathes; they took with them a mulato child, named June about four years old. Any perfon taking up and fecuring faid Negroes and Child, fo that the owner gets them again, fhall have the above reward and all reafonable charges paid by,

JAMES FRAZER.

N. S. All mafters of veffels and all others are hereby forbid to harbour, employ, carry off, or conceal, faid negroes as they will be profecuted in the hgneft manner, the faid James Frazer hath the Protectional Government for faid negroes.

Current of St. Marys near Montreal, Auguft 12th 1798.

Some slave advertisements published in the *Montreal Gazette* in the 1790s. The one dated 18 January 1798, for "An excellent Negro Wench aged about 30 years," was the last to offer a slave for sale in Montreal.

had bought Robin in New York on July 10, 1773. Ten years later, when the British left New York to the Americans at the end of the Revolution, he had sailed to Nova Scotia with his slaves Robin and Lydia. Then, in 1784, he had moved to the Island of St Johns (Prince Edward Island), and later to Montreal.

The court looked at his papers, listened to the arguments, and, on February 18, Chief Justice Monk and Justices Isaac Ogden and Pierre Louis Panet (who had a sister in Missouri married to a founder of St Louis, Auguste Chouteau; you may have heard of him) ruled that Robin "be discharged from his confinement under the said warrant." In the court's view, all of Frazer's papers didn't add up to 100 per cent solid proof that he owned Robin.

"Bull!" the slave owners said, though they said it in a nice round-about way in their complaint to Lower Canada's Legislative Assembly: "The petitioners tho' they entertain a high opinion for the authority of that Honourable Court, cannot but remark that the evidence produced on that occasion was, in their apprehension, the best which it was possible in any case to produce, and that the Court in desiring more, have asked what it would be impossible almost ever to obtain, and in this manner have divested all the owners of slaves of any property in them."

It was as if the court had been as tough as that Vermont judge, Harrington, who a few years later refused to send a runaway back to slavery, saying that nothing less than "a bill of sale from God Almighty" would convince him that one person could own another.

Monk and company didn't go that far, but they came close. They ruled that a British law of 1797 denying you the right to seize the slaves of a master who owed you money had "repealed all the laws respecting slavery." Wherever they got that idea, it certainly wasn't from the law itself. It just wasn't true. All the slaves down to Demerara and back could have told them so. And the slave owners of Montreal knew better, which is why they kept trying to get the Assembly to lay down the law on slavery. It never did.

Those court rulings of 1798–1800 didn't abolish slavery overnight, but they gave it a death blow. See, the slave owners, being law-abiding men and women, no longer had power over their slaves. The laws said one thing, but the judges said another.

Slaves, too, must have wondered where they stood. Some, like Henri McEvoy at Rivière-des-Hurons, got wind of what the judges had said and took them at their word. Any slaves who decided to walk, walked – there was no legal way of stopping them. Others, too young to know, or too sick or old or wary to take advantage, stayed put. That's why you still saw the odd slave around in the first ten years or so of the nineteenth century.

One sign that it was "game over" for slavery is that the last advertisement offering a slave for sale in Montreal was published on January 22, 1798, just before Charlotte started the ball rolling. "For Sale," the ad in the *Gazette* said, "An excellent Negro Wench aged about 30 years, can do all kind of work belonging to a house particularly washing and ironing. She has no fault, and is very honest, sober and industrious."

It was 1821, more than twenty years after Charlotte had stood her ground, when Jane Cook, her former owner, popped back into her life. Charlotte was married by then, the wife of John Trim. They lived on the east side of McGill Street, below Notre Dame Street, at the head of St Maurice (there's a bistro terrace there now). Jane Cook needed her help.

Jane's sister Elizabeth had died abroad, a widow with no children. As the last of the Cooks, Jane laid claim to her sister's estate.

The site of Charlotte and John Trim's home on McGill Street. When the land was sold to pay off debts of the Trim estate in January 1850, the new owner put up a building, of which all that remains is the stone façade. Before it was gutted in the late twentieth century, the building's address was 445–51 McGill. It bears no civic number now.

But there was no record of her parents' marriage, nothing to prove she and Elizabeth were their legitimate daughters or their only children. Jane Cook needed proof.

Two Montreal men had sworn in July 1821 that she was the daughter of George Cook and Margaret Rafter, and the sister of Elizabeth. But their affidavit gave no hint of how they knew this. They might just have been repeating what Jane Cook had told them, so their statement proved nothing.

If anyone had known the family, it was Charlotte. Maybe she needed coaxing or maybe it was Jane who needed time to swallow the humble pie. Anyway, five months passed between the time the two men gave their statement and the day Charlotte gave hers. It was on December 17. It's short, written in legal language (see how neatly it avoids mentioning slavery), but it's the closest we come to hearing Charlotte herself:

Charlotte, a native of Guinea, in Africa, and wife of John Trim of Montreal ... declared, and affirmed upon oath: that from the age of twelve Years, until she had attained the Age of thirty Years, She was in the Service of George Cook, and Margaret Rafter, both of whom are deceased; that the Said George Cook and Margaret Rafter were considered by every person who Knew them to be lawfully Married, and highly respected as Such by the Officers of His Majesty's Sixtieth Regiment, of which the said George Cook was Quartermaster Serjeant, and the said Margaret Rafter was Nurse in the Hospital, that they had two Daughters named Jean [sic], and Elizabeth, who were considered to be the legitimate Children of the said George Cook, and Margaret Rafter, and were brought up in a decent, and genteel manner, one of whom (Jean Cook) now resides in the City of Montreal. That after the death of the Said George Cook, the Said Margaret Rafter married a Serjeant McKenzie also of the Sixtieth Regiment, who was sent home to England by the Colonel of the Regiment by reason of his Cruel treatment towards her. This done, declared, and affirmed at the Said City of Montreal.

So the onetime slave owner was at the mercy of her former slave. For Jane Cook, it was about property, an inheritance, things, just as Charlotte had once been a thing she inherited. For Charlotte, it was about something else.

6

ONE
Amazing
AMAZON

☞

THE WINTER THAT CHARLOTTE RAN OFF, Rickett's Circus
from Philadelphia played Montreal. It wasn't a Big Top with tigers
and trapeze artists. It was an equestrian circus – horses, with trick
riding, skits, and such. Come May, it was time to move on to their
next stop, Quebec. John Durang, one of the performers, and four
circus hands set off ahead of the rest to scope things out. They
made Berthier (Berthierville) the first night; the next evening they
stopped at a farm at Rivière-du-Loup (Louiseville).

That's where it happened, according to Durang, on their second
day out, May 11, 1798, as the farm wife cooked their supper:

After we had smoked a segar and took a drink, a black lady entered
the house in great stile. She was dress'd in a blue riding habit, black
hat and feathers, a whip in her hand, gold watch, gold chain and lock-
et round the neck, lacet boots, a red satin under west [vest], her figure
tall, slender, and well shaped. She had a polite address; and she talk'd
very familier and ask us where we come from and our business. We

33

told her that we had dispatches from the United States government to the British government. She made her exit with a swiming courtsey; who she was I know not. By this time supper was on the table.

No doubt about it, that black lady was something else! A vision in her riding clothes and jewellery, waltzing in and out of a white man's house, quizzing those strangers about their business.

Feeling small but wanting to look tall in her eyes, they could think of nothing better than to string her a line about, ahem, having important government papers to deliver.

You can almost hear Durang's mind slip into overdrive – Whoa! lady, could the circus use someone like you! But before he can get his act together, she's gone. He doesn't even get her name.

Is she slave? Is she free?

Is that really a whip in her hand?

If you've ever travelled the road between Montreal and Quebec and stopped for a meal that you'd rather forget, you'll appreciate what happened next. As the lady exits, Durang and his crew turn to the supper laid out on the table and find – what's this? Instead of roasting the ducks and boiling the water for tea, their hostess has boiled ducks and tea together in one pot. *Canard à l'orange pekoe*, ugh!

Life's one crazy gallop, isn't it? Up one minute, down the next.

7

Charity
DIDN'T DO IT

ABOUT ALL THAT CHARITY HAD to her name was her name. All that's left of her now is three scraps of paper. Tie them together, why don't you? Make a small bundle, give some weight to her memory. She'll just blow away otherwise.

She worked as a tavern servant at Coteau-du-Lac, where the boatmen coming down from the Great Lakes stopped before shooting the rapids down to Lachine and Montreal, and where travellers heading upriver paused before crossing Lake St Francis to Cornwall and beyond. The place was run by a Scottish couple, John McIntyre and his wife Sophia Murchison. Charity landed a job with them July 14, 1798.

A tavern was more than a beer hall in those days. You could get a meal and a room, or at least a place to sleep even if it sometimes was just the floor. Some taverns also served as meeting halls and grocery stores – the only ones in the area. Out in the country, tavern and inn were the same thing; in town, the place was sometimes called a coffee house or even a hotel. Unless the tavern was a one-horse operation where the owners did everything, from stabling horses to waiting on tables, there were servants or slaves to carry some of the load.

There were no black tavern keepers in Montreal at that time. Jeanne Bonga might have managed it, but her tavern-keeping days were over. She and her husband Jean had kept one at Michilimackinac (Mackinac Island, Michigan). The place was the upcountry hub of the Montreal fur traders and an important military post. The Bongas (like Hilaire L'Amour and his wife Catherine) had been slaves of Daniel Robertson. He had freed them and their four kids in 1787, before heading back home to Montreal after five years as commander of the post.

The Bongas ran their tavern until Jean Bonga died in January 1795. The next year, the area was turned over to the United States, and the Montreal fur traders shifted their depot to what is now Thunder Bay, Ontario. Jeanne Bonga moved down to Montreal with three of her children, Charlotte, Étienne (Stephen), and Rosalie, all in their teens; her son Pierre (Peter) stayed on to work as an interpreter for the fur traders. Once she got to Montreal, Jeanne Bonga was done with tavern keeping.

If there were no black tavern keepers in Montreal, there were black tavern workers. At the eastern tip of the island, Phoebe and Sampson, both slaves of a Mr Dumont, worked at his tavern in Pointe-aux-Trembles. Jacqho, about 38, and Rose, about 27 (close to the same age as Charity), worked closer to town, at John Brooke's tavern, sign of the Black Horse, on St Mary Street (now Notre Dame Street) in the east-side Quebec Suburb. Brooke had bought the two of them together in the fall of 1796, Jacqho for £100 and Rose for £50.

In town, there was Manuel Allen, whose status was up in the air. Remember him? Thomas John Sullivan had bought him in 1797 to work at his Montreal Coffee House, but Allen had run off in March 1798, claiming to be free. He may have gone back to working at the coffee house as a servant, though; because when Sullivan closed up shop in 1799 and moved to Pointe-aux-Trembles to run a tavern there, Allen and his family moved out there too.

Lydia Saunders worked at Thomas Powis's Montreal Tea-Gardens on Côte-St-Antoine. She'd been there since the end of November 1797, but for how much longer was anybody's guess. Her master, an ex-army officer, had left her there before sailing for

Halifax. He owed Powis £27 4s and gave him Lydia Saunders and her baby boy as his marker. He'd done the same five days earlier with Ledy, "a Mulatto wench," parking her with Richard Dillon of the Montreal Hotel, to whom he owed £20. The deal in both cases was that he would get his human IOU's back if he paid his debts in eighteen months.

Lizette Lewis might have been working in Montreal then, too. It's hard to say. In the fall of 1789, she'd been sold at Detroit to a fur trader, who brought her to Montreal and sold her to a merchant. The merchant had shipped her off to Quebec in the spring of 1792 to the auctioneers William Burns and John William Woolsey. And on May 9 that year, Burns & Woolsey had sold her to an innkeeper for £25. Then – maybe a little after the "revolt" of 1798 – she made her way back to Montreal. She was here by the summer of 1801 when, as a free woman, she was hired by Robert Walker to work at his inn in Kingston for £18 a year, plus room and board.

Now, Charity was a free woman, or said she was, when she went to work for the McIntyres at five shillings a year, plus room and board and clothing. She claimed to be about 26 – Who knew? She didn't carry much weight and it showed in scrap of paper no. 1, her contract. She had a roof over her head, but the pay was nothing to write home about. She signed on for ten years, accepting that the McIntyres could hand her off to anyone they pleased if they had no need of her.

She'd been working at Coteau for just seven months when the axe fell. It was February 1799, the dead of winter. Someone stole a wad from one of the guests. Which guest? Somebody from Cornwall. How much did he have on him? Don't know. Who did it? The finger pointed at Charity. She might have said, "No Sir, I didn't do it." She might have screamed in big black capital letters with exclamation marks, "NO SIR! I DIDN'T DO IT!" Her words didn't carry much weight. She was locked up in the Montreal jail to wait for her day in court.

If the details are skimpy, it's because no account of her case has survived beyond scrap no. 2, two lines in the *Montreal Gazette* of March 17: "Charité, a Negro woman, was tried for compound larceny, and acquitted for want of evidence." The court records aren't there to tell us more. Is Charité our Charity? What was that "compound larceny" exactly? Had she been accused of stealing a whole pile of things? And what about "want of evidence"? Was there no evidence against her at all? Then why was she charged and put through the wringer?

Scrap no. 3 answers some of these questions. Tie it in with scraps 1 and 2, and you'll see. It's a notice that ran in the *Montreal Gazette* on August 26 (by mistake, the paper left out the signer's name):

Whereas it has been reported that I suspected the servant of Mr John M'Intire, at the Coteau du Lac, Innkeeper, to have taken a considerable sum of money from me at his house, in the month of February last, and as such a report might injure the repute of his servants and hurt his custom, I do therefore in justice to him and his family, hereby publicly declare, that I am fully convinced, that it was not any person belonging to his house or family, who took the money from me. Given under my Hand at Cornwall, this 11th day of July 1799.

There! Without naming her, even the victim denied that Charity was the crook. So in case you hadn't heard, Charity didn't do it. Spread the word. The thief is still out there. No, not the one who took the money – that's ancient history. I mean the one who pointed the finger at her and stole her good name.

8

The World Turned Upside Down

☞

YOU THINK SLAVES WERE SLAVES, masters were free, and that's all there was to it? Don't be so sure. Slavery had a way of turning the world upside down.

Take Harry. He was like a keychain or a fridge magnet – a little black souvenir of the American Revolution picked up by Michel Eustache Gaspard Alain Chartier de Lotbinière, son of a marquis, seigneur of Vaudreuil and much else besides. Was Lotbinière a free man when he bought Harry? Not exactly. He was a prisoner of war.

At 27, he'd been one of the British defenders captured in an American attack on Saint-Jean in November 1775. He was held for a while at Albany, New York, then in Pennsylvania, at Bristol on the Delaware River north of Philadelphia. As a white gentleman and all, being a military prisoner didn't stop him from playing tourist – a little sightseeing, a little schmoozing, some shopping. On one shopping trip, on July 16, 1776, he bought Harry, just a boy, for £45.

Blacks rarely appear in pictures of early life in Canada, but George Heriot put three into this view of a French Canadian party in 1807: the tambourine player, the one standing near the wall to his right, and another whose upturned face is just visible below the tambourine.

So there was Harry, slave to a prisoner. But that changed soon enough. In December 1776 the Americans and British swapped some prisoners, and Lotbinière went free. (Harry must have breathed a sigh of relief to know that he was, at last, the slave of a free man, don't you think?) After spending the winter in New York City, which was in British hands, Lotbinière returned to Canada in the spring of 1777 with Harry, his souvenir.

At the manor house of Vaudreuil on the Ottawa River, just off the western tip of Montreal Island, where Harry lived for the next twenty-two years, he was known as Henry or Henri, even Michel Henri. Michel Eustache Gaspard Alain Chartier de Lotbinière certainly had enough names that he could spare him one.

But all bad things must come to an end, and the end for Harry came in the fall of 1799. After all those years, he stepped out of line somehow and got on his master's bad side. Maybe he'd picked up that "revolt" bug from the slaves in Montreal. Maybe, knowing he'd soon be a member of the quarter-century club, he pushed a little too hard for a gold watch. Who knows?

His master, a heavyweight in the colony, member of the Legislative Council, was so upset over Harry's *mauvaise conduite*, whatever it was, that he decided to inflict the ultimate penalty.

Death? No, freedom.

What?!

Yeah. Harry, too, probably scratched his head over that one, till the day he died – To punish him, his master set him free.

On November 26, 1799, he sent Harry packing. Gave him twelve shillings and a load of clothes: eleven new shirts, twelve vests (some of silk, one of gold cloth), flannel underwear, cloaks, coats, jackets, five suits, a red riding coat, several pairs of pants, stockings and socks, buckles, shoes, hats, caps, mittens, belts, two silk cravats, and a silk handkerchief. You name it.

Harry must have looked a perfect clotheshorse leaving. In case anybody on the road took him for a thief with all that loot, or a runaway, he carried papers explaining the situation. The certificate Lotbinière had written said that he'd given Harry the boot, banished him from Vaudreuil for life, and it listed every single item in Harry's severance package, down to his underwear.

Only the previous summer, Lotbinière's old mother had made her will, leaving Harry a little something to be paid to him every year as long as he stayed put and behaved. Now that he was out on his ear, he'd never see that money. When she rewrote her will in 1803, there was no question of a gift to Harry. He was gone.

Oh well, win some, lose some.

As for Lotbinière, when you come down to it, any man who could see freedom as a punishment – slavery as a favour? – had to be a slave himself to some pretty twisted notions.

———

9

THE KING OF
FRANCE

☞

THE PAPINEAU NAME IS SACRED HERE. (The name of Prince is not, but we'll get to that in a minute.) At the turn of this century, if you followed the news, you'd have seen how prickly people could be about it when Quebec's place-names commission decided to rename the Papineau-Leblanc Bridge over to Laval. In the face of the outcry, the commission backed down, and two months later the old name was back.

"The Papineau name, at least, must remain," the president of the patriotic Société Saint-Jean-Baptiste de Montréal had insisted in a piece he wrote in the Toronto *Globe and Mail.* Leblanc, the name of a Laval pioneer, might go, he seemed to imply, but removing the Papineau part was like wiping out "the memory of one of this province's proudest names."

"The name Papineau is very important in our history," he wrote. "The father and son are interchangeable in our collective memory."

The bridge, built in 1968–69, and the long Papineau Avenue running up to it from clear across town, were named after the father, Joseph, a notary and sometime politician. His son, the career politician Louis-Joseph, is much better known because of his leadership of the Patriote party right up to the Rebellions of 1837–38. In Quebec's collective memory he's a star, and a bright one. Almost our Ogyasefo (as President Kwame Nkrumah of Ghana was known), almost our redeemer. There's an old Quebec expression, *la tête à Papineau* (Papineau's head), meaning bright. As people sometimes say about a dim bulb, *ce n'est pas la tête à Papineau* – he's no Einstein.

Papineau Avenue and its bridge are not named after Louis-Joseph, for all his brightness and fame, but after his father, for the simple reason that he owned land at the south end of the street in 1810 when it was given the name. After the rebellions, with Louis-Joseph a wanted man, the authorities wiped the Papineau name off the map and called the street Victoria, for the Queen. It didn't matter to them that the street had been named for the father, not the son. They made no distinction – the names were interchangeable to them. A few years it took for heads to cool, and the Papineau name returned. (Prince still had nothing named after him, but we're coming to that.)

About the father. The day his son was born, October 7, 1786, he had him baptised at Notre Dame Church. The priest he got to do the job and also to be godfather to his boy was the slave-holding Louis Payet – not one of the regular Sulpician priests at Notre Dame but a backwoods reverend who always kept a slave or two. To be blessed at birth by a buyer and seller of bodies and souls, and saddled with him as your spiritual minder, wasn't the most promising start in life for freedom's coming champion. More like a curse.

It gets worse. On September 15, 1792, Louis-Joseph's father – who was elected that summer to the very first Legislative Assembly of Lower Canada as one of two members for the County of Montreal – bought himself a slave. Prince was a steal at 300 livres (£12 10s). This probably had to do with his age (he was about 54); maybe also with the fact that Joseph Benoit, dit L'hyvernois, the Montreal tailor who sold Prince to Papineau, was going through a nasty breakup with his wife, trying to do her out of her share of the property.

Being a notary, Papineau knew how crucial it was to nail down his property title so no one could deny that every bit of Prince was his. He made sure he got the full ownership record, the way you

43

might do if you were buying a used car. All the sales slips, going back to when Prince was imported, told a tale. L'hyvernois had bought Prince on May 31, 1787, from the distiller John Lagord, who had bought him on December 18, 1786, from Elisha Yeoman, who had bought him six days earlier from Martin McEvoy of Saint-Jean, who had bought him a month before that, on November 15, from Elisha Fullman of Walpole, New Hampshire. Papineau had himself an iron-clad chain of titles there.

His son Louis-Joseph was about to turn six. He was a bright boy, so what did he make of Prince? Maybe then or maybe later, as he preached liberty up and down the land, an old black shadow crossed his mind. Who can tell? In all the reams of stuff written about the Papineaus, there's not a word about Prince.

When slavery was close to extinction, getting snuffed out by the courts, Joseph Papineau filed two petitions in the Assembly to try to keep it alive. Help! he pleaded as slavery's mouthpiece in the spring of 1799 and again a year later. Pass a law! Do something! The judges are letting the slaves go, robbing the owners blind.

Or, as he grumbled about slaves in August 1800, "Given the lack of means in this province for safeguarding this kind of property, it is considered precarious and uncertain." He wrote that on an inventory of the property of Michel Eustache Gaspard Alain Chartier de Lotbinière, which he'd drawn up, giving the value of each item. It was to explain why no value was set down for Pompé, Lotbinière's last slave. (His other slave, Harry, he'd sacked the year before.)

A while back, the author of a sketch of his life wrote that from the works of the great thinkers of his day, Joseph Papineau had picked up liberal notions:

Thus he brought before the Assembly a petition from the electors of Montreal to abolish slavery. The practice of it is not widespread, but it does exist. Papineau finds it abhorrent that men can be bought and sold like cattle, proof of the humanity of this cooper's son, Seminary-educated, stoutly Catholic, who cannot abide the idea of human bondage. He is horrified that high officials in the judiciary and members of the Assembly and of religious orders are slave owners.

The "Prince-Papineau Bridge" looking towards Montreal from Laval

Ah … yes … and Prince, you know, was the king of France.

About that bridge. Now that we've come to it, we will have to cross it. It doesn't take *la tête à Papineau* to see a way. Make it the Prince-Papineau Bridge, and put up a plaque explaining the name and its place in our collective memory. Do it on some October 7, Louis-Joseph's christening day, and lift that curse.

10

JUST JULIA

FIRST THEY WERE BAPTISED in the spring together. It's not often you see that, two grown-ups on one baptism record. But there it was on the books of Christ Church: "John Flemming, a black man living at Mr Shuter's of Montreal, Aged Twenty two Years, and Julia Johnson a black Woman, Aged Twenty Years, were baptised the Twenty ninth of April, one thousand seven hundred & ninety eight." Sarah Jackson, Manuel Allen's wife, was a sponsor, making her X.

Eight months later, when he was still a slave of John Shuter's, John married Julia. That was no match made in heaven, more like a job cooked up in slavery's kitchen at closing time. You get the feeling it never should have happened, but it did, at Christ Church, December 16, 1798.

Anyway, slavery died out, and it was as a free man that John Flemming got himself some land, two lots in Griffintown, in May 1804. That was under the old seigneurial system, so he didn't have to come up with a big down payment and a mortgage – just payments of a bit over £3 a year. He put up a house, and in 1811 the fact that he owned his own place was enough to get him, a "Negro Servant," on the jury lists, even if he never was called for duty.

He had three kids by his wife Rose in those years, the first in 1802.

Wife Rose? What about wife Julia?

Julia didn't share his Griffintown home and his family was not hers. She had kids of her own (they all died young) but with Joseph Pierson, a pastry cook.

If Pierson was her man, imagine how she felt when he married another. That was on September 13, 1809 – a grey day for French Canada, it being the fiftieth anniversary of the Battle of the Plains of Abraham. Not the brightest day in Julia's life either.

By then, she and John Flemming had made their break official. They could have gone their separate ways and just let it go at that. But for some reason, one of them at least wanted their split on record. They couldn't ask a priest to un-marry them, and divorce was beyond their reach, way too messy and expensive, if not impossible: it would have taken a special law. So John Flemming and Julia Jackson (she was Johnson when they married, Jackson when they split) went before a notary and pretty well un-married themselves:

On the sixth Day of february of the year one thousand eight hundred & nine … Personally Appeared John Fleming of said Montreal yeoman, and Julia Jackson his wife, which said John Fleming & Julia Jackson for divers considerations them moving mutually consented and agreed to live separate and apart from this day henceforth and for ever, without the one having any claim or demand whatever against the other or for any property or effects whatsoever, or for the support or maintenance of one another, hereby formally renouncing to cohabitation with each other and all matrimonial rights and rights whatsoever in future.

Maybe it was his idea, to make sure Julia couldn't claim a piece of him now that he had assets to his name. Or maybe Julia wanted a clean break, maybe she had in mind setting up house with Pierson – but he went and married Mary Rusk that year.

Jackson or Johnson, Juliet or July or just Julia – whatever name she went by, she had no luck with men, no luck at all.

11

Isaac the Impossible

YOU MUST KNOW A FOUR-YEAR-OLD BOY. Think a minute. A four-year-old boy is real and he's unreal. He's an angel, a handful, a food processor that can't be filled up (but no peas, please; he hates peas). He's a deep thinker without a thought in his head, shakes like a leaf but steady as rain, three feet tall, ten on the Richter scale … He's all this and none of it, because what he really is is the future, and the future is – Who knows? Not real, just possible – one big candyshop/toystore/hall of mirrors of possibilities.

That said, it doesn't take an Einstein to figure that a four-year-old boy giving 100 per cent isn't worth two bits as a servant. That's just too real. But that's what happened to Isaac Wily.

Isaac Newton Wily, to give him his full name, was born on December 17, 1804, to William Wily, a labourer who'd come from Philadelphia, and his wife Margaret July (sometimes called Peggy Christie). They named the boy after their friend Isaac Newton, who had come from England and worked for a spell for Sir Alexander Mackenzie at his farm on the mountain.

You know Mackenzie, the fur-trade explorer – first European to cross what we call Canada (it wasn't real then either, just possible) and reach the Pacific? When he got there, he mixed red dye and animal fat and put his tag on a rock: "Alexander Mackenzie, from Canada, by land, the twenty-second of July, one thousand seven hundred and ninety-three." That Mackenzie.

In Montreal in the summer of 1809, Isaac Wily's father packed him off as a servant to George Clark, a furrier, and not just for a few months but until he turned 21 – sixteen and a half long years down the pike. The deal was that Clark would take care of all Isaac's basic needs – house him and clothe him and feed him – and at the end of it, round about Christmas 1825, Clark would send him on his way, with $40 and two new suits of clothes.

What kind of a heartless father would do such a thing to a four-year-old? You don't have to be a professional child-care worker to know that the boy belonged at home. But don't be hard on William Wily, he had it hard enough. And he was no Abraham ready to sacrifice his Isaac, and nothing like those wicked fairytale dads who try to lose their kids in the woods.

The thing is, when he made the deal with Clark, they didn't meet at home, in a shop, a notary's office, over drinks or dinner, on the street, or in any of the usual places. They were in the Hôtel-Dieu. If you summoned a notary to the hospital to draw up a contract, it usually meant one thing: you weren't coming out.

If William Wily had known how to write, if he'd had some of Mackenzie's red dye and grease, he might have scrawled on the hospital wall: "Take care of my boy. William Wily, the third of August, one thousand eight hundred and nine," or something like that. That's what you read between the lines of that contract. Because William Wily had reached his Pacific and he wasn't going to make it back. He died in the Hôtel-Dieu on August 28.

That's how reality got hold of Isaac Wily.

12

COLD
CASE

☞

THE SILENCE OF THE MONTREAL PAPERS on the murder of
Joseph Pierson was something else. Nothing like the moment of
silence that honours the dead.

In March 1815, the *Courant*, the *Gazette*, and the *Herald* could
chatter on about the war just ended with the United States, or what
Napoleon was up to in France, or some joker going around stealing
door knockers – but they never breathed a word about the black
man stabbed in the street by men of the King's Regiment. As if in a
town of 15,000 or so, murder was an everyday thing.

It wasn't so to Jane Wilson. She'd popped into Pierson's cook-
shop the night that four soldiers ate there and then ran off without paying their bill. Pierson had chased after them, and ten
minutes later he stumbled back in, stunned and covered in blood.
He asked her to feel if his head was cut. No it wasn't, she said,
though it was bloodied.

"I'm a dead man," he said as he fainted and fell to the floor. She
then checked his stomach, as he'd asked, loosened his clothes, and

saw his innards busting out of a deep cut by his navel.

He made it through that long Wednesday night. Young Robert Nelson, the doctor, was called. Using bloodletting and other tricks of his trade, he tried his best to get the swelling in the belly down.

Police Magistrate Mondelêt was on the case by morning. Jane Wilson told him her story and gave him a cap that one of the soldiers had left behind, with two calico handkerchiefs and a pair of mitts in it, and she gave him a brass chip (from a bayonet sheath) that she'd found on the ground by the door.

Pierson, writhing in pain, was clear-headed enough to speak for himself, though in no shape to sign his statement. If he'd signed it, they'd have known his name was Pierson, not Pearson. It said:

Joseph Pearson of Montreal, Pastry Cook being duly sworn on the Holy Evangelists deposeth and saith, That Yesterday Evening between the Hours of Seven and Eight oClock, there came into the House of Deponent in Notre Dame Street four soldiers of the 1st Battalion of the Kings or Eight Regiment and asked Deponent to give them Supper, that Deponent did so and after demanded payment of the four men for the supper he had furnished them, which they refused and on Deponents following them out in the Street and demanding his payment – one of the said soldiers struck deponent over his head with his Bayonet, and another of them at the same time struck his Bayonet into the Beley of Deponent and immediately ran way – Deponent then came into his house and fell on the floor – Deponent does not Know the name of the Man that Stabd him, but thinks he should Know him again if he saw him. Sworn before me at Montreal 9th March 1815

JM Mondelêt J.P.

Joseph Pierson.

The 1st Battalion, 8th (King's) Regiment, veterans of the Upper Canadian front in the War of 1812, was in barracks by the Quebec Gate, east side of town. Magistrate Mondelêt told the officers there what was up.

"Find out who's missing a cap," he suggested. He held onto the cap but gave them the white-blue-and-brown handkerchiefs so that they could find out who they belonged to. Then he went back to Pierson's with a soldier in tow:

And the said Joseph Pearson being duly sworn deposeth and said that William Thompson a private soldier in the first Battalion of his Majesty's eighth regiment or Kings, now being present and shewn to the said Joseph Pearson, is one of the four soldiers mentioned in the preceding Deposition, who had supper at the deponent's house Yesterday evening, that it was not the said William Thompson who stabbed the said deponent with the bayonet – but the said William Thompson was present.

About midnight that Thursday, Dr Nelson opened the wound a bit to push the gut – the *omentum*, he called it – back in, and Pierson breathed more easily for an hour. But then he sank, and just before two o'clock on Friday morning it was over.

Magistrate Mondelêt, who was also the coroner, collected twelve men for a jury and held an inquest at Pierson's that day. They saw the body laid out, saw the bayonet wound and the cap Jane Wilson had found. They heard her account and what Pierson had said on his deathbed, and they heard Dr Nelson's conclusion: "From the examination of the body after death, it appears beyond a doubt that the wound was the cause of his death." They had no trouble reaching a verdict: murder by a soldier unknown, of the 8th (King's) Regiment.

Still no word in the newspapers.

At the barracks that Thursday, Private James Douglas of the Light Company of the regiment had quickly come under suspicion. He'd been absent at roll call just before eight on Wednesday evening. And when they held an inspection on Thursday at noon to check for a missing cap, he'd borrowed the cap of a soldier laid up in the sick ward (though that wasn't known until later).

But George McCollough, pay sergeant of the Light Company, showed around one of the handkerchiefs that afternoon and was told it belonged to Douglas. Douglas denied this, but a soldier was eventually found who swore it was part of a piece of cloth, "white ground, brown and blue spot," that he'd given Douglas in December.

At noon on the Saturday, with the case no longer one of assault but of murder, Sergeant Major John Binns, with Sergeants McCollough and John Kennedy, paraded the whole 1st Battalion to get to the bottom of the matter. When he came to Douglas, Binns stopped. Something fishy about Douglas's hat. McCollough swore that this wasn't one of the hats he'd issued to his men. It was

The east end of Montreal in 1824. The soldier at lower left is walking on Notre Dame Street where Joseph Pierson operated his restaurant.

made by Hicks, Keats & Co., not by Bicknell and Moore like the others. And instead of fur lappets or trim, it had ribbons, and a different cockade, and strings to tie under the chin. Kennedy, sergeant of the Light Company, had never seen Douglas wear anything like it before.

Douglas was thrown into the guardhouse. Later, they led him to his bunk to check his bayonet and scabbard. When he pulled them out, it turned out that the bayonet was his but the scabbard was one he'd borrowed from soldier James Hinds. Pressed, he pulled out another bayonet and scabbard, with the scabbard missing a brass bit. This time it turned out that the scabbard was his but the bayonet in it belonged to Hinds.

On the Monday and Tuesday a succession of soldiers paraded before Magistrate Mondelêt at the police office, giving their statements. On Wednesday the fifteenth, he had the prisoner brought in. But Douglas knew nothing about nothing anything – or so he said.

As for William Thompson, who'd been fingered by Pierson as present at his stabbing, he had an alibi. A fellow soldier swore that Thompson had been with him at the barracks all evening the Wednesday before, except for a few minutes – never long enough to have gone out for supper.

Nobody stepped forward to explain or confess. So Douglas alone stood charged. He was held till September, the next sitting of the Court of King's Bench. The grand jury convened then, studied the charge, and on September 7 found "No bill."

It's true, strictly speaking, that the evidence showed only that Douglas had been at Pierson's the night he was killed and that he'd done his best to hide the fact with his lies and denials and tricks. It was awfully suspicious behaviour but it didn't prove he was the killer. They didn't have the science then to take fingerprints, match the blade to the wound, test for blood on the bayonet or on Douglas's clothes, etc. So the grand jury decided there wasn't enough evidence for a trial, and that was that. Two days later, the court had to let Douglas go.

Still no word in the papers.

So this is the news, almost two hundred years late, about the latest late news you'll ever get: Montreal, March 8, 1815. Joseph Pierson, who ran a restaurant on Notre Dame Street, was stabbed in the gut with a bayonet by an unknown soldier of the 8th (King's) Regiment, who got away with murder.

13

HOME
at Last

☞

WILLIAM WRIGHT HAD CAUSE TO celebrate the Fourth of July, and here's why.

He'd been the slave of James Dunlop, a Scottish Loyalist who fled Virginia during the American Revolution. Dunlop had set up in business in Quebec, then moved to Montreal in the early 1780s. He became one of the richest men in the city – shipbuilding, finance, import-export, all sorts of things.

Maybe Dunlop brought William with him from Virginia, or maybe he bought him after he reached Canada. The first we hear of William (that's what he was called then, just William, "a Negroe belonging to James Dunlop of Montreal Esq.") is on December 17, 1799, when he was baptised. Almost three years later, in August 1802, his name was recorded as William Dunlop at the christening of his friend John Flemming's first son. And in 1804, at the baptism of another Flemming boy, he was called William Wright.

They said William was about 30 when he married Catherine Guillet on May 26, 1806. She was from Haiti, about 18, the daughter

55

of African parents. She worked as a household servant for John Trim, the black entrepreneur, and his wife Charlotte; she'd been with them for a year or so. William Wright was no longer a slave then but was still with James Dunlop, as a servant.

William Wright and Catherine Guillet had three sons and three daughters. When it came to religion, where many Protestants and Catholics ragged on each other, the Wrights were Presbyterian Catholics: all the boys were baptised Presbyterians, all the girls Roman Catholics. Whatever side God was on, they had the bases covered. But only their last child, John, born October 15, 1823, lived to be an adult. He became a gilder, painting with gold leaf on fancy furniture and picture frames, in mansions and churches and steamboats.

James Dunlop died in the summer of 1815. He didn't leave anything to his ex-slave and servant, but he did order that all his debts be paid. That must have included back pay to William Wright, because on July 4, 1820 Wright was handed sixty-two pounds, fifteen shillings, and ninepence "for as much due to him for wages from the estate of the late James Dunlop."

Five years is a long time for a servant to wait for his pay; if the estate owed him that much, it must have meant that he hadn't been paid for some time before Dunlop's death. In the meantime, he probably lived at John Trim's, because that's where his wife lived and worked, right up to 1820.

If Catherine Guillet left the Trims in 1820, was it because her husband had suddenly come into a pot of money on the Fourth of July? Well, £62 15s 9d was a nice nest egg, but it wasn't a million dollars. What probably made her jump was the nest that came with the egg.

That's right, somebody gave William Wright a house. Not a rat trap either. They built him a brand new house. On June 26, for £50, businessman Charles Frederick Hoofstetter and his friend Adam Ann Gordon bought a vacant lot at the southwest corner of Inspector Street and College Street (St Paul, west of McGill). Four days later they hired a carpenter to put up a house there for £100. It was to be a square building, 30 x 30 ft (9 x 9 m), split into two dwellings side by side, each with three rooms on the ground floor and an attic. College Street ran by the front, and the Little River ran out back. This is how Hoofstetter and Gordon put it on the fourth of July when they gave Wright house and lot:

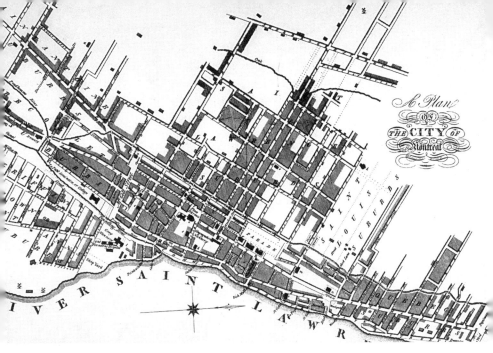

William Wright's house stood in Récollets Suburb, just east of where three
streams converged to flow into the harbour of Montreal. The St Martin,
or Little River, ran east to west along Craig Street (St Antoine); the
Prud'homme River came from the northwest, and a branch of the
St Pierre River from the southwest.

Feeling a friendship for William Wright, a negro, of this city, and
commiserating his helpless state after spending … his life as a servant,
they the said Adam Ann Gordon and Charles F Hoofstetter of their
free will have determined to ensure as much as in their power a com-
petency against too great distress in his said William Wrights old age;
moved by these motives they have and do hereby give … unto the said
William Wright … a lot of ground situated in the recolet suburb …
with a wooden house thirty feet square to be erected on the said lot
of ground.

But, it wasn't all free and clear. While Wright would not have to
pay a cent for the house, he would have to pay the £40 still owing
on the lot, plus the yearly seigneurial dues. He couldn't sell the
property without permission, and if he died before his wife he
couldn't will the property to anyone he pleased – it would belong

to her during her lifetime. If she decided she didn't want it, then it would be sold and the money used to set up "a sufficient life rent to support her."

Hoofstetter threw in a few trimmings. He had the contractor fence the lot, run a small dividing fence down the middle of the yard from the house to the Little River, and put in a double outhouse to serve two families. This cost an extra £15 10s.

Everything was finished by September 19. How strange it must have felt for William Wright and Catherine Guillet in those first days, masters in their own house when they'd never been masters of anything before. Did they rush in, eager to take possession? Or did they pause outside, hesitate a second, almost afraid to look, shy to open the door? They still had their living expenses to pay, but that £62 15s 9d would have gone a long way, plus the money they could make by renting out the other half of the house.

You might say the system was rotten that made some people so well off they could afford to give away a house while William Wright and his wife were so hard up they couldn't hope to own one any other way. But Hoofstetter and Gordon didn't invent the system; they just worked within it.

The point is, there was no law that said they had to be kind. And if you think kindness is too strong a word, call it reparation for William Wright's years as a slave. Any way you look at it, something good happened.

William Wright lived in his house less than five years. He died on February 10, 1825. If he really had been about 30 when he married in 1806, he would have been about 50 at his death, though they said he was "about 66." His widow was much younger and she lived almost another forty years, thirty of them in that house.

———

14

A WHOLE NEW *LIGHT*

TO WORK WITH LIGHT IS TO PLAY with shadow. You can't have one without the other. They're the two sides of the coin, like sound and silence. Warren Glossen knew both sides. He was a lamplighter for a while.

The newspaper was pretty clear about his fate: "Yesterday, at 10 o'clock A.M. *Warren Glossen* and *Jean Baptiste Albert*, for burglary, and *Abraham Paradis*, for sheep stealing, were executed upon the Drop in rear of the Gaol, agreeable to their sentences at the last Court of King's Bench." It was more like 10:20 A.M., and Paradis had actually been convicted on two counts that had nothing to do with sheep; he'd been stealing cattle and horses. But who had time for little things like that at a time like this? The records of Christ Church confirm the essentials: "Warren Glossen, a Negro, was hanged on the 24th of October 1823, aged 35 Years, and was Buried on the same day by me, John Bethune, Rector."

Amen.

And what had he done to deserve that? He'd walked into the shadows and fallen in with thieves.

He'd already had brushes with the law for stealing, in early 1818 and in 1819 and 1820, but always seemed to get off. The one time his luck had failed him was in mid-July 1819. For running a brothel, he had been locked up till the end of the month, then put in the pillory in the marketplace for an hour. The pillory!

Not that that did any good.

On the night of January 4, 1823, his gang cut a hole in the window of a shop on McGill Street and snatched £15 worth of black satin cloth and other things on display. Small potatoes, you might say. Not to Mr Hitchcock the shopkeeper, not in 1823.

Four nights later they struck again, out in Lachine. There they broke into the offices of Whiting & Crane, a forwarding company shipping goods up and down the river. Warren Glossen and his crew boosted some clothes – about thirty blue army fatigue jackets – but what really hurt Whiting & Crane is that they took their books. Without those business records, the company couldn't tell whether it was coming or going. Two thousand pounds in accounts was up in the air.

Whiting & Crane offered a $100 reward for information, and within a day or two they got results. They found their papers stashed at a scuzzy tavern in Récollets Suburb, west of McGill Street. The gang was caught, tried after some delay, and on September 10, three of them – Warren Glossen, Jean-Baptiste Albert, and Peter Johnson – were sentenced to death. A few days later Johnson's sentence was commuted to five years on the treadmill at Quebec, so Glossen and Albert were the only members of the gang to hang.

Stealing cloth and old account books is no hanging offence, you might say. But burglary was a capital crime then – breaking and entering, stealing from a home, sheep stealing, horse stealing, and hundreds of things we think of as petty crimes. That same September, in two separate cases, the court sentenced two white men to death for breaking into a house and stealing a watch.

And it's not as if Warren Glossen didn't know the rules. After all, he'd been busted before. He'd also been a member of the night watch, the police force that worked dusk to dawn. Not a full-fledged cop – none of them were – he was a lamplighter, one of four black men hired to mind the street lights when street lights were the latest thing.

It was a white businessman on St Paul Street, then the main commercial street, who'd had the bright idea of putting oil lamps on the streets of Montreal. In October-November 1815, Samuel Dawson and some fellow businessmen had put up twenty-two on the stretch of St Paul between the Old Market (Place Royale) and McGill Street. They cost just under $7 apiece. The idea caught fire, and soon people were collecting money to pay for lights farther east on St Paul, and on Notre Dame Street, which was uptown then, downtown now.

All of a sudden, everybody wanted lights. From being a private idea, lighting became a public service. On April 1, 1818, the governor in Quebec approved a law giving the city the power to set up a night watch and organize street lighting. Magistrates ran the show (there was no mayor and council until 1833). The magistrates sprang into action as soon as the law passed, and the watch was up and running by May 1.

By law, the force was limited to twenty-four men at the outside. As foreman, or chief, of the watch, they hired Emmanuel D'Aubreville, a French-born soldier of fortune who'd served with armies in Europe before winding up a captain of the Voltigeurs Canadiens in the War of 1812. Hard up in 1818, he had written to the magistrates begging for the chief's job. They handed it to him on April 18 at a salary of £75 a year. Six days later they hired Antoine Lafrenière as his deputy at £60.

D'Aubreville then rounded up twenty men – fourteen labourers, a butcher, a carpenter, a shoemaker, a river pilot, a voyageur, and a gardener – to work for six months as watchmen at three shillings a night. So they were twenty-two in all. Off they went, pounding the beat with whistles and sticks, sounding off the hours, one by one: "Past one o'clock, and a starlit morning!" Try that today, and it's called "disturbing the peace": Then it was maintaining the peace.

Six months on, those watchmen who had pulled lamplighter duty had had enough. Too messy, maybe – handling that fish oil, trimming the wicks, cleaning off the soot. Probably thought it beneath them. You know: "I didn't join the force to be a damn wick-trimmer!"

On November 17, D'Aubreville tells the magistrates that seeing as how none of his men want to be lighting technicians, "he has selected four Negroes for this object." Then and there, the magistrates resolve "that the Foreman of the Watch hire these

Récollets Church in Récollets Street, 1865, two years before
it was demolished. In 1818 Warren Glossen and his fellow
lamplighters worked out of the former monastery which then
adjoined the church.

four Negroes to be paid two shillings for each lamp per month."
That's how Warren Glossen, Peter Dago, John Hyers and Prince
Thomson, labourers all from the Quebec Suburb, came to be
public servants, hired as the lamplighters of the night watch for
the winter and spring of 1818–19.

No whistles and clubs for the Negroes. From the two-room watch
headquarters in the old convent of the Récollet priests behind John

Trim's place, they set out on their rounds with funnels and ladders, jugs of whale or cod oil, loads of cotton wick, and soap and water and turpentine for cleaning. One of them always stayed back at headquarters in case someone reported a light out somewhere that needed quick fixing.

There was light then, and Warren Glossen and his buddies made it happen.

In fact, by February 1819, there were 174 street lamps in town. At two shillings a lamp per month, that means the team would have been paid £17 8s a month, or £4 7s apiece. The other watchmen were paid three shillings for every night they worked, so if they worked, say, thirty nights a month, that gave them £4 10s. But with the odd night off, they made a little less than that. So the lamplighters were paid about the same as regular watchmen.

So much for wages. Working conditions were another matter. For one thing, Warren Glossen and the lamplighters were hired under different terms from the rest – as a crew, instead of one by one – and paid not per working day but according to the number of lamps in use. But maybe that wasn't so bad. The number of lamps kept going up. By February 1819, the magistrates were already saying they needed 502 more!

If the watchmen's duty was to stroll about and keep an eye out, the lamplighters had to hustle. One by one, all those lights all over town had to be lit, seven nights a week, and promptly; and one by one, they all had to be killed come morning.

And if a lamp was damaged, the lamplighters had to cough up for repairs or pay for a new one, unless they found a witness to swear that the thing had broken through no fault of theirs. What if somebody smashed a lamp for kicks when no one was looking? Ah well, that was one hard rule. But it was typical of working conditions then.

Look at St Antoine Suburb. When residents there asked that the night watch cover their area, they struck a deal. Six of them would be allowed to join the force and, as they wished, they would patrol only their own turf, but they wouldn't be paid a cent. No three shillings a night, no two shillings per star in the sky. Nothing. Pounding the beat for free sounds crazy now, like hanging Warren Glossen for burglary. But that's how things stood.

Warren Glossen knew the score all right. He worked with the lights, but the shadows drew him. And that last day, walking to the platform behind the jail, "The Lord have mercy on my soul!" he kept saying, like he couldn't believe how dark it was for a morning.

The lighting's much different in Montreal now. You look at street lights and maybe you don't think twice about them. And maybe you think, the way their heads are bowed, kind of sad-looking ...

Many early street lights, like the one at left, were attached to buildings – a cheaper, less obtrusive arrangement than lampposts. This view of Notre Dame Street, looking west from near Berri Street, shows the funeral procession of Sir Benjamin D'Urban, commander of the British forces in Canada, in May 1849. Before coming to Canada in 1847, he had served as governor of the Cape Colony in South Africa, where the city of Durban was named after him.

15

Trim the Gardener

THERE'S PROBABLY MORE THAN ONE WOMAN, slave or free, who made eyes at John Trim. About 40 when slavery peaked and then crashed, he was free, self-employed, unattached, dabbling in real estate … You could say "most eligible bachelor" and you might not be far wrong. He would have been a catch.

He owned a place at Côte-St-Catherine (Outremont) with his friends the Moores, Henry and Margaret. The house was no palace, but it stood on a really large lot, like a farm lot, planted with fruit trees. They'd paid cash for it too, 600 livres ($100), when they bought it in April 1796. Then in the summer of 1798 (the year Charlotte had started the slave "revolt"), he moved back to town. For $350, paid off over five years, he and Henry Moore's wife, Margaret Plauvier, bought an old wooden house on the east side of St Augustin Street on a lot backing onto the property of the Récollet priests. Henry Moore had rented that same house for a year before the three of them moved up to Côte-St-Catherine. And in May

John Trim

1799, on his own this time, Trim bought a vacant lot in St Antoine Suburb for 170 livres ($28). So by 1800 he owned one property and a big chunk of two others.

He would have been a catch all right – or had Charlotte already claimed him? That might explain some puzzling things about her "revolt." Like, what kept her in town to face the music rather than run clear after she'd fled from her mistress Jane Cook? And if she'd stood twenty years as a Cook family slave, why did she have to run off in freezing February instead of biding her time till April or May or June?

Anybody who knows February in Montreal knows it's no time to make a run for it, with no money and no place to stay. Judith Gray and Manuel Allen, who followed her lead, had family to hold them. Charlotte had none – but a well-heeled lover who could give her shelter and get her a lawyer? Maybe.

All we know for sure is that John Trim and Charlotte married sometime between the late 1790s and September 25, 1808. That was the day Ann Ashley was baptised. She was the baby daughter of Robert Ashley and Margaret Pierce, a black couple who had moved to Montreal from Quebec City a couple of years earlier. Charlotte was a sponsor at the baptism, along with Margaret Plauvier and Alexander Valentine, and she gave her name as Charlotte Trim.

Charlotte and John Trim lived out their lives in that house on St Augustin Street. The old city walls were being torn down at the time, and St Augustin, which ran along the southwest wall, was broadened and renamed McGill Street. As late as 1813, Charlotte and John Trim's house was one of only five on that new street.

Someday, someone may dig up Trim's past. He was a little older than Charlotte when he surfaced in Montreal. The records usually refer to him as a gardener. From that, you'd think he was some poor Joe with a hoe, tending the flower beds of the rich. But the fact that he was buying up land, paying cash in some cases, suggests something else.

And here's another sign that he was no run-of-the-mill labourer. In 1805 and 1806, lawyer James Reid, the future chief justice of the Court of King's Bench, gave him two promissory notes (like post-dated cheques) "for value received," one for £220, the other for £233 4s, either of which would have been more than enough to buy Trim's house on McGill Street twice over.

How did he make his money? In the case of Reid's debt to him, at least part of it may have been payment for laying out gardens or orchards on Reid's east-end property. The fruit trees on the Côte-St-Catherine property give us another hint: he grew fruit and probably vegetables. But market gardening hardly seems like a big money-maker. John Pruyn, Rosalie Bonga's husband, grew fruit and vegetables, in the 1820s and never got rich. Unlike Trim, he never had land of his own; he leased it, in St Louis Suburb northeast of town, under a deal where his rent amounted to half of what he got for his produce over the year.

Now, Trim may have been more careful with his money than John Pruyn, but there had to be something else he was doing that gave him that extra cash, and it was probably his ham business. There's the odd reference to him now and then as a "dry salter" or "curer of hams." This seems to have been his specialty. In fact, at his death, seven hams found at his house were snapped up like prizes by friends and neighbours at a sale of his belongings.

Trim's prosperity was no secret. When in 1821 a dividing wall was built between his property and that of his neighbour Simon Clark, one of the workmen reported that Clark's son had instructed them to build it more than a foot inside Trim's property – because even if Trim lost a bit of land, "he is rich enough that it will hardly hurt him."

What with all that, you'd expect Trim, with Charlotte by his side, to cut quite a figure among blacks in Montreal. So he did, and the house on McGill Street was the closest thing to a black community centre.

There were blacks who boarded there. Robert Moore, for example, at different times a labourer, servant, and waiter, lived there for about six months in 1815, probably until his marriage to Sente Williams on November 4 that year. Trim was a witness at their wedding. Abraham Low was another who lived there around that time. He had served in the militia up around Quebec City during the War of 1812 before moving to Montreal at the end of 1814.

67

Then there was Catherine Guillet, William Wright's wife, a live-in servant of the Trims for fifteen years. In 1820, around the time she and her husband moved out, Jacob Abdella, a native of Malta, moved in. He stayed about three years. He married an African American, Mary Downing, in 1823 but she died just five months later. And after William Wright died, Abdella married Catherine Guillet in Notre Dame Church in 1826.

Trim was a witness at William Wright's funeral, as he was at the baptisms, weddings, and funerals of many other black Montrealers. He was there, of course, at the burials of his old friends Henry Moore and his wife Margaret Plauvier, who had shared the house on McGill Street. Moore had died there in 1803, supposedly at the age of 42. His widow was said to be 80 when she died in September 1827.

Mary Ann Drummond from Jamaica was another in his circle. Trim and William Wright had stood witness at her wedding to Jacob Grant on August 8, 1815. The least that can be said about her is that she had staying power. She lost her husband, a waiter on the steamboats to Quebec, in 1841, but she lived another thirty-five years, never remarrying and with no children to help her out. A widow had to be pretty hardy and resourceful to go it alone in those days, when there were no government old age pensions and no social welfare benefits of any kind. For practical reasons, most widows didn't stay widows long.

Mary Ann Drummond was definitely resourceful: In September 1829 it was she, not her husband, who had bought their house and paid £150 for it, cash! It was a two-storey wooden house on St Constant near Mignonne Street (de Bullion near de Maisonneuve). The money probably came from her laundry business. After her husband's death, she survived by renting out one floor of her house. Jean François, a cook from Haiti, was her tenant right through the 1840s.

Then she lost everything in a fire that swept through town on July 8, 1852. It broke out in a building on St Lawrence Street: "Within half an hour a hundred houses were on fire. They were generally the dwellings of poor artizans and laborers, and it was a heart-rending spectacle to see the poor people gathering their few household goods together, and carrying them perhaps to some place where the fire reached them a few minutes after, perhaps to a place of safety."

16 July 1838

Negro waiter on board the "British America" Steamer

Like this unidentified man sketched aboard the steamer *British America* in 1838, Jacob Grant, Mary Ann Drummond's husband, worked as a waiter on the steamboats sailing between Montreal and Quebec.

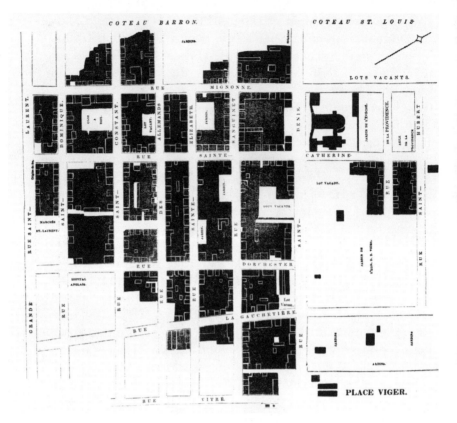

La Minerve of July 15, 1852, published this map showing (in black) the area
swept by the fire of July 8 which destroyed Mary Ann Drummond's house
and many others.

The fire razed everything from St Lawrence east to St Denis, and
from Mignonne down to Craig (St Antoine), except for the odd
stone building like the Montreal General Hospital on Dorchester
at St Dominique. In a flash, Mary Ann Drummond's house and
hundreds of others were turned into a vacant lot.

In one of those weird jokes that fate likes to play, after the fire
she went to live with the Ashes, Joseph and Lucinda. That's where
she was in the early 1860s anyway, in the east-end St James Ward.
Joseph Ash and his wife were among the many African Americans
who had fled to Canada after the Fugitive Slave Law of 1850 turned
slave catchers loose on the free states of the North and opened the
door to the kidnapping and enslavement of free blacks.

When Joseph Ash died in 1863, his wife remarried, and Mary Ann Drummond found refuge at the Ladies' Benevolent Institution on Berthelet Street (Ontario Street), where she died of old age on February 18, 1876. She was buried in the institution's plot in Mount Royal Cemetery.

These were some of Trim's friends and acquaintances, many of whom lived on long after his death. The love of his life did not. Charlotte died on September 20, 1823. She was 61, so they said. He never forgot her, though he might have been trying hard to when he took up with Fleurie Deniger. She was a white girl, only 16. Tongues must have wagged! Trim, about 70 then, and Deniger had a child: Mary Ann Shuter Trim. She was born on April 6, 1825, and named after the wife of one of Trim's white friends, merchant Joseph Shuter.

A psychiatrist could have a field day trying to figure out what made Trim tick. He certainly seems to have been caught up in the idea of his own end. You may think Fleurie Deniger was just an old man's fling, but there was more to it than that.

Look at it this way. He's a successful entrepreneur, with the real estate to prove it. In September 1808 he and the widow Margaret Plauvier had sold the property at Côte-St-Catherine which he and Henry Moore had bought in 1796. That left him with the house on McGill Street and the lot in St Antoine Suburb which he had picked up in 1799. But then he had acquired more land. In April 1809 he had bought a sliver of land in St Antoine Suburb for 102 livres, paid in cash. It was so small it might have done as a garden patch, not much else, but Trim was probably thinking ahead. Sure enough, five years later, for £100, he bought the lot next to it – a proper lot with a house and stable on it. It ran along Cemetery Street (de la Cathédrale). Then in July 1818 he added to his McGill Street property, buying an adjoining lot there too. It cost him £110, which he paid cash.

These were his holdings at the time Charlotte died. But with her gone, what was the point? You don't buy land just to buy land. He'd be gone soon enough himself, he couldn't take it with him, and he had nobody to pass it on to. Looks as if he badly wanted an heir. It also looks as if he wanted to make sure that no Trim heir would want for anything.

So he took up with Fleurie Deniger, and the birth of their daughter Mary Ann in the spring of 1825 gave him an heir. By the following winter, he and Deniger had decided to marry. They struck a deal. If Trim died before her, as was likely, she'd get a one-time payment of £10, plus £24 a year for life. But if she remarried, she kissed the money goodbye and it would be up to her new husband to support her.

There was nothing unusual about this, except that few blacks bothered to draw up a prenuptial agreement, or "marriage articles" as they were called. Most blacks, when they married, had little or no assets, though some acquired property later on. Before Trim, the only other black Montrealers who had signed a marriage contract were shoemaker Narcisse Coudrin and Violet Jones, in the spring of 1807. He'd come from New Orleans, after France sold the Louisiana territory to the United States in 1803, and she was from Leicester, Massachusetts.

Their contract was in French, and since she didn't understand a word, Coudrin's black friend Joseph François – who farmed up at Saint-Eustache, owned 128 ¼ arpents (about 45 ha), bought and paid for in 1802 – interpreted for her. Coudrin's assets at the time may have boiled down to little more than the tools of his trade, but he hired two apprentices that year, white boys, so business and prospects must have been good.

One interesting point about Trim's marriage contract is that he made sure Mary Ann's rights would be protected after his death. Even though she'd been born before the marriage, she would have the same inheritance rights as any "legitimate" kids he might have with Deniger. In the words of the contract:

The issue of the said Fleurie Deniger being by the said John Trim prior to the said Intended Marriage, shall be held and considered as fully entitled to all rights, claims & pretentions as well in the Estate of the said John Trim as in the Estate of the said Fleurie Deniger, equally with the Issue of any there may be by & subsequent to the said Intended Marriage.

Trim and Deniger were married on the following April 2. Maybe he had hopes that they'd have a son to carry on the Trim name. No such luck. They had two more children in the next three years, but both were girls: Henriette, born on May 8, 1827, and Charlotte, on August 9, 1829.

All the while he kept buying up land in St Antoine Suburb. In

July 1827 it was a house on Janvier Street (Lagauchetière between Mountain and Peel) for which he paid 1,500 livres. At a sheriff's sale in February 1828, he picked up another lot that backed onto his Janvier Street property, for £55. Then on September 2, 1829, for £275, he bought a property on St Antoine Street – a big lot that included a house, stables, a shed and a well.

Trim and his family didn't move to any of these new locations, but in a will he made out on December 7, 1829, he ordered that the McGill Street house be sold at his death and that his family move to one of his houses in St Antoine Suburb. He asked to be buried "at the old burying ground of this City alongside of his first wife Charlotte." He named three white men as his executors: merchants Joseph Shuter and William Forsyth, and grocer Nicholas Peter Mathias Kurczyn.

Trim was not done yet. He dictated a new will in the fall of 1831, repeating his wish to be buried beside Charlotte but dropping the requirement that his family move from McGill Street. Mistrusting his wife's abilities to manage things, or perhaps worried that if his daughters married their husbands might squander their inheritance, he left all his properties to his "lawfully begotten" grandchildren; his daughters had only the "usufruct" (the use, the interest on the revenues from the properties) during their lifetimes.

In other words, his daughters could live in his houses, but the houses would belong to any "legitimate" children they might have. And if there were no grandchildren, the use of the properties was to go to two of his white connections; and at their death, the properties were to be sold, the proceeds going to the poor of Montreal. Trim again named three white executors: Forsyth, Kurczyn, and the Connecticut-born merchant Jacob DeWitt, who was a Reform member of the Assembly. (Only Kurczyn accepted.)

In an addition to his will, on February 9, 1832, he asked his three executors, along with "my reverend friend" John Bethune, rector of Christ Church, to act as guardians of his children. Oh, and he specifically said: "I desire that my wife Flavie Deniger shall have no controul whatsoever over the property or person of either one or another of my said Children." Cutting her out of the administration of his estate was one thing; denying her the right to raise her own kids seems outrageous – what you might expect from a crochety old man – and that part of his will was ignored.

But at least Trim had made some arrangements for the disposal of his property instead of leaving everything up in the air. Wills, like marriage contracts, were not common among black Montrealers. One of the few to make out a will was the widow Marie Élizabeth Charles, at Saint-Philippe-de-Laprairie, across the St Lawrence, who had done so as far back as 1799; she also made out a new one in 1803 when she was living downriver at Saint-Sulpice.

Then there was Pierre Bonga, the North West Company interpreter, who had dictated a will on a rare visit to town in 1815. He might have spared himself the trouble. When he died out in the field, in what is now Minnesota, in 1831, no one knew or remembered about his will. Everything ended up going to his kids, more or less as he'd wanted; it just took a lot of needless expense, paperwork, and time. For instance, they paid £11 to his two widowed sisters, Charlotte and Rosalie, in Montreal to buy out any claim they might have to his estate. But under his forgotten will, Charlotte and Rosalie had no such claim.

As for Trim, with his last will signed and sealed, he bought one last house in St Antoine Suburb, this one on St Marguerite Street (Ste-Cécile), on September 19, 1832. He got it at auction for £96.

That fall, a young man called Paola Brown passed through town, seeking donations for the black refugee settlement of Colbornesburgh in Upper Canada. On November 20, he held a public meeting at John Bruce's English and Classical Academy. Trim couldn't have missed it – it was next door to his house. They sang something called the "African Appeal." Among the voices raised in song that night, you might imagine Charlotte's calling to him, like a siren, from the coast of Guinea or wherever her spirit had flown. Trim died two months later, on January 26, 1833, at 78. He was laid to rest beside her, as he wished, in the old Protestant burial ground.

A sale of his household goods on February 10 brought in £53 3s 10d. Among the buyers were James Rollings, Alexander Grant, Jarrad Banks, and shoemaker John Patton who, four months earlier, had married Ann Ashley, the girl at whose baptism Charlotte had acted as a sponsor twenty-five years before. Several whites were there too, including Dr Daniel Arnoldi, who had probably tended Trim in his last illness. Rollings, a barber, was obviously setting up house. The biggest buyer there, he picked up furniture, dishes, appliances, cutlery, and engravings, clothing, not to mention a huge slab of bacon and a cow. Grant, a clothes cleaner, bought a big copper kettle and other odds and ends, including a sword. Arnoldi picked up "a large Siringe."

Trim left three young daughters – three heiresses. How valuable were the assets he left? When his McGill Street property, by then a vacant lot, was sold on January 8, 1850, to pay off a judgment against his estate, it went for £1,100. And that was only one of his properties.

Less than five months after his death, his young widow married widower Robert Moore, Trim's former lodger, giving up her right to the sums mentioned in her marriage contract. And Trim's three girls grew up. We'll leave them to it.

—

16

AGENT OF THE
Liberator

PEOPLE WERE DROPPING LIKE FLIES in the streets in John
Trim's last summer. It's a wonder the cholera didn't get him, old as
he was, or one of his daughters, young as they were. It came in at
Quebec on the ships full of immigrants. It started in June and
spread through the river towns and up around the Great Lakes.
Thousands died. It had eased some by midsummer when Paola
Brown travelled down Lake Ontario, down the St Lawrence to
Montreal and on to Quebec, but death must have crossed and re-
crossed his path many times. The summer of 1832 was a good time
to go that way if you were looking to die. Otherwise, it was the worst
time. It's a wonder Paola Brown was spared.

He wasn't after dying. He was after money, maybe a little respect.
Officially, he was collecting funds to build a church and school at
a settlement of black American refugees called Colbornesburgh.
Ever heard of Colbornesburgh in Upper Canada? No, not many
people have. Some have heard of Wilberforce and Buxton or the

Elgin Settlement, and the Dawn Settlement and Oro Township and places like that, but Colbornesburgh always draws a blank.

Some people have heard of Paola Brown. He was an American who turned up in Upper Canada in the late 1820s. What they mostly know him for is one double-barrelled speech he published in 1851 called *Address Intended to Be Delivered in the City Hall, Hamilton, February 7, 1851 on the Subject of Slavery*. The reason for the "intended to" in the title is that he had barely launched into his long speech – it ran to 64 printed pages – when some joker killed the gaslights in Hamilton city hall, and that was the end of that.

In his speech, Brown railed like a preacher against the brutality of American slavery and against the whites who supported it – ministers, some of them. He spoke of the need for blacks to stop bowing and scraping, and to stand together and strike without flinching, when they would see the path to freedom open before them. He invoked the mercy of God upon the oppressors, but prophesied that blacks would one day be avenged and whites would be sorry.

"Slave-holders," he wrote, "I call God, I call Angels, I call Men, to witness, that your destruction is at hand, and will be speedily consumated, unless you repent." Here are a few other examples:

[On the day of reckoning]
The south wants slaves, and wants us for their slaves, but some of them will curse the day they ever saw us, as true as the sun ever shone in its meridian splendour. My color will root some of them out of the very face of the earth; they shall have enough of making slaves of, and butchering, and murdering us in the manner which they have. Now, some may say that I, being a black man, wish these things to occur. I say, if these things do not occur in their proper time, it is because the world in which we live does not exist, and we are deceived with regard to its existence.

[On interracial marriage]
I would not give a pinch of snuff to be married to any white person, I ever saw in all the days of my life. And I do say it, that the black man, or man of color, who will leave his own color, (provided he can get one who is good for anything) and marry a white woman, to be a double slave to her, just because she is white, ought to be treated by her as he surely will be, viz., as a nigger!

77

[On slavery and ignorance]
Do you suppose that one man of good sense and learning would submit himself, his father, mother, wife, and children, to be slaves to a wretched man like himself, who, instead of compensating him for his labor, chains, handcuffs, and beats him and family almost to death, leaving life enough in them, however, to work for and call him – master! No, no: he would cut his devilish throat from ear to ear; and well do slave-holders know it. The bare name of educating the colored people, scares our oppressors almost to death ...

Some people know the speech better than they know the man. One historian who read it, misled by Brown's first name, gave him a sex change and called him a "remarkably large-lunged young woman." (We think of Paola as an Italian girl's name pronounced Pow-la, but Brown's name was probably pronounced Pey-ola.) He was no woman and he wasn't young either, by 1851.

Not many Americans know of Brown or his speech. But some of them know David Walker, the Boston tailor, son of a North Carolina slave, and his famous *Appeal to the Coloured Citizens of the World.* Three editions of it were published in 1829–30, more than twenty years before Brown's speech. The *Appeal* is an antislavery classic, which you can still find in bookstores. Here is a sampling:

[On the day of reckoning]
The whites want slaves, and want us for their slaves, but some of them will curse the day they ever saw us. As true as the sun ever shone in its meridian splendor. My colour will root some of them out of the very face of the earth. They shall have enough of making slaves of, and butchering, and murdering us in the manner which they have. No doubt some may say that I write with a bad spirit and that I being a black, wish these things to occur. Whether I write with a bad or a good spirit, I say if these things do not occur in their proper time, it is because of the world in which we live does not exist, and we are deceived with regard to its existence.

[On interracial marriage]
I would not give a *pinch of snuff* to be married to any white person I ever saw in all the days of my life. And I do say it, that the black man, or man of colour, who will leave his own colour (provided he can get one, who is good for any thing) and marry a white woman, to be a

double slave to her, just because she is *white*, ought to be treated by her as he surely will be, viz: as a NIGER!!!!

[On slavery and ignorance]
Do you suppose one man of good sense and learning would submit himself, his father, mother, wife and children, to be slaves to a wretched man like himself, who, instead of compensating him for his labours, chains, handcuffs, and beats him and family almost to death, leaving life enough in them, however, to work for, and call him master? No! no! he would cut his devilish throat from ear to ear; and well do slaveholders know it. The bare name of educating the coloured people, scares our cruel oppressors almost to death.

As you can see, Brown's big speech of 1851 was cribbed from Walker's *Appeal*. The line calling on "slave-holders" to repent, that's Walker's too, only he wrote it: "O Americans! Americans!! I call God – I call angels – I call men, to witness, that your DESTRUCTION *is at hand*, and will be speedily consummated unless you REPENT." Brown did make slight changes to Walker's text and added a little material about Canada and about the Fugitive Slave Law of 1850 to make it sound up to date and to make up for sections of Walker's work that he had to drop because they were outdated or otherwise unsuitable.

One man who saw through the scam right away was Thomas Smallwood, an ex-slave from Maryland living in Toronto. In the same year that Brown published his speech, Smallwood came out with an account of his work on the Underground Railroad. Apart from a few quotations and some bits in his preface, it was entirely written by him, he said, and he felt obliged to say so:

From the fact that I have seen a book for sale in this city [Toronto] purporting to be a production of Mr Paola Brown, of Hamilton; but the fact is, it is a copy, almost verbatim, of a book known as "Walker's Appeal," written by a coloured man of that name. And in order to shew the reader more plainly the diabolical attempt of P. Brown to rob the memory of an estimable man, of one of the boldest productions against slavery ever written and published in America, I will give the preface to a brief sketch of the life and character of David Walker, together with the sketch itself, written by Henry Highland Garnet, and published with the second edition of the book referred to in 1848.

Hence it will be seen that Mr Brown is not honest in putting forth a work like the one in question in his name and as his own production.

Some people might say that in "borrowing" Walker's words, Brown was paying tribute to him. Maybe so. He had to think the book was pretty hot to copy it out and make it his own. But he obviously counted that no one in his audience knew Walker's powerful words (according to him, 210 people of Hamilton had signed the invitation for him to speak). He never mentioned Walker, never hinted that his speech was anything but his own; and many of the changes he had made were simply to mask the true identity of the author as someone living in the United States and writing in 1829.

You could spend hours analysing all the changes Brown made to Walker's text. But it's Montreal we're concerned with, so his cribbing is of interest only in that as it gives us a fix on the man who visited the city in that terrible year, collecting for Colbornesburgh.

Obviously it tells us that he wasn't above putting one over on people. And that he was proud of himself, publishing "his" speech rather than hiding it away. And the name under which he published it – Paola Brown, Esq.! Esq. (short for Esquire) was tacked onto the names of men of standing: professionals, public figures, men of means, which Brown was not. Was he just putting on the dog, or was this his way of claiming to be a somebody in the face of a world that too often looked on him and blacks generally as nobodys?

One other thing this speech tells us, of course, is that he had a way with words. There weren't many Canadians, black or white, who could go through a 20-year-old book with a fine-toothed comb and copy it out by hand while making all the fiddly changes needed to pass it off as a new one.

So this was a foolhardy, flim-flam man from Upper Canada with above-average reading and writing skills (who might have rated an Esq. if he'd been white) who defied death to travel down to Montreal in the cholera year.

The previous February 20, a small group of black refugees, most of them from Ohio and Illinois, and now living in Woolwich Township near Guelph, had met to plan the building of a church and school and also to give a name to the place they were setting up. It was at his suggestion, Brown claimed, that they decided to call the place Colbornesburgh, for crusty old Sir John Colborne, lieutenant governor of Upper Canada. That was smart PR. The walls of church and school were raised on June 26, and for help in completing the work, the settlers counted on God, said Brown, and on "the kind christian aid of our former friends, and those who may by our perseverance and success, feel favourably disposed in our cause."

He left on his fundraising trip probably in late July, and by August 8 he was in Brockville. After passing through Montreal, he reached Quebec by September 8. There he presented a petition to Governor General Lord Aylmer, explaining his purpose and asking Aylmer to add his name to the subscription list, "with such a pecuniary consideration as to your Excellency may seem fit."

Brown got good write-ups in the newspapers. You had to be impressed – a lone man on a selfless errand in such a dreadful year. Besides publishing the text of his petition, the *Quebec Gazette* reported that he showed "a warm zeal in the cause of his brethren."

Just before leaving Quebec at the end of September, he sent a copy of the petition and his "Circular Address, to the Free People of Color Throughout the United States" to the *Liberator*, William Lloyd Garrison's abolitionist newspaper in Boston. It published both documents on its front page on October 27. In his circular, Brown explained what Colbornesburgh was about; he urged downtrodden American blacks to move to Upper Canada and reported: "In Quebec I received much encouragement from Lord Aylmer, the Governor in Chief, from the Reverend the Clergy of all denominations, and from influential inhabitants."

At the beginning of October, on his return to Montreal, where he spent two months, the *Montreal Gazette* and the *Canadian Courant* endorsed his efforts. "We recommend his cause to the inhabitants of Montreal," the *Courant* said, "and hope that the appeal, which he intends to make in a few days, will not be made in vain."

So how much money did he raise? He never gave a figure. In the *Liberator* he did say he had been "very successful." And in early December, when he passed through Brockville on his way back to Colbornesburgh, a paper there reported: "We understand from him that he has received enough to finish both the Church and School-house commenced in that settlement."

Brown had picked up more than money. A bachelor when he came down, he had a wife on his return. He married Catherine Lloyd in Montreal on October 27. That must have taken some fast footwork, considering that he had nipped through Montreal on his way down to Quebec and returned to the city less than a month before his wedding.

He was married "by Licence from His Excellency Mathew Lord Aylmer." That saved time. Normally the banns had to be read in church, which meant announcing the intended wedding three Sundays running. Brown had also won the support of Alexander Grant, a black Montrealer whose abilities as a writer and speaker were at least equal to his own. Grant was a witness at Brown's wedding, along with Jarrad Banks, another Montrealer.

With money raised, a wife, and helpful new friends, could Brown wish for more? Well, on November 24, before he left Montreal, his name began appearing in the *Liberator* as its representative in Upper Canada. One big feather in his cap. Brown's last public function in Montreal was a meeting he called for the evening of November 20 at John Bruce's English and Classical Academy on McGill Street, next door to John Trim's, to thank all those who had helped him.

It was a little more than a month after he'd gone when word got around that he'd snowed everybody. He was put on the spot on January 11, at a meeting he called in Hamilton to discuss further fundraising plans for Colbornesburgh. People naturally wanted to know how much money he had raised on his trip and where it had gone. He couldn't say, or wouldn't.

They scolded and groused. They got so worked up, they went public and told the press: "We consider him an unfit person to be entrusted with such contributions, as he has not applied them to the purposes for which they were intended, and that we publish him to the world as an impostor." The *Canadian Wesleyan*, a Methodist church magazine, chimed in calling him "an impostor, collecting money for which he has not accounted."

In Montreal, the *Courant* carried a report on the Hamilton meeting and threw in its own two cents' worth:

When Mr Brown was in this City, we had reason to fear his conduct was not such as became the representative of the Colbornesburgh Settlement of colored people. His breath often smelt of intoxicating liquors in the forenoon, his habits were little marked by economy, his verbose conversation on religious subjects, and his importunity, appeared too urgent for real merit. After advising with friends on the subject, we stated our doubts to Mr Brown, and proposed that he should submit

Alexander Grant and Jarrad Banks witnessed Paola Brown's wedding to Catherine Lloyd at St Andrew's Presbyterian Church on St Pierre Street in 1832.

his subscription list to the scrutiny of two respectable gentlemen, who should take charge of the sum collected, and deposit it in the Montreal Bank. This he refused to do, but promised to forward for insertion in the *Courant*, a statement of his collections and disbursements. Our readers will now perceive the reason for his so refusing.

Now they tell us!

The *Courant* had never breathed a word about its suspicions before. It had recommended Brown to the charity of Montrealers and never cautioned people against him while he was there. Cholera, and now this! A bad year had just got worse.

For black refugees in Upper Canada, it was even worse than Montrealers knew. Israel Lewis, agent for Wilberforce colony, was in the same hot water as Brown. A founder of that black settlement in 1829, he had gone fundraising in the United States but had pocketed or spent most of the money. The Wilberforce managers sacked him and notified the press, but he wouldn't quit. In fact, he'd been in this kind of trouble in 1831, and he kept it up for years. He was special, Lewis was. Montreal would get a taste of him later.

The *Liberator* reproduced the bad news about Brown in its edition of February 23, 1833, but it went on listing him as an agent right through to the end of the year, as if nothing had happened.

As for Colbornesburgh, it just died. Who ever heard of it?

17

The Valentines' Day

ALEX VALENTINE HAD AN ESTATE. Put it that way, it sounds so grand, as if he owned a plantation in Trinidad or a ten-chimney mansion on the slopes of Mount Royal. But, all it means is that he left stuff behind when he died. Like his house. That was the main thing. No. 7 St Charles Borromée (Clark Street). It was built of squared logs, with a shed out back. He'd bought it for 3,000 livres (about $500) in 1803, around the time he left Judge Davidson's service to work as a carter. He and carpenter Augustin Labadie had gone halves on it. Then in 1804, with a loan from the judge, he'd bought out his white carpenter friend. It was all paid off by the end of 1814.

For twenty-six years he and his wife Catherine Mayson lived there, renting out rooms to make ends meet. When he died on November 18, 1829, Catherine Mayson could thank her lucky stars she had the house. Not that she planned to go on living there. On the day of his funeral she moved in with Mary Ann Drummond and her husband Jacob Grant, who'd just bought a place on St Constant

Street (de Bullion). But the house at 7 St Charles Borromée was Catherine's meal ticket; going on 70, she had no other means of support. "She wishes the House to be let immediately," said George D. Arnoldi, the notary who helped her settle her husband's estate, "the rent to be paid punctually every Month that she may pay for her Lodging and Board."

You know how sometimes when you're riding the bus home at night, a light in a window catches your eye as you pass. And without thinking, you pry into somebody's life for a second, see a TV screen flickering, the glow of a lamp, knick-knacks on a shelf, shadows moving in a room that looks golden through the curtains.

You get a peek like that at Alex Valentine's life if you look at the list, made up at his widow's request, of all that their house contained. There wasn't much there; still it was more than she needed, boarding at Mary Ann Drummond's. Planning to sell most of it, she had Arnoldi draw up an inventory. Two trusted friends – John Patton, the shoemaker, and William Goodrich, a hairdresser born in Barbados to a slave and a white businessman – were there to price everything. Here's what they found:

	£	s	d
Nineteen Plates	2	2	6
Fifteen tea cups & four saucers, Coffee Pot Cream Pot & sugar Dish	–	3	9
A Basin & Lot of crockery ware	–	2	6
Two Lanthorns five jars &c	–	4	–
A lot of Glass ware	–	–	7
Four pitchers tea Pot & case Bottle	–	2	6
Ten puter Spoons	–	–	3
Two earthen Dishes Canister &c	–	1	–
A Large Jar	–	3	–
Two Kettles a Lanthorn & rat trap	–	3	–
Eleven Pictures & frames	–	3	–
a lot of Bottles	–	1	3
a Chest of Drawers	–	10	–
a lot of tin ware &c	–	1	–
Two Looking Glasses	–	15	–
Three Trays	–	2	–
a Blue Chest	–	–	3
a Mattress & two feather pillows	1	5	0

a lot of old clothes	–	–	6
Two large trunks	–	15	–
Two cloth coats	1	–	–
Two Surtouts	1	5	–
Three pr pantaloons	–	10	–
Three vests	–	7	–
a trunk	–	5	–
Nine chairs	–	2	6
Knives & forks &c	–	2	–
a lot of Tools	–	1	3
Two Saws	–	2	6
Three Iron Pots & a tea Kettle	–	7	6
Dog Irons shovel tongs & bellows	–	3	–
two Smoothing Irons & a lot of Sundries	–	2	–
a Small table	–	1	–
a Double Stove & pipes	2	10	–
A cherry Table	–	5	–
a feather bed four blankets, bolster & two counterpanes	1	5	–
a Bedstead & two water casks	–	6	–
a tub & pr of Sabeau	–	–	7½

It came to £13 11s 5½d all told. The estate sale took place on November 26 and brought in £8 2s 7d. Catherine Mayson had pulled from the sale the things she wanted to keep:

A Bedstead Feather Bed, 1 Bolster 2 Pillows &c
A Chest of drawers
A Small table
4 Chairs
A Small Looking Glass
A Tea Canister
A Candlestick
A Tea Kettle
A tea Pot Sugar dish & Milk Pot
2 teacups &c
Two Plates
2 Glass tumblers
A Large Earthen Crock
A small Lantern
A Mouse trap Iron Skillet

This and her clothes were all that she owned. And the house. In March 1831, she mortgaged it to Dr Daniel Arnoldi because she owed him £12 10s for "medical attendance during several years past." Then she sold it, on May 1, 1834, to his son George D., the notary. He was to pay her £20 a year till she died. She lasted nine years. Since she and Valentine never had kids, January 28, 1843, was the end of the line. ➤

18

Messing with
Dragons

☞

IF BLACK PEOPLE AS A WHOLE counted for something in Montreal in the 1830s – and there are signs that they did – Alexander Grant was a big part of it. Why a man would leave New York City and move to Montreal, God knows. But that's what Grant did in 1830, when he was 29. And what's one of the first things a New Yorker with smarts does when he sets up shop in a new place? He advertises.

That's what Grant does. "Economy and Elegance" his ad in the paper said, "Old Garments cleansed and made to look as well as new, by Alexander Grant, from New York, at No. 80 St Paul Street nearly opposite Mr Rollings, Barber. Orders will be received at Mr Rollings' Barber, St Paul Street."

So he's a dry cleaner or laundryman or something – that's it? Well, they called it scouring. He was a scourer. But don't go judging a man by what he does for a living. You can't confuse a living with a life. A living is something you do for money; a life is something else – spent or given.

The look of Montreal as it was when Alexander Grant arrived in town is captured in this 1830 view of St James Street, looking west from Place d'Armes. The first building on the right is the original Bank of Montreal. Next to it, across St François-Xavier Street, is St James Street Methodist Church.

From May 22, 1830, Alexander Grant made his presence known. He was the first black person to advertise in a Montreal newspaper.

ECONOMY AND ELEGANCE.

OLD GARMENTS cleansed and made to look AS WELL AS NEW, by ALEXANDER GRANT, *from New-York*, at No. 80 St. Paul Street nearly opposite MR. ROLLINGS, Barber.

☞ Orders will be received at MR. ROLLINGS' *Barber*, St. Paul Street.

22d May, 1830.   7—am, w.

In fact, there's more to Grant's newspaper ad than meets the eye. For one thing, it was probably the first time black barber James Rollings had seen his name in print. And another thing, it was the first time a black had advertised his services in a Montreal newspaper. Go ahead and look – you won't find any earlier.

So "I'm here," his ad says. Then what? It's all a bit of a blur for a couple of years. He came with his wife Celia, Celia Farley, though you don't hear much of her. But it looks as if James Grantham lived with them, at least for a while, maybe up to the time he married in 1835. Grantham was a bit younger than Grant, an Englishman, who for years was the only black tobacconist (wholesale and retail) in town.

The fact that Grant was a witness at Paola Brown's wedding in 1832 may give us a hint that he was into black causes (Brown having been fundraising at the time). But it's 1833 before we really get a fix on Grant, the summer after he bought that sword at the sale of John Trim's things.

In London, British members of parliament, inspired by the old antislavery champion William Wilberforce, who was on his death-bed (he died July 29), were pushing hard to get a bill passed to abolish slavery in the West Indies. Grant called a meeting of the "Coloured brethren" of Montreal at his home on St Paul Street for July 23 to hash it out.

Twelve black men took part, counting Grant. It took some doing. Not all of them were the best of friends. Peter Dago and Jacob Abdella, for instance, had had a big blowup three years earlier when Abdella had ended up jabbing Dago pretty hard with a fork. But Grant brought them together (and maybe Celia hid the cutlery, just to be sure). Being a New Yorker, he knew about blowing your horn and using the media, so they put out a press release saying they had adopted these resolutions:

1st. – That as British subjects we duly appreciate the blessings of the constitution under which we have the happiness to live – a constitution which will ever be dear to our hearts – a constitution, which the march of *chastened* intellect has stamped with its highest approbation, and which is the envy and admiration of the civilized world.

2nd. – That as men and as christians, we must naturally feel anxious that the sacred blessings we enjoy should be extended to the habitable globe; consequently we are *peculiarly* anxious that our brethren of the "British West India Colonies," should fully participate in the glorious privileges we are so justly proud of.

3rd. – We, therefore, contemplate with *intense anxiety*, the progress of the bill which His Majesty's Ministers have introduced into Parliament, for the "Total Abolition" of slavery in the West Indies; and we wish it complete success, conceiving it to be the harbinger of *light* and *life* and *liberty*, to all of our fellow brethren and subjects; and we hereby most respectfully tender to His Majesty's Ministers, and to all the friends of humanity, our heartfelt acknowledgments for their benevolent and God like exertions.

They all put their names to it (most with an X), Grant first. The others were Jacob Abdella, Jarrad Banks, John Broome, Peter Dago, Jacob Grant (no relation), Louis Greene, Anthony Hinksman, Abraham Low, John Russell, Joseph Shaw, and Thomas H. Smith.

The abolition law passed that August and was scheduled to come into effect on August 1, 1834. Of course, twelve black men meeting in Montreal, even if they'd been the Twelve Apostles, weren't going to make much difference to what happened in the British parliament. But that isn't the point.

The point is, they were speaking to the hometown crowd, like Grant when he advertised his scouring business. It was the first time that black Montrealers had held a formal meeting and issued a public statement on a public issue. And it wasn't about themselves or some neighbourhood squabble. It was about abolishing slavery in the West Indies, where some of them had connections. "We're here," they were signalling, "but we've got our eye on the world," in case anyone figured that blacks couldn't see beyond their own backyard.

That's the kind of thing Grant was up to. So how come nobody's heard of him?

Well, he didn't stay around long – only eight years. But that's not it. One reason is that when people today look back at the Quebec of the 1830s, or Lower Canada as it was called, they see white and nothing else. They get wrapped up in the old news of white-on-white violence (Patriotes vs Tories, French vs English, reformers vs bureaucrats – two sides but with many different labels) that bubbled for years before boiling over in the Rebellions of 1837–38, when a lot of people died for nothing.

Another reason why Grant is forgotten is racism. Racism in Montreal was not upfront like in the United States. It was quiet and lawless, you might say, because nobody talked about it much and there were no racist laws and no laws against racism. In the "free" American states, you had segregation, with laws that said blacks couldn't marry whites, couldn't testify against whites in court, and couldn't vote in elections. Even churches boxed blacks off in "negro pews." There was none of this in Montreal, and blacks did marry whites, did take whites to court, and did vote. There were no hard rules to fight against. Only attitudes.

If you've ever had to fight an attitude, you know it's not like fighting a law. You can't take on a state of mind(lessness) the way you can fight against official segregation or apartheid. It's one thing to fight the dragon when it's out in the open. You can slay it with your sword, and you've got the body to prove it's dead. But when the dragon is a bad idea in people's heads, how can you tell it's a dragon? How can you even convince people it's there? To kill it, you've got to get inside people's heads and make them think. And there'll always be some who will say that there never was any dragon except in your head. That's what Grant was up against.

But back to that meeting in 1833. You see how pro-British those resolutions are? That wasn't the kind of language the British brass in Lower Canada was used to hearing. The contrast between pro-British blacks and anti-British whites was even heavier in 1834, the year the abolition law took hold.

In February that year, the Patriote majority in the Assembly, led by Louis-Joseph Papineau, rammed through their own resolutions – 92 in all, a long list of complaints. The government in Lower Canada, they insisted, should be redrawn along American lines; it should be more democratic, better suited to Canadians than the British system, with its king and lords and ladies and class distinctions. All spring, summer, and fall the Patriotes called meetings to rally public support and to dump on the Tories. The Tories called counter-meetings to damn the Patriotes as traitors. It went on like that until the elections in October.

While the whites were fixing for a fight, the blacks were in a party mood, preparing to celebrate the historic First of August. In Montreal, they booked the public hall upstairs in St Ann's Market (Place d'Youville).

Then the cholera stepped in. It wasn't as bad as in 1832, but it was still a killer. It's probably what hit the five black Montrealers who died that year – all in July and August. At just eight months

94

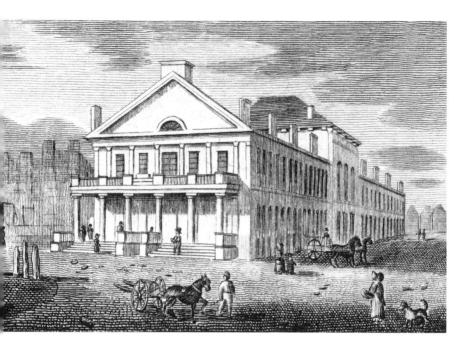

Black Montrealers met in the hall above St Ann's Market to celebrate the
coming into force of the British act abolishing slavery on August 1, 1834.
The market stood in what is now Place d'Youville.

old, Jacob Abdella Jr was the youngest and the first to go, on July 8.
He was the last of the three children of Jacob Abdella and Catherine Guillet; none of their kids made it to age two. Othello Keelings,
about 60, once a tenant of Catherine Guillet's, died on July 29;
John Pruyn's widow, Rosalie Bonga, in her fifties, died on July 30;
and Catherine Crowell, twice widowed, died on August 2 at the age
of 37, leaving William Fortune, her 16-year-old son from her first
marriage, to fend for himself. Servant John Broome and his wife
Jane Wilson didn't quite die but probably wished they had. Being
from the West Indies (she from Bermuda), they would have been
looking forward to the day of liberation. But on July 31, the eve of
the great day, their Mary died. She was their first child, all of one
and a half years old. If John Broome drank to freedom the next
day, his arm may have shaken as he raised the glass. And Jane Wilson never would forget that summer of death and freedom, you
can bet.

Finally, the big day dawned and the men gathered at St Ann's Market. John Patton, the shoemaker, opened the meeting with a psalm and a prayer. Alexander Grant gave the keynote speech, and then "the Brethren" trooped over to St George's Tavern on the waterfront for a dinner full of toasts and songs. The ships in the harbour hoisted their flags. "The day has at length come when England, and not America, is entitled to the undisputed honor of being 'the land of liberty,'" gloated the *Gazette*.

In his speech, Grant gushed over Britain for dealing "the death-blow to slavery all over the world," and he roasted the United States for its hypocrisy. While its 60-year-old Declaration of Independence proclaimed the equality of all men, and its people proudly sang of their country as the land of liberty, two million Americans languished in slavery, he said.

But he never breathed a word about parts of the British law which some abolitionists found hard to swallow – that slaves above the age of six were to continue working for their masters for a six-year period as "praedial apprentices" before being fully free; and that £20 million in compensation was to be paid – not to the slaves for their pain or to help them make a fresh start, but to the masters for their loss of human property. Grant wrapped up his speech with a call for "three hearty cheers for Old England, the true 'land of the brave, and the home of the free.'" Everybody cheered.

You would think that with their experience of slavery, blacks would have backed any call for freedom. And there were issues on which they and the Patriotes could see eye to eye. Reform of jury selection was one. Grant had brought the subject up in an open letter to "The Colored Brethren Residents of Montreal" in May 1834. There were privileges of citizenship, he said, which the laws "strictly entitle us to, such as serving on Juries &c. but which, from some unexplained cause have not been extended to us." There was no law barring blacks from jury duty, yet no black had ever served on a jury.

Here was Grant messing with the dragon, making people think about that, maybe for the first time. He could have shouted, "We know why no blacks are called for jury duty – it's because of all you racist pigs!" But then everybody would have tuned him out. So he blamed "some unexplained cause," leaving people to figure out the "unexplained" bit for themselves. He was smooth.

Maybe it was Jacob Grant, one of the "twelve apostles," who

brought the matter to his attention. In 1833, Jacob's name had been on the list of people who were qualified to sit on juries because of the property they owned; but he had never been called. (In fact, it was his wife Mary Ann Drummond, who should have been listed, because she had paid for their house. But she was a woman, and who'd ever heard of a woman on a jury!)

The *Vindicator*, a Patriote newspaper, picked up Alexander Grant's letter and used it to stick it to the Tories:

Being advocates for the extension of Civil Rights to all persons without difference of color or creed, we cannot but regret that Mr Grant's Brethren should have to complain of the partiality of public officers. As far as the Jury Law provides, there is *no distinction*. If the colored men are excluded it can be attributed only to those who are intrusted with the execution of the Law and of which officers the House of Assembly complain.

We repeat, the men of color, if qualified by property, have an equal right to be Jurors as any other of His Majesty's Subjects.

So there were grounds where blacks and Patriotes could meet. But the big stumbling block to their getting together was the spectre of slavery. The Patriotes raved about the United States as the home of free institutions; to blacks, it was the den of slavery. And it so happened that as the Patriotes began dropping hints that a U.S.–style revolution might be in order, Britain abolished slavery. Easy to see why blacks might figure: "What good is democracy to me? Monarchy is best." No wonder the *Vindicator*, while presenting Grant as "an intelligent, industrious, and humane man of colour," slipped in that he was "differing with us in politics."

It wasn't only in Montreal that blacks and white reformers were at odds. The same thing happened in Upper Canada. William Lyon Mackenzie, who would lead the rebellions there, deplored the fact in answering a questionnaire from the American Anti-Slavery Society in 1837. He said of the blacks in Upper Canada:

Nearly all of them are opposed to every species of reform in the civil institutions of the colony – they are so extravagantly loyal to the Executive that to the utmost of their power they uphold all the abuses of government and support those who profit by them ... I regret that an unfounded fear of a union with the United States on the part of the colored population should have induced them to oppose reform and free institutions in this colony, whenever they have had the power to do so. The apology I make for them in this matter is that they have not been educated as freemen.

The apology we can make for Mackenzie is that he was not black.

As a spokesman for Montreal's blacks, Alexander Grant warmed the hearts of the Tories with his praise for England. Here was proof, from the mouths of those who had known real oppression, that Britain was ... well ... Great. If blacks were all for British rule, what did the Patriotes have to complain about?

In the elections for Lower Canada's Assembly in October 1834, some whites tried to draw the blacks into their fight. The Patriotes' candidates for the two seats in the West Ward of Montreal (the west side of Old Montreal) were Papineau himself and city councillor Robert Nelson, a doctor who had trained under Dr Daniel Arnoldi.

Tory newspapers reported that at his nomination meeting, Nelson had really stuck his foot in it. In putting down Irish voters who claimed that only an Irishman could represent them, he was supposed to have said: "As well might our German fellow-citizens insist upon our nominating one of them, or I will go further and say that if we are to yield to the pretensions of the Irish, the *Niggers*, who are numerous likewise, would have an equal right to send one of their body to the House." Now there's a pretty kettle of fish! And Nelson couldn't plead that he didn't know the microphone was switched on, because microphones didn't exist in 1834.

After criticizing Nelson for the way he spoke of the Irish and Germans, the *Gazette* went on:

As to the coloured portion of our community, they are not so numerous nor so wealthy as the others we have mentioned, but they have never forfeited their right to a decent and proper regard for their feelings, by any set of misconduct. Here they are freemen, and fully entitled to the exercise of their privileges as British subjects in whatever way it may suit their inclination. The colour of the body can have no effect on the qualities of the mind, and the sons of Africa will ever receive in this Province, the respect that is their due, so long as they support the laws and the constitution which confers upon them all the blessings of British liberty. While they are persecuted almost to death by the free and independent citizens of America and debarred of their privileges, here they are really equal, and no doubt at the coming elections, such of them as have votes or influence, will show their disapproval of a party by whom they are contemned and despised, by voting against Dr Nelson.

The warning to blacks to hang with the Tories, or else, was none too subtle. Had there been signs that they were leaning the other way? Was the claim that "here they are really equal" meant as an answer to Grant's open letter of the previous spring, in which he had dared to suggest that some "unexplained cause" denied black people their full rights? Who knows? The Patriotes insisted that Nelson had never put down the Irish, Germans or blacks – it was all just sliming by those slime-bucket Tories.

Whatever the truth of the matter, it was the first time black Montrealers were acknowledged as a political force. In an election where every vote counted, especially on the greatly outnumbered Tory side, the Gazette had made a pitch for the black vote. But the Patriotes swept the province, and Nelson and Papineau both made it. Tensions between the Patriotes and Tories continued to mount, and they lent a political edge to what turned out to be the high point of Grant's career, the Betsy Freeman affair.

Betsy was a black teenager from the United States who accompanied her mistress on a trip to Montreal in the spring of 1836. The black grapevine hummed, and the question on everyone's mind was, Is that girl a servant or a slave? Grant heard that Betsy was a slave, that her mistress's husband, Ebenezer Marvin of Charlotte, North Carolina, was a slaveholder. To make sure, he called on Betsy, on Sunday, June 12, and she told him that, yes, she was a slave and wanted to leave Ann Gelston, her mistress, who had abused her. But where could she go, a 14-year-old girl in a strange country, without friends or work? Grant told her she could stay at his place and his wife would take care of her. Betsy went along.

The next day, Ann Gelston filed a complaint that Betsy had deserted her service. High Constable Benjamin Delisle showed up at Grant's house with a warrant for Betsy's arrest, made out by magistrate Dr Daniel Arnoldi – the same Dr Arnoldi who had bought the big syringe at John Trim's estate sale, where Grant had bought a sword. As Grant soon learned, Arnoldi acted not only in his capacity of justice of the peace but as doctor to Betsy Freeman's mistress, who was in an "advanced state of pregnancy."

"The land of the free & the home of the brave," a touring British officer wrote at the bottom of this sketch he drew in 1833 at a slave market in Charleston, South Carolina. Abolitionists like Alexander Grant often cited this line from "The Star-Spangled Banner" to shame Americans into recognizing the hypocrisy of claiming to cherish freedom while abetting slavery.

Instead of taking the girl to the police station, Delisle took her to Arnoldi's, and Grant went along too. The doctor gave Betsy a tongue-lashing and threatened to lock her up. He was the prison doctor besides being a magistrate, so he had the power to do so. "Upon my endeavouring to plead for the girl," Grant said, "the honorable Magistrate took me by the collar and degraded himself by kicking me."

"Breathe we in a Christian land?" the *Vindicator* sputtered. "Is this the sort of justice that 'our Magistrates' are sworn to administer?"

Betsy was returned to her mistress, who was staying with her in-law, the jeweller James Dwight. And Grant swung into action. On the Sunday of Betsy's arrest, he filed a charge of assault against Arnoldi. He also swore out an affidavit that unless the courts stepped in, Betsy might be spirited back to the States. Grant's lawyer, Charles-Ovide Perrault, age 26, was a rising star of the Patriotes, elected to the Assembly in 1834 as the member for Vaudreuil. He filed the affidavit in the court the next day, asking that a judge look into Betsy's case. The court issued a writ of habeas corpus, ordering Gelston to produce Betsy without delay. But Arnoldi replied that Gelston was bed-ridden and couldn't comply. This made things dicey. There was talk that Dwight's son was planning to sneak Betsy out of the country before the court had a chance to hear the case. So Grant and other blacks set up a round-the-clock watch outside Dwight's house on College Street. On that Monday night, June 13, a commotion there led to Grant and two other black men, Moses Powell Wormley and George Nixon, being charged with causing a riot.

So Betsy Freeman, a black girl, comes to town and – boom! – all hell breaks loose and three court cases result. Not many girls, black or white, ever caused such a stir.

The habeas corpus case, being the most pressing, was the first to be heard, and it went ahead on Wednesday, June 15, without Ann Gelston. U.S.-born lawyer Charles Dewey Day, a Tory who knew the Gelston family, appeared for Ann Gelston and presented her statement – sworn before Justice of the Peace Daniel Arnoldi. According to Gelston, Betsy Freeman was no slave; the girl was her husband's indentured servant. She also claimed that Betsy "is desirous of remaining in the service of the said Ann Gelston and of avoiding all communication with the said Grant and the people of her own colour by whom he is supported and encouraged in his attempt to seduce the said Elizabeth from the care & service of the said Ann Gelston."

Since Gelston had no papers proving Betsy was a servant, not a slave, the court couldn't take her word for it. Everything depended on what Betsy had to say. But Betsy froze – who can blame her? She gave her name, her age as about 15 or 16, and told the court that she was from North Carolina … and she wanted to go back there with her mistress. The court told her she was free to do as she pleased, and she did go back to Gelston. The fullest account of the case appeared in the Patriote newspaper *La Minerve*, and no wonder: Grant's lawyer wrote for the paper, which was published by his older brother.

The next case to proceed was the assault charge against Arnoldi. He'd had to post a bond of £10 until his trial. On July 12 a grand jury headed by the Patriote hero and *Minerve* editor Ludger Duvernay indicted him. The next day he pleaded not guilty, and his trial followed on July 19. He was convicted and fined ten shillings.

This pleased the Patriotes no end, not so much because Grant had been vindicated, but because it confirmed their view that rotten Tories were picked as magistrates over better-qualified people. Here was a perfect illustration: – a magistrate convicted of assault. "We should think that it is full time to purify our Commission of the Peace," the *Vindicator* commented. Arnoldi was stripped of his magistrate's commission (but was reinstated a few months later).

Finally, after a summer on pins and needles, Grant, Wormley, and Nixon went on trial on September 7 in the Court of King's Bench. They were accused of leading a noisy five-hour protest outside Dwight's house on the day of Betsy Freeman's arrest. They were said to have cursed him, threatened to shoot him, and actually fired a shot through his window. But the evidence all went to show that Grant and the other blacks present had staged a peaceful demo and that the ruckus had been caused by a rowdy sailor, name unknown, who had shown up brandishing sabre and gun. Verdict? Not guilty. Not guilty. Not guilty.

Black Knight: "It does appear, Doctor, that your large syringe has lost its sting."

Dr. Arnoldi: "Curse you, Alex Grant!"

Again *La Minerve* carried the fullest report, retelling Betsy's saga from beginning to end. Noting that she had chosen to return to North Carolina, the newspaper concluded: "Notwithstanding that, it appears to us that the conduct of Mr Grant as a friend of humanity is deserving of praise; and we are pleased to see that despite the obstacles with which he met, he has triumphed over his adversaries and accomplished his honorable purpose."

Certainly, if Betsy Freeman was a slave and had been persuaded, out of confusion and fear, to stay a slave, Grant had cause for regret. But two out of three ain't bad. He had made a charge stick against Arnoldi, a big wheel in town (a few years later Arnoldi became the founding president of Quebec's College of Physicians and Surgeons). And Grant, Wormley, and Nixon had beaten the riot rap. That had to count for something. Still, he must have wondered whether all that mattered to the whites was that once again, the Patriotes had nailed the Tories.

In court, Grant had given his occupation as hairdresser. In fact, he'd worked at that business practically from the moment he arrived in town, but he kept up the clothes-cleaning side too. After that stormy summer of 1836, he billed himself as a "fashionable hair cutter, perfumer and peruke maker," but he also advertised: "Wearing apparel renovated on a new improved principle." Maybe his wife Celia handled that side of the business (she did work as a laundress after his death).

In a letter he wrote that summer, Grant had mentioned one detail of his efforts on behalf of his fellow blacks: "Being, what is termed, a man of colour, and extremely anxious that all my friends should enjoy the same degree of liberty and happiness which I possess, I have always been active in promoting the permanent settlement of them in the Canadas." He didn't say how he encouraged black immigration and whether he'd had any luck. Too bad.

From his home and shop at 80 St Paul Street, Grant moved in the mid-1830s; he even lived for a while in part of John Trim's old house on McGill Street. In 1837 he rented a place on St Urbain Street near Craig (St Antoine) and kept shop on Notre Dame Street. That's where he was when the rebellion broke out in November. Perrault, his lawyer, was killed that month, fighting British regulars at Saint-Denis. There are no letters that might tell us how Grant felt about that.

There are no letters, either, to give us a glimpse inside his home or shop. But the hairdressing must have gone well because in February 1838 he advertised for an apprentice. He wanted a boy of 14 or 15, he said, someone who spoke French and English: "A Canadian [i.e., French Canadian] boy would be preferred."

Here was another affirmative step – a black man who not only hired whites (he'd had several apprentices before) but broadcast to the world that he would be the master of a white boy. In Betsy Freeman's North Carolina – in most states, in fact – whites wouldn't have stood for that. In Montreal, there was not a peep.

Full freedom came to the slaves of the West Indies in the summer of 1838. The six-year apprenticeship system launched in 1834 had turned out to be pretty much an extension of slavery in all but name, and it was cut short. The last slaves were released at midnight on July 31. It was the First of August all over again.

A few weeks after this, Grant's turn on stage came to an end as absurd as it was abrupt. August 20 was a big day at the races. Lord Durham, the new governor general sent by England to pick up the pieces after the shoot-out of 1837, was there with all his gleaming crew. You'd have seen the ladies in their jewels and fine dresses, and all the army and navy brass. And everybody who was anybody had turned out to see and be seen – including Grant. That night as he rode home, his head full of the spectacle and the sport, his horse was spooked by a cow; it reared and threw him. He died in a couple of hours. He was 37. Done in by a cow. Not a dragon, a cow.

A newspaper editor paid tribute to him: "Mr Grant was a man of color, but respectable and very upstanding." He might have left out the "but" – that loaded little word which implied that Grant, unlike other blacks, was respectable. The editor was well-meaning, but in praising one dead black man, he insulted all live ones. It was enough to make Grant turn over in his grave.

They buried him in the protestant Burial Ground on Dorchester Street. His body was laid in the same lot as Mary Broome, John and Jane Broome's daughter. Jacob Grant, like Broome one of the "twelve apostles," was later buried in that lot too. It was called Wilberforce Lot 913, after William Wilberforce, the British anti-slavery hero.

Henry Clay of Kentucky arrived in town on July 30, 1839, less than a year after Alex Grant's death. It was lucky for him Grant wasn't around. To skim parts of the letter he wrote to a friend in the United States the next day, you would think Clay was a runaway slave, with hounds at his heels: "I arrived here last evening, worn down and prostrated by the incidents of the Journey ... I escaped to the Provinces to find that freedom of which I found myself deprived in my own Country."

But Henry Clay was no slave. The U.S. senator and former secretary of state had his eye on the presidency. With the Whig Party convention slated for December, he had been glad-handing his way through New York. And if you read through his letter instead of just skimming it, you get the picture:

I arrived here last evening, worn down and prostrated by the incidents of the Journey. After you left me at Rochester the same enthusiastic demonstrations which you witnessed there marked my progress. Quasi public dinners, suppers, vast concourses of people, Committees, & Speeches completely prostrated me. I escaped to the Provinces to find that freedom of which I found myself deprived in my own Country.

So the freedom he was after on a short side trip to Canada was a rest from political stardom and too many dinners. No slave ever fled the United States because of either.

If Grant hadn't been killed by that cow, Clay's visit might have turned into another Betsy Freeman case, because travelling with him was his slave, Charles Dupuy. This time there were no court cases, no noisy protests. But some blacks, it seems, did make a quiet stab at rescuing Charles Dupuy. A pro-slavery paper in Baltimore later reported:

At Montreal, we believe it was, some of her Brittanic Majesty's subjects approached Charles with assurances that he was as free in Canada as Mr Clay, and that he could now leave him without the least fear of being compelled again into his service. For some time Charles listened to these suggestions with silent disregard – but, as they were pertinaciously pressed upon him, he at length put a stop to the entreaties of his philanthropic friends, by telling them that he was as well aware as they were of the ease with which he could now gain his freedom; but that, in fact, in the service of Mr Clay, he had as much liberty as he needed or desired; that he preferred to remain with him, and that, in short, *he would not leave him for both the Canadas.*

Abolitionists wondered about that. How could a slave turn down freedom? Maybe he was a "pampered menial ... who might actually prefer the lazy indulgences of a waiter on Henry Clay to the necessity of earning free bread by honest industry." Or maybe he had a wife and children, parents, or other relations that he knew he'd never see again if he skipped. On the other hand, maybe he stuck by Clay out of plain loyalty. In that case, Clay owed him. Clay never got to be president. But he did eventually pay Charles Dupuy back for his "fidelity, attachment and services." Five years later, he set him free.

19

Things You've Got to Wonder About

THERE WAS THIS BLACK MAN AT Berthierville, a tavern cook called William Thomson, much appreciated by the gentlemen of the place for his skills in the kitchen. He had a wife, a white girl from Yamachiche named Desanges Blais, who he'd married in 1818. They had two daughters, Marguerite, turning nine in a couple of weeks, and Eléonore, age seven.

It was a fine June evening in 1828, and William Thomson was dancing – dancing! – on a tightrope. You have to wonder what the devil he was up to, him a cook and family man, doing his highwire act out there in the country as the sun set. Was this some circus trick he'd picked up as a boy? Was he out to prove he still had it in him at 32? Or was he drunk or what?

Oh, but he misses his step and loses his balance, and, oh my God, he's falling! You want to stop the tape right there, rewind, reach into the past and break his fall. You can't.

He hit the ground and cracked his skull. Someone ran for the doctor. The doctor did his best, but William Thomson was past saving. A few hours later and he was dead.

Poor man. Poor wife. And good luck to his daughters. You can't help but hope that Marguerite and Eléonore made out better in the country than Martha Hyers did in town after she lost her father.

You have to wonder about Martha Curtis Hyers, a Montreal girl just a few months younger than Marguerite Thomson. Her father, John Hyers, was a lamplighter for the city when he married her mother, Catherine Salter. He couldn't write, but his wife could. When they married at the Presbyterian Church in St Gabriel Street on April 1, 1819, the church register noted that there were "a number of Blacks present but could not write." (It's thanks to Catherine Salter that we know his name was Hyers, not Airs, and that hers was Salter, not Alter, as their marriage record called them.)

Martha Hyers had a brother, briefly. He was born two years after her, on May 8, 1822. He was christened Francis Zbana Hyers. Zbana is not an English name, and it's not French – it has an African ring to it. You have to wonder what that meant. There weren't many echoes of Africa in the names of Montrealers by then, except in those of the *Bonga* sisters, Charlotte and Rosalie, and maybe *Sente* Williams and Peter *Dago*, and Catherine *Cora*, who usually went by the name Catherine Guillet. Francis Zbana was just over a year old when he died on May 30, 1823.

So Martha Hyers, born in Montreal on February 28, 1820, lost her baby brother when she was too young to know what hit her. And sometime within the next few years she lost her father too, and her mother married again, a man called Edward Beard (or Baird). So by the summer of 1833, when Martha was 13, it was she and her mother and her stepfather against the world.

The three of them were among a group of eight people arrested on August 6 that year for keeping a "bawdy house" – a brothel. It was a first offence for Martha, but some of the blacks arrested with her were old hands at the game. As a matter of fact, one of them, Jeanie Martin, had just been released on July 19 after spending two and a half months in prison for being a brothel keeper, along with her husband, Jacob Simpson.

Thomas Cockburn, veteran of the War of 1812, also knew the ropes. His wife Mary McArty, and Jeanie Martin had spent a month in jail in the summer of 1828 for keeping a bawdy house. The following spring, Cockburn, McArty, and Martin had been among 22 people jailed for "aiding and assisting in Keeping a Bawdy-house" or "aiding & assisting in their debaucheries."

Now, in August 1833, while her mother and stepfather, along with Cockburn, Martin, and the rest, were up on the charge of keeping a bawdy house, Martha Hyers was convicted of larceny too. (She had probably pinched something from a john.) On August 26 the eight of them were sentenced to a month in the old prison that stood near where the city hall is now.

Maybe a month in that hole was enough to shake Martha Hyers. She went straight for a while, or at least kept clear of the law. And when she was 15 she got married, with her mother's permission (her stepfather, Beard, had died a year earlier). She married Richard Jackson, a man twice her age, at the First Baptist Church on August 5, 1835.

You have to wonder whether "respectable" types like Alexander Grant had any time for people like Martha. Where slavery and the big issues of race and rights were concerned, he made speeches, wrote letters. He flew to the rescue of Betsy Freeman, and he connected with Paola Brown on his mission. But we don't know that he ever connected with the likes of Martha Hyers. Though maybe he did.

One criticism levelled at white abolitionists in the United States and Britain, mostly by defenders of slavery but also by some champions of the working class, was that they got all worked up over the slaves in other people's yards but ignored the "wage slaves" in their own factories. There was some truth to this. Was something similar at work among "decent" black Montrealers – that they would go the distance for a Betsy Freeman but would let the "indecent" Martha Hyers of this world go hang?

On the other hand, did Martha Hyers have any time for the big issues? For instance, was she in the crowd of blacks who followed Betsy Freeman to court on that June day in 1836? Was she among those who showed "the greatest zeal and the warmest sympathy for one they supposed to be a slave?" The two girls were close to the same age, and you'd think that the heart of a free black girl would go out to Betsy Freeman. Still, you have to wonder how free Martha Hyers was.

That year, 1836, they opened a spanking new prison at the Foot of St Mary's Current. It was a T-shaped three-storey building. The men were kept in the main part – the bar of the T – and the women in the leg of the T at the back. The cells measured 8 feet by 5 ½ ft (about 2.5 x 1.5m). At 17, Martha Hyers got to try one on for size.

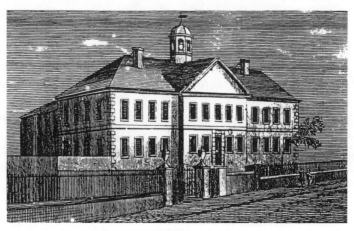

The old jail (top) on Notre Dame Street, approximately where the city hall stands today. It was used from 1806 to 1836, when the new jail (bottom) was opened at what is now the northeast corner of Notre Dame and Delorimier streets. Martha Hyers knew both.

She was sentenced on April 21, 1837, to a month's hard labour as an "idle and disorderly person" – a hooker.

Once, long before she knew what hit her, she'd had a life. From around the time her husband died on February 12, 1839, she went to pieces. She'd just done a month inside when he died. In the next two and a half years, she was back behind bars seventeen times – twice for theft, but mostly for vagrancy and disorderly conduct – always at hard labour. For women, that meant cooking, washing, starching, and cleaning for the inmates and the staff.

Take 1841. Big changes were afoot that year. In a kind of prelude to Confederation, Lower Canada and Upper Canada ceased to exist as separate colonies, each under its own government. As of February 10, they were united as the Province of Canada, under a single government, and were known as Canada East and Canada West until they were renamed Quebec and Ontario in 1867.

You think that made a bit of difference in Martha Hyers's world? She was locked up at the time, serving two months for disorderliness. Freed on February 22, she was sentenced two days later to another two months. She came out on April 24 and was sent back to prison on the twenty-sixth, to be let out on May 15. Four days after her discharge, she was sentenced to two months. Released on July 19, she went back in again on the twenty-seventh for another two months. She got out on September 27, only to be hauled back in October 9, this time for just ten days. She was out on October 19 – then back in on the twenty-third for a month.

It makes your head spin to see her dancing on the highwire like that, her life spiralling out of control. She was due to be released November 23, but she gave everyone the slip. She had a friend on the outside. In the prison log there's a note about that, about who she'd been freed by and when. It says: "By Death on the 25 Novr."

You want to stop the tape right there, rewind, reach into the past and break her fall. You can't. She was 21, officially an adult. You have to wonder where her childhood went.

20

Gabriel, Be an Angel and Blow That Horn

YOU WERE WONDERING, WERE YOU, why they closed the street to traffic? It's for the parade. I'm just going to borrow a piece of your stoop and sit awhile and watch, if you don't mind. You have to see this. The black men of Montreal who served their country in the war are going to march. Well, I mean, their ghosts are, because the men themselves are long gone. I'm talking about the War of 1812. Look, here they come.

That one in front, carrying the flag, that's Hero Richardson, 17 when he joined. Born in Green Island, wherever that is; only Green Island I know is near Troy, New York. It was end of May 1814, almost two years into the war, when he enlisted as a private in the 1st Battalion of Select Embodied Militia. Most of the action was over. He got no bounty when he signed up. The others got up to £5, but Hero got zip. He did get some extra pay his first month, though. He joined on May 30, but he was paid from the twenty-fifth, making five extra days' pay at sixpence a day – all of 2s 6d.

He wound up in Captain Faribault's company, the same outfit as

Gabriel Johonnot. We ought to see Gabriel soon. Hope he plays that bugle of his. Nothing kills a parade like having the music die just as it's passing.

Hero enlisted for the duration. He even promised to serve for six months after the war if he was needed. But the war ended officially in December 1814, and everybody was discharged by the following March.

They didn't have a black veterans' association, nothing official anyway, but the men kept in touch. So Hero was there as a witness when Robert Williams, who was in the Voltigeurs, got married in 1816. And when Hero married Dinah Morrison in 1820, Abraham Low, who'd been a drummer in the war, was one of his witnesses; the other was old John Trim.

Poor Hero. We used to kid him about being the only Hero of the war. He must have liked the ring of it because when he and Dinah had a son, they called him Hero too, Hero Alexander. Charlotte, John Trim's wife, was his godmother. Dinah died a week after he was born in the summer of 1821. Then Hero Alexander died too, not two months old. We kind of lost track of Hero after that. He vanished.

Now, see this fellow driving the cart? That's Bill Feeler. He gets to ride instead of marching because that's what he did in the war: he was a private in the Royal Artillery Drivers. He was in his early thirties, almost twice Hero's age, twice as lucky in the family department too, in a way. He was five years married when the war broke out, and he and his wife, Tibby Prejumier, already had three kids. They had another two later. After Tibby died in 1819, Bill married Nancy Bradshaw, a widow, but they didn't have any kids.

I don't remember much about Bill Feeler, how long he served or anything. In peacetime, he worked as a servant or labourer, like Hero. He died in 1828. His second daughter, Nancy, who was 17 by then, got into a heap of trouble – in and out of jail for vagrancy in the early thirties. I kind of figured she was daddy's girl, and when daddy died, she was nobody's.

Oh, but look now, here come the Voltigeurs. For my money, they were the sharpest-looking outfit in those grey uniforms, with that black trim and the bearskin hats. What do you mean, "They look kind of small for soldiers"? When there's guns going off, you don't want to be a seven-footer, believe me. Besides, the rules said you could join as long as you were 5 foot 3.

Black Voltigeurs. Heroes of the War of 1812, the Voltigeurs Canadiens are invariably depicted as white, yet blacks served in this and other Lower Canadian militia units. Several of them were buglers or drummers.

The big guy there, walking beside the rest and keeping them in line, that's Jacques Williamson.

Sergeant Williamson, all 5 foot 7 of him. He couldn't write but he had a head on him, maybe from all the figuring he'd done as a carpenter. He almost didn't make the cut, on account of his age. You had to be between 17 and 35 – and he was just about 35 when he joined.

He started as a private, signed up in May 1812, a month before the war broke out, and picked up his £4 bounty. He told them he was 34. You couldn't say he joined for a lark; he was too old for that – married fifteen years, to a French-Canadian from Mascouche, Marie Louise Bleau was her name. And you couldn't say it was because he had no job and nothing better to do; he had a good trade.

Maybe his age and level head and his early sign-up helped him get promoted. If you ask me, his light skin didn't hurt. And he spoke French, like most of the Voltigeurs. Anyway, he served from before the beginning until after the end of the war, starting off as a private in Duchesnay's company and ending up a sergeant in Captain William Johnson's.

Next to him is Robert Williams, a couple of inches shorter and a lot darker. He was a tenant at Alex Valentine's on St Charles Borromée for a while. Funny thing, Williamson joined before the war started, and Williams joined after it was over. The thing is, no one on this side of the water knew it was over because they signed the peace in Belgium, Christmas Eve 1814, and it took forever for word to reach us. That's why the big, bloody whipping we took at New Orleans on January 15, 1815, was such a waste. Not that we heard about that for a while either. Bob Williams signed up the day after New Orleans, for as long as the war might last, and Lieutenant William Clark paid him his bounty, which was £4 7s 6d.

He was about 25 when he joined. I seem to recall he came from Quebec. He was friends with the Ashleys and they were from Quebec. Ever hear of Robert Ashley? Used to work as steward on the *Adeona* when she ran between England and Quebec. Then he moved his family to Montreal. Worked on John Molson's first steamboat, the *Accommodation*, in 1809–10. His daughter Margaret was born here; when she was baptised in the summer of 1816, Bob Williams and Esther Thomson were the sponsors. And wouldn't you know it, a couple of months later Bob and Esther got married, and Robert Ashley was their witness along with Hero.

Oh, I know why Bob Williams makes me think of Quebec. It's not just the Ashleys. There were a couple of other Williams men from Quebec who served in the Voltigeurs. One was John (he'd moved up from Boston), probably over the age limit, but what the heck! He started off with Duchesnay's company, the same as Jacques Williamson. I think he died during the war. And there was Thomas – that's it! – Thomas Williams. He must be the one marching beside Robert. I can't say the face is familiar, can't tell from here whether they look alike. He signed up in February 1815, with Captain Johnson's company or John McKay's. He moved to Montreal later: I don't recognize him but I remember his wife Sarah Johnson was Mary Ann Trim's godmother.

The two men behind them I recognize: John Dolphin and Henry Thomson, the farmers from around Saint-Michel. They were buddies, signed up together in February 1813. John was in his early thirties, as tall as Williamson. Henry, the shorter one, well, he said he was 35, but he was more like 45. When he died at the beginning of 1819, some of us figured he was at least 55. So they must have winked at him being over age when he joined. Just as they overlooked the rule that you had to be Canadian-born to be a Voltigeur. I mean, Hero wasn't born here, and Cockburn came over from Ireland and never tried to hide it.

John and Henry lucked out. The bounty was up to £5 when they joined. That was the highest it went, so maybe that had something to do with Henry enlisting. But really, I think he just tagged along with John, even though he was older. John needed a change. His wife Lydia had died the summer before and he was pretty shaken up. When Henry and his wife had a daughter the year after the war, they called her Lydia. That was a nice thing to do, don't you think? But then she died, not half a year old.

I don't think Henry stuck it out to the end of the war: I heard he was working a farm at Saint-Michel by the spring of 1814. John joined the regular army for a spell, as I recall, then went back to farming.

Speak of that devil Cockburn! There he is, and with Castor Jay – what a pair! They were rough and ready those two, what you might expect from raftsmen. Cockburn, he'd worked up on the Ottawa for Cameron & McMillan, making up timber cribs and taking them down to Quebec. And Jay had done the same thing for the McNabbs on the Bay of Quinte. That was dangerous work. Soldiering probably looked a picnic to them, compared to that.

Remember what I said about Cockburn not being Canadian? Well, Jay he was from around Albany, New York (Betsy, his woman, was from Connecticut). So there's a couple of rascals who weren't Canadian-born who still made the Voltigeurs. They were scrappers and that's what you need in a war – never mind where you were born. Of course, since we were fighting the Americans, some people might have worried that Jay would pull up short, going up against his countrymen. But it's not as if he had much reason to love the States. I mean, they still had slavery in New York.

Cockburn and Jay joined in December 1812 and served in the same company at first, Captain Jacques Viger's. They were in Upper Canada in the summer of 1813, at Gananoque near Kingston. Jay we never saw again after the war. Cockburn served down along the border in the last year under Captain Emmanuel D'Aubreville, and then came back to Montreal. He and his wife Mary McArty – they'd married at the end of the rafting season in 1809 – joined the booze-and-bawdy house crowd. One freezing night in February '41 down in Griffintown, they found Cockburn lying drunk out of his head in the street. They took him to the police office in McGill Street, and he died there. Died of "misery and intemperance," the inquest said.

But will you listen to that music! Now that's what I call war-dance music. Bugles and drums will do it for me any day.

The bugler on the far side is George Crozier, a friend of Joseph Pierson – you know, the cook who was stabbed to death by a soldier. Crozier he was with the Voltigeurs, started in May 1812 in de Rouville's company as a private, then became company bugler. From Christmas Day 1814 until his discharge in March, he was bugler in the company of Captain d'Estimauville.

And the bugler in the middle is William Thomas, who volunteered in March 1813 with the 1st Battalion of Select Embodied Militia. He lived in Quebec then, but moved here later. That's why he's in the parade. I think he was the only one of them who was at the Battle of Châteauguay in October 1813, with Captain Panet's company.

And the one closest to us, you recognize – Gabriel Johonnot, Caesar's son. He enlisted in March 1814 and started off as bugle in Captain Faribault's company, Hero's outfit. In June, he was made a private and I don't think he cared for that. Buglers and drummers were paid more than privates. They got 7 ¾d a day and privates got 6d, meaning that in a month of thirty-one days the musicians got £1 and the privates were 4s 6d short of that. But I don't think it was the cut in pay that bothered Gabriel so much as that he was born to play the horn.

He stuck it out as a private for seven months before pulling a switch. Around Christmas time, we heard he was laid up sick in Beauport. Lovesick's more like it – he'd just married a Quebec girl,

Madeleine Maréchal, and he was blowing his horn … in Captain Finlay's company – right to the end of March, when the regiment was disbanded. Tan-ta-ra.

And bringing up the rear is "Lie Low," the drummer boy. That's what I called him. His real name was Abraham Low, from the West Indies, I think. He was living in Quebec at the end of 1812 when he joined Captain Christie's company of the Quebec Volunteers. He stayed with the company when it became part of the 4th battalion, Select Embodied Militia. He hung in till November 1814.

You'd think that in the two years that he served, they would have got his name right. But no, from start to finish, he was Abraham Volunteer to them. No wonder he de-enlisted before the war was over. He deserted on November 4, 1814, and hightailed it to Montreal. He lived here the rest of his life, at first at John Trim's, later on St Dominique Street and on St George (Jeanne Mance). I never heard a bitter man who could play so sweet on a flute.

But here's the sweetest part. Years later, the government comes up with this plan to reward the men who'd served in the war by giving them grants of land. Almost thirty years have passed, and many of them are six feet under. But Lie Low's still kicking, and he figures he's entitled to his 100 acres. Of all the men marching today, he's the only one who filed a claim. He spells it out for the clerk filling out his application that he is "Abraham Low, who was called Abraham Volunteer during his Militia services, now of the city of Montreal, trader and labourer, formerly of Quebec." This is in May 1844.

But he can't very well show his discharge papers to prove that he served. So he comes up with this dog-ate-my-homework story that he was regularly discharged but somehow lost his papers. Ha! He crossed his fingers and in September 1845 he got £20 in scrip "in Commutation of my claim for One Hundred acres of Land." They must have let him know the cheque was in the mail, because a week before he got it he'd sold it for £9 17s 6d. Strapped for cash, I guess.

There's no excuse for lying, I know, but he had served two years, after all. And you can't help but feel they owed him for never bothering to get his name straight. It wasn't just during the war; all through his life he was called Abel Low here, Abraham Lawson there, Abraham OLoan – all kinds of things. I mean, even when he died they couldn't get it right. That was November 19, 1846: the church record made it December, and the cemetery put him down as A. Lance.

He never had to cover his tracks – they did it for him. See, that's why we had to hold this parade. To uncover his tracks, all of their tracks. I say, go on, Gabriel, blow that horn, and Abraham, beat that drum. No more reason to lie low now.

21

BAD NEWS LEWIS

☞

THE CONSULTATION COMMITTEE OF Coloured People of Montreal met in early 1846 – or did it? That's the question. If there really was such a body, it was the first black organization formally set up, with an official name, in Montreal.

The people who are supposed to have attended were real enough. Moses Carter, who kept a hairdressing shop at St François-Xavier and Commissioners Street (de la Commune), apparently was the chairman, and Peter Jarard Lee, a bit of bad apple and a hairdresser too, acted as secretary. Two others who are supposed to have played minor parts were William Paul, at different times a tavern keeper and engineer (in charge of a steam engine), and Peter Dago, dyer and scourer.

The man who did all the talking was Israel Lewis, and that's the problem. He's the only one who left a record of the committee's existence. We have to take his word for it, and his word isn't worth much.

You could shout it on TV, you could post it all over the Internet that Israel Lewis was a snake in the grass, and no one would give you an argument. Historians will tell you he was bad news. Of course, Lewis would deny it if he could, but he died long ago, in 1847, the summer of the big typhus epidemic when thousands of starving Irish, driven from home by the famine, sailed to North America on filthy ships, dying on the way or on landing. Moses Carter died that summer too, on July 31.

Lewis didn't make his name in Montreal. His bad reputation came from his association with Wilberforce, the black refugee settlement he had helped found in Biddulph Township, near London, Upper Canada, at a place now called Lucan. He spent only the last few years of his life in Montreal. But two things that he did in this city – publishing a record of that CCCPM meeting and making out his will – can give us the key to understanding where Bad News Lewis was coming from.

What makes a man like Lewis go bad? Slavery. Look no further. He'd been a plantation slave in the American South, where sneakiness, faking, and masking the truth were survival skills. If the law made it illegal for you to learn to read and write, you wanted to keep your book and pencil stub out of sight. If you were bright and the whites were dumb, you played dumber. If your masters were beasts, you bowed to them. If you had ambition, too bad.

Lewis escaped to Cincinnati, in the free state of Ohio. The constitution of the free state of Ohio denied blacks the right to vote, to hold public office, or to serve in the militia. In 1804, the first session of the Ohio legislature passed "An Act to Regulate Black and Mulatto Persons," requiring all of them living in the state to have a court certificate proving they were free. No certificate meant no job. The law made it illegal for anyone to hire you.

If you were a runaway slave, the law made it illegal for anyone to help you in any way. In 1807 they increased the penalties for helping a fugitive and added some new twists. All blacks settling in Ohio had to get two whites to post a bond of $500 guaranteeing their good behaviour, and no black or mulatto could testify against a white in court.

Enforcement of these "black laws" was slack – until June 29, 1829. Then the trustees of Cincinnati Township, responding to calls from whites to do something about the growing black population, cracked the whip. Blacks had thirty days – later extended to about sixty – to line up $500 bonds if they hadn't done so already.

The stage was set for Israel Lewis. "The colored people had a meeting and talked about a court of appeals to test the law," James C. Brown, a former slave, recalled years later:

Some talked of going to Texas, – we knew not what to do: we were sore perplexed. I spoke to them of Canada, and we formed a Colonization Society, of which I was President. I wrote for the Board to [Lieutenant Governor] Sir John Colborne, at Little York, now Toronto, to know if we could find in Canada an asylum for ourselves, our wives, and children. Two members of the Board went with the letter to Toronto, and were well received by Sir John.

Lewis was one of the two sent to Upper Canada, and he arranged to buy a whole township from the Canada Company. But when the time came to pay for it, there was no money, and the Canada Company became so frustrated at its dealings with Lewis that it refused to sell land to blacks from then on. Some land was purchased anyway, with money from Quakers in Indiana, and a colony was begun with a dozen or so families.

The board of managers, under Brown, named Lewis its agent to raise funds in the United States. In 1831 the settlement's residents elected a new board, with Austin Steward as president. He'd been a grocer in Rochester, New York. This new board also gave Lewis the power to go fundraising in the States. Fundraising he did go, all right, and lived high on the hog, but sent precious little money back.

People started asking questions that first year, and after trying many times to call Lewis to account, the board sacked him early in 1832. But he wouldn't quit and went on passing himself off as the agent of Wilberforce settlement. On Christmas Day 1832, the board warned its well-wishers not to give Lewis any more money because "he is now practising a deception upon our friends in the United States by taking up donations, pretending that such gifts will be faithfully applied to our relief."

In New York, Arthur Tappan, one of the white founders of the American Anti-Slavery Society (he'd been in business in Montreal up to the War of 1812), published a notice in February 1833 that Lewis "had obtained in this city, at different times, upwards of Fifteen Hundred Dollars, for the above named Settlement; of which money he has paid over short of One Hundred Dollars."

Three years later, Lewis was still at it, and on March 28, 1836, the Wilberforce board issued a notice saying: "We deeply regret the manner in which our Friends in the States have been imposed upon by ISRAEL LEWIS, and that we hereby inform them, that as a Board of Managers or otherwise, we have received less than One Hundred Dollars of all the money borrowed and collected in the States."

In April that year, the "colored citizens" of New York, after sending somebody to check out Wilberforce, held a public meeting and concluded that Israel Lewis had "abused their confidence, wasted their benevolence, and forfeited all claim to their countenance and respect." On May 20, Philadelphia blacks, who had been stung too, met to discuss the Lewis case. Recalling the misery the blacks of Cincinnati had known in 1829, they said:

With persecution behind and suffering around, and want and uncertainty before them, an individual, in the stolen garb of philanthropy, addressed himself to their peculiar and painful condition, and in order that he might carry out more fully his knavish and corrupt designs, he insinuated himself into their confidence, and obtained their recommendation to solicit from the public such aid as their pressing demands called for … His appeal was successful as has been evinced by his extravagant mode of living ever since this fatal and misconfided mission … We say to the public, that we have not the remotest degree of confidence in said Israel Lewis, or any of his appointed agents.

On it went until the late 1830s, when Wilberforce itself was in a shambles. Steward, the Wilberforce president, later wrote that Lewis had tried to frame him on a charge of stealing money; he'd had two of Steward's horses poisoned, had him poisoned too, and when that didn't finish him, he'd ambushed him on the road one night and tried to shoot him dead. Lewis's wife was so disgusted by his antics that she left him.

Steward had a lot to say about Lewis in his memoirs, *Twenty-Two Years a Slave and Forty Years a Freeman* (1857). In a chapter called "Character and Death of I. Lewis," he tried to explain what made the man tick. Lewis had "a natural energy and strength of character," Steward said. He had "quick perception," his personal appearance was "prepossessing; his manner and address easy and commanding." And while he had little education, "he had managed to gather a sufficient knowledge of the sciences to enable him to read and write, together with quite a fund of general information; and then his shrewdness and tact accomplished all the rest." Lewis had once addressed the New York legislature with "eloquence and marked effect." He was, you might say, exceptional.

But the worm of slavery had eaten him up inside. As a plantation slave, he had been: "subjected to all the cruelties and deprivations of a bondman. His natural abilities were above mediocrity, but having never had the advantages of an education, or the privileges of a society calculated to cultivate and refine his natural aspiring intellect, and to direct his indomitable will ... he had come to manhood with a determined, selfish disposition, to accomplish whatever gratified his vanity or administered to the wants of his animal nature."

Neither Steward nor anyone since seems to have considered the possibility that Lewis was insane. But then, no one seems to have taken note of the pamphlet he published in Montreal in April 1846 called *Crisis in North America! – Slavery, War, Balance of Power and Oregon*. Taken together with Steward's assessment, this pamphlet suggests that while its author (whom the cover identified as "Israel Lewis, Colored Man!") was sharp, he also suffered from delusions.

The first part of the pamphlet is billed as a report, signed by Moses Carter as chairman and by P.J. Lee as secretary of the Consultation Committee of Coloured People of Montreal. It's about the "preamble and resolutions" that Lewis submitted to a meeting of the CCCPM on how to end American slavery (no date is given for the meeting.) Lewis's main resolution was "that we, the Consultation Committee of Coloured People of Montreal, will petition Her Most Gracious Majesty Queen Victoria, to authorize the assembling of 100,000 coloured men, and all others who may feel disposed to join us, at Niagara, Upper Canada, for the purpose of putting an end to slavery."

Crazy idea! And anyone who wondered how this righteous army was going to wipe out slavery was referred to the Bible: "Jeremiah, chapter 47, concerning the destruction of the Philistines, also the 48th chapter, same book, against Moab ... We would likewise call the attention of our readers to the 5th chapter of the epistle of Saint James."

Never mind all the problems and expense of trying to muster, house, feed, arm, and drill 100,000 people in the boonies of Canada, there wasn't the ghost of a chance that anyone in their right mind would buy the scheme. And if they had, did Lewis think the United States would stand by and watch as a black army massed on its doorstep? Needless to say, abolitionists never fell for it, and the press didn't breathe a word. Lewis says nothing about how the CCCPM reacted – no word of any discussion or any vote on his proposals. There's no voice heard but his own.

In an appendix he wrote of the sabre rattling going on between the United States and Britain over the Oregon Territory on the West Coast, which both countries claimed. Lewis saw this as a symptom of the real issue, which was monarchy versus democracy in North America and the coming showdown between them:

I feel it a duty that I owe to my God, and my coloured brethren, bond and free, to intreat them speedily to decide which side they will take in this great struggle, I hope you will permit me to say that you ought, by all means, to go heart and hand for a Monarchal form of Government … I hope we, one and all, will rally round the British flag, and put an end to this base and foul traffic in HUMAN FLESH; and that every African or descendant on the American continent, in fifty years, will be governed by British law.

Alexander Grant and others had expressed strong pro-British views before, but Lewis seems less pro-British than hurt deep down – eager to see Queen Victoria grind Uncle Sam into the dirt the way Uncle Sam had ground him down. And down. And down.

If Lewis was deranged, it is not hard to find a cause. If slavery and racism could make a man go bad, they could just as well make him go mad. You hear a lot about how slavery broke the bodies of slaves, but what about their minds? And what about the lingering hurt of those who got away? Or the dread that free blacks lived with every day, knowing that slavery lurked in the shadows, ready to jump them if they came within reach?

Lewis never really escaped slavery: it had entered his soul, and he felt it there. He knew he was born to shine, but he wouldn't. He had the talent to go far, but he went nowhere.

There's some pretty strong language in his pamphlet. Take this passage, only a sentence long: "The ungodly slave-holder, seduces the helpless unoffending slave-woman, and she is compelled to act as the lamb who licks the knife of its bloody slaughterer!" The sexual abuse of slave women by their masters was commonplace, but Lewis put it in a way that still jolts. Here's another passage:

Another of the horrifying evils of slavery is amalgamation, and cohabition between father and daughter! Mother and son!! Sister and brother!!!
These occurrences happen in consequence of the manner in which they are separated, sold when they are young, and sent into various parts of slave holding countrys, where they grow up without any knowledge of their relationship; and then amalgamate in the way above mentioned. Good God! stop the institution of slavery for the sake of thy Son!

Is "thy Son" Jesus Christ or Israel Lewis? Had Lewis lived these things himself? That would have been pretty traumatic. Maybe he hadn't; maybe he was speaking from hearsay or reaching for effect. But he sure knew the words to make you squirm.

Five days before his death, on June 5, 1847, at the age of 52, Lewis made out his will in the Montreal General Hospital. To Peter Albert O'Connell Lee, first son of P.J. Lee, he left 50 acres in Biddulph Township. He left other lands in that area to his executors to be sold to "establish and support as long as possible a school or some other such Institute for the purpose of conferring the blessings of education on the colored inhabitants of this Province of Canada." He also asked his executors to patent "my invention of Fire screen and the Escape Ladder," any benefits to go to the school.

Lands and inventions seem to have been all in his head. Steward wrote that Lewis died "leaving not enough of all his gains to afford him decent burial." He was buried in the "Poor Ground" of the Protestant cemetery on Papineau Street.

No doubt Lewis gave Wilberforce a bad name and damaged the cause he claimed to champion. He was bad news. But to all who condemned him as the devil in disguise, it may be time to say, "Yes, but…" It may be time to appeal the verdict of history and to enter a plea of insanity on his behalf. Of course, he'd kill you if he knew.

22

Taking
Care of
ROBERT

☞

WHERE I GREW UP, THE GREY NUNS RAN a place that was a combination of grade school, orphanage, and home for old folks who were crippled or handicapped. Théophile was one of the old folks, but he didn't know it. He had a dried-apple kind of face, with a hook nose that he blew often, no teeth to speak of, and his eyes were kind of milky. The nuns would send him on errands – to the post office maybe, to pick up the mail, and he'd go off, wearing short pants and a cap, with a boy's schoolbag on his back. He was pretty lively for his age – sometimes rode a bike – but he walked with a shuffle. Being schoolkids up on our figuring, we got a giggle out of asking him his age whenever we saw him. He'd cock his head and answer "five" sometimes, sometimes "seven," and give us candy.

More than a century before, in Saint Laurent, there had been a black man called Robert who was a bit like that – not as old, but just as slow and trusting. Five, seven, all the same to him, it meant nothing. He did odd jobs and he got stiffed. People hired him and

127

didn't pay, or paid him way less than they promised. One cent, two cents, two dollars – he didn't know the difference.

Work as he might, Robert couldn't earn enough to make ends meet. Gabriel Roy, a merchant and militia officer, saw what was happening. He took Robert under his wing, made him his personal servant. In 1815 Roy was 45. He had lost one wife, married another, and had just come through the War of 1812. He knew he wouldn't live forever – and who would take care of Robert then? So he made out a will, leaving Robert a pension of £12 10s a year, which was to start the moment Robert couldn't work any more.

But life didn't end then for Roy. In 1818 he got himself appointed Robert's curator, or legal guardian, meaning that he had a duty to watch over Robert's interests and make sure he didn't get shortchanged in anything.

When the cholera hit in June 1832, Roy thought his hour might have come. So he made out a new will, this time saying he was leaving 300 livres a year to Robert. But, again, life didn't end then for Roy. He lived to cancel that will in 1847, the typhus year, and make another – again keeping Robert in mind.

By 1848 Roy, who was then 78 and had been a member of the Legislative Council of the Province of Canada for seven years, knew that death wasn't any longer just a possibility but a sure thing. He was sick, and he made out a new will, repeating that Robert was to get his £12 10s a year for life. Roy died that December.

A few years later, his widow Sophia Bagg made out her will, and to keep faith with her husband, she ordered that her relatives go on paying Robert's pension out of the money she left them. She died in November 1860.

Robert had been in his seventies when, after Roy's death, he was placed in the care of the Grey Nuns at the Hôpital Général in Montreal. In 1851 they said he was 77. Ten years later, in January 1861, they made him out to be 85, and when he died that April, suddenly he was 89. He wasn't the only one who couldn't keep count.

23

Philomène's Third Birthday

☞

IF SNAPSHOTS HAD BEEN AROUND – and dirt cheap – back then, Peter Dago might have had a collection. A stash of old black-and-whites, maybe not going way back to the 1790s in New York State (his folks would have kept the baby pictures and the ones of him as a boy) but from his early days in Montreal. And on the back of them, somebody might have scrawled things like:

- Charles Whitemore funeral May 1817. Found Drowned
- Peter Dago, Jn Hyers, W Glossen, Prince Johnston, lamplighters 1818
- 12 of us at Alex Grant's, St Paul street, July 1833
- Mary Scholastique Philomene Dago one week old and parents Peter and Scholastique, Aug 19 1843
- "For Better or for Worse" Peter & Scholastique Wedding Day 18 Sept '51
- Philomène cradling cousin Johnny Sept 30 1853. Parents John Taylor, Caroline Diller, Godfather Mathew Bell

- Howling Isaac T baptised with godparents P. Dago, Mary Ann Trim (Mrs Brooks), parents Isaac Taylor and Henriette Trim. Jany 21 1855
- 18/03/58 funeral of Peter Jr, 3, Notre Dame
- Francis, 12, off to school, January 1861
- Philom and Wm Moseley married 20 Oct (1862), best man Edm. Turner
- Bristol Bosworth and his Mary Ann, godparents of Peter Jr, mother Hellen, Notre D, June 21 1863
- With Meads cousins Mary 12, Charles 9, Ann 13½, outside Courthouse March 28 1863. On steps Ch. Meads, Wm Jackson, Sheddrak Minkings, and John Jones
- Wedding party Aug. 7/65. Philomene bridesmaid, Hellen Coffey, PD, Francis
- Marie Jeanne, 2 days, bapt 28 Oct 66 with proud parents me and Hellen, godparents Sam and Em Anderson

Well, relax. You won't have to sit through an evening of boring old Dago family pictures, with Peter D. yammering on about the Taylors and the Meads and all those names that don't mean a thing to you – Sam Anderson, and Bristol this, and thingummy Jackson, and that black crowd on Wolfe Street … Don't bother even looking, because there were no "photographists" around till Dago was close to fifty and then they weren't so cheap he could afford them. No, all those snaps were in his head. They died with him in 1868.

Some pictures he had no mind to show, especially when the kids were around. Like the one of him looking beat after three days in jail for selling liquor without a licence. It had taken him three days to come up with the scratch to pay the fine – £15 3s 8d! Plus court costs, that was a year's rent! It was pay up or six months inside – who needed that? The note on the back of that one just said, "Sept 1840. Damn law." There were more like that.

Then there were the really lousy ones, the ones that are nothing but a blur, like somebody walked in front of the camera and jostled you as you clicked the shutter. The kind you toss – except that this one taken on August 12, 1846, had sentimental value. It was the one shot he had of Philomène's third birthday. On the back, someone had written, "Mary Ann Trim what have you done," and it wasn't a question.

In that birthday snap he saw the three of them at home, him and Scholastique and their Philomène, when Mary Ann burst in and dropped her bomb. In a flash, everything that should have stood still for the time it took to snap the picture – the world, people, time – had started sideways twenty years or more, then back. It would take that long for the dust to settle. No wonder it had turned out a smudge.

A few things you should know about Mary Ann. Twenty-one that April, she was going the way of Martha Hyers. Not in trouble with the law, no, in trouble with herself, into the sauce in a big way. She was no stranger to Dago's house: for some time, she'd been by every day, all the way to eastern Lagauchetière from her home on Mountain Street, for a nip and small talk, and another nip (oh make it a double). But most of her day she spent nearer home at James Grantham's on McGill Street, at the Haymarket (Victoria Square). He had his tobacco shop there, with his bar and rooms above. And he kept her liquored up – because he had a plan.

Don't know how Mary Ann explained to Brooks, her husband, how she'd spent her day – if he ever asked her, coming home bushed from the printing plant. Five years they'd been married, but she ran rings around him, and he never did catch on till too late.

None too swift, Tom Brooks. That was Dago's opinion. Like he'd used up all his sense getting clear of Virginia. Thought he was pretty sharp, though. That's the thing about Brooks that rubbed Grantham the wrong way. Truth is, Grantham really didn't need rubbing. A born wheeler-dealer he was, always with some scheme on the boil. And in Mary Ann he saw easy pickings.

Everybody knew the Trim girls were sitting prettier than most, living off the fat of their father's estate. In the half-light of the bar, her lips loosened by liquor, Mary Ann opened up to Grantham – how she wanted more, she needed more, they were being sued for debts owed by her father's estate, blah, blah. Most people would have told her, "Look be happy with what you've got."

Not Grantham. He was all ears. He was on her side. He even got hold of her father's will and studied it closely, even though he couldn't read (may have got his white pal George Fax, the tailor, to give him a hand with that). With his English accent, his big deals and big talk, Grantham was a gentleman, sooo different from all the rest, so different from Tom Brooks.

St James and McGill streets, 1858. It was at this corner that in 1846 Mary Ann Trim often came to drink and chatter at James Grantham's shop.

Brooks needed taking down a peg – that was Grantham's excuse – so he'd teach Brooks a lesson by fleecing his Mary Ann. He worked on her for more than a year.

So Mary Ann turns up at Dago's on Philomène's birthday with a yarn about how she'd sold her inheritance for £300 to Bill Forsyth, a businessman friend of the Trims from way back. Brooks had had to sign the papers with her, but she'd snowed him and got him to make his X (he couldn't read or write), telling him it was nothing important, just paperwork. "Sign here."

Even she wasn't sure what she'd done, but after she'd done what she'd done, she had this awful feeling that this time she'd really done it. She ran to Dago's in a flap. No way she was going back home after that. Where was home anyway? The house she and Brooks shared on Mountain Street belonged to her father's estate. She and Brooks had no claim to live there now.

She stayed at Dago's for a week and a day, and he pried the truth out of her. No, she hadn't sold out to the trusty Forsyth, she admitted. She'd sold out to Grantham's friend George Fax. It was Grantham who'd set up the deal. And the money? Well, she hadn't been paid her £300 yet, but the cheque was in the mail.

Mary Ann Trim, what have you done!

On August 20 she left Dago's, left town. That too was Grantham's doing. A few days later, Brooks came knocking at Dago's door, looking for his Mary Ann. She stayed away till wintertime.

She was back by February, a changed person. Sobered, maybe. Soured on Grantham for sure, because she knew by then that he'd conned her. The truth is, she never saw a penny of that £300 he'd promised her. And her share in the estate went the rounds, sold and transferred from one person to another – to Grantham for a while.

That made for all kinds of legal problems over who owned what of John Trim's estate. The estate itself was never well managed. Nobody seemed to have a handle on it: lawsuits for back taxes and other debts and no end of lawyers' fees and court costs ate away at it. Mary Ann's stunt only made things worse. And it poisoned her family. Her sisters Charlotte and Henriette and their husbands Tom Tinsley (a white man) and Isaac Taylor (a black man) never trusted her again.

As for Mary Ann and Brooks, they made a stab at starting a family, had three daughters between 1848 and 1859. Two died in the fifties; only Mary Elizabeth, born in 1856, survived. Then Mary Ann left Brooks and took up with Samuel Ransell, a steamboat engineer from Philadelphia. She passed for Ransell's wife, and Mary Elizabeth for Ransell's daughter. And on the very day her Mary Elizabeth turned six, she had another daughter with Ransell. They called her Marie Anne.

Considering that John Trim's will left all his property to his "legitimate" grandchildren, this caused more headaches, especially after Brooks and Mary Ann died. He went first, May 11, 1866; she followed him to the grave three months later. Then Mary Ann's sisters claimed that both her daughters were illegitimate and out of the running for whatever was left of the Trim pie.

All the belongings that Brooks and Mary Ann left behind boiled down to a silver watch and chain worth $7; a chest of drawers, $2; a small clock, $1.50; four wooden chairs, 80 cents; and a mirror, 25 cents, plus $105.24 stashed at the Bank of Montreal. Not much to show for a life, even less for two. Not much of a picture for Dago to keep, but he kept it because it showed his Philomène on the day she turned three.

24

Jericho!

☞

LOCATION, LOCATION, LOCATION, THEY SAY. Find the right spot for your shop, and you're laughing. Clarence Selden set up his hair salon on Notre Dame in 1857 – shop on the ground floor, home on the floor above and to the rear, away from the clatter of the street. Notre Dame just east of Place d'Armes was a good spot. Everybody, but everybody, shopped on Notre Dame.

Before that he'd lived uptown on St Charles Borromée and plied his trade at Coleman's Montreal House on Custom House Square. Nice spot for a hotel, that, down by the water, with a view of Victoria Bridge going up. And he and Coleman, the hotel keeper, had at least this in common: they were both from Troy, New York. But when a hairdresser's day could stretch from 6 AM till 9–10 at night, there was something to be said for having your home and shop in one place, view or no view.

One problem with 157 Notre Dame, though. It was next to the ghost of Christ Church Cathedral. The church had burned down

Christ Church Cathedral burned down at midnight on December 9, 1856. Early in 1857, Clarence Selden set up shop next door to the ruins of the cathedral, on Notre Dame Street east of Place d'Armes.

two weeks before Christmas. As locations go, next door to a burnt church might not be ideal but it beats being next to a burning one. Selden moved in around February. The place suited him, so in March he signed a lease for a cool £100. The lease was to run for a year from May 1, with the first of four payments due at the beginning of August.

Boot and shoe makers J. & T. Bell bought the prime lot where the burnt church stood, planning to put up a shoe factory. Workmen went to work clearing the rubble and starting to dig.

Now get this. It's mid-July, 4 o'clock on a Sunday afternoon as sunless and stormy as all get-out. Selden's at home with his wife, windows shut tight … no one coming in, no one going out. He's nodding off maybe when

BLAMBABLAMBLAM!

"What the ...?

BABLAM!

His eyes open wild and he can't believe what he sees: the wall's gone. The back wall's come tumbling down. Oh my sainted Anna! Look, that's it, a heap of rubble – down in the pit the Bells dug ...

You can imagine, Selden or Anna, his wife Anna Watkins, one of them, would have been on the blower pretty quick to their landlord if they'd had phones then. And words might have passed in the heat of the moment about getting the place fixed on the double or you can forget your £25 due in two weeks, Mr Arthur Webster, sir. But there were no phones, not for another twenty years, so Selden had a chance to cool down.

A week later, he did go after old Webster in writing, claiming damages and demanding repairs right away. Of course, Webster had an interest in having the place fixed up, but the damage wasn't his doing. It was J. & T. Bell that Selden had to go after, because their workmen were to blame, "excavating on the site of the late Christ Church, adjoining ... without propping the walls."

Going after the Bells took some doing. Joshua Bell put him off, claiming Selden hadn't suffered much – "a few days inconvenience" is all, he said – while the wall was rebuilt. So Joshua fit the battle. But Clarence could fit it too.

In the end, rather than go to court, they agreed to binding arbitration, "binding" meaning they had to abide by the outcome or fork over £200. That was in April 1858. Selden picked his man, Joshua chose his, and the two arbitrators named a third to act as umpire, to be sure the whole thing didn't end in a deadlock. They had twelve days to reach a decision. Right on deadline, April 20, they ruled two to one that J. & T. Bell owed Selden £36 5s in compensation, no ifs, ands, or buts.

LADIES'
HAIR DRESSING ESTABLISHMENT.

MRS. C. F. SELDEN

BEGS leave respectfully to inform the Ladies of Montreal that she has opened a LADIES' HAIR DRESSING ESTABLISHMENT at No. 292 Lagauchetiere Street, three doors from German Street, where by strict attention she hopes to merit a share of public patronage. She will be also prepared to restore Hair to its original colour by the best improved Hair Dyes and Cosmetics, and cleanse the Head of all Dandriff by a New Vegetable Wash, made by herself, and can furnish everything that will complete a Lady's Toilet.

Ladies will be attended at their own Residence, by leaving their address at Mrs. Selden's Private Room, or at C. F. Selden's Hair Dressing Saloon, 194 Notre Dame Street.

Montreal, Nov. 23, 1858.   175-6m

Anna Selden opened her first hair salon in the fall of 1858.
She later had a salon on Place d'Armes.

So the sun shone on Clarence Selden and 157 Notre Dame that spring, and maybe 157 wasn't such a bad spot. But now he'd found a better one at 194, for a whopping £150 a year. He was about to move. And Anna, no slouch in the styling line, was thinking of opening her own salon for the ladies, which she did that fall on Lagauchetière, near German Street.

25

The
CENTAUR

OSBORNE MORTON LOVED HORSES FROM the day he was born. So much so that as a slave kid in Lexington, Kentucky, he'd wait till dark, sneak out to his master's stables and steal a ride, even though he knew he'd catch hell for it when he got back. You might figure, because of those joyrides – but mostly because he was sold to the owner of a Louisville track along with a horse whose name, Glencoe, was the name of a massacre in Scotland – you might figure two things about Osborne Morton. One is that horses would be his life; two is that horses would be the death of him. And another thing – Scotland would come into it somehow. You might have figured that.

His fate was sealed the minute his master sold him and Glencoe to Campbell, who owned the track in Louisville. Lumping horse and man together like that, they were thinking livestock. Fate had another idea and cast a spell then and there, turning Morton into one of those centaurs of legend, half man, half horse, who knows the secrets of both. Does the man ride the horse or is it the other way round? Slavery had a way of turning the world upside down.

On September 18, 1850, President Fillmore approved the Fugitive Slave Law, the man stealers' charter passed by the Thirty-First Congress of the United States. It gave black people the willies because it made slave catching the patriotic duty of all good Americans, so they were told. North, south, east, and west, in free state or slave state, no place was safe for black people, freeborn or fugitive. No one was safe under that law, but it took most whites fifteen years and a civil war to catch on.

Osborne Morton didn't need catching, he was long caught. But fate gets tired before long, then fate grabs the reins, and look out! Give a centaur his head and he's gone. There was no stopping Morton. It was in the early 1850s when he was about 25. He slipped out of Louisville – left a wife and child – and flew clear across the free states, where the Fugitive Slave Law applied, to Canada, where it did not. First, to Canada West, and when he got there he hung a right and ran to Canada East.

So here he is in Montreal, a centaur in a strange city, panting, slick with sweat, pretty cut-up about losing his loved ones, feeling spent, feeling free. And those men in calèches calling "Hue donc!" to their nags – Do horses speak a different language here? No time to wonder or regret when all you own is the shirt on your back, give or take a button. Got to make a living.

Morton lands a job as servant to Harrison Stephens, a Vermonter who had moved to Montreal in the 1820s and done very well, importing rice and tobacco and stuff from the States. Morton is there about a year when the past comes calling in July 1854 in the shape of Mr Otts of Campbell & Otts, owners of that Louisville track. Yes, that Mr Campbell. You might have known that word would get back to him that the centaur was living in Montreal.

Now, Otts has to be cagey. He can't let on what he's up to. He knows that all the blacks in town, the antislavery types too and God knows who else will come down on him if they get wind of his purpose. So he sends a man to sniff out Morton on the quiet – but he points him at the wrong door! "You've got the wrong Mr Stephens," a kitchen servant tells the man snooping around Romeo H. Stephens's place. "You want his father, Mr Harrison Stephens." And he takes him there.

Slavers offer livestock – human and animal – for sale in this sketch, which appeared on the masthead of the Boston abolitionist paper, the *Liberator*, from 1831 to 1838.

So Otts has tracked Morton down, and Morton agrees to a meeting. "Look, Osborne," Otts lays it on thick, "come back to work for us and we'll give you all the liberty papers you want. We'll set you free, free your wife and kid, freedom all around, OK? And how much they paying you here? That all? We'll pay you three, no, four times as much, think of it. And the money you make at the track, all yours to keep. Whaddya say? Deal?"

And Morton buys it, poor sap. He's packing his bag, ready to go. Can you blame him? All that trouble they took to find him and get him back, all that expense. In a few days he'll be with his wife and baby again and they'll all be as free as the birds. He must have felt wanted. You couldn't help but feel wanted. Every man, woman, and child likes to feel wanted. But feeling wanted and being WANTED! under the Fugitive Slave Law are opposite things, like saying good evening when you mean good night.

Lucky for him, Romeo Stephens figured that. He smelled a rat and did some checking. "Fortunately, Mr R.H. Stephens was informed of what was going on," the newspaper said. "He was aware

Osborne Morton in 1863

that the law of Kentucky prevented the manumission of a slave unless he was sent out of the State, and that the poor fellow's wife and child had been already sold to some man living in one of the back counties of Missouri."

Imagine the reaction when word got out. It would have been all the buzz in every black home and shop – from Shadrach Minkings's in the heart of town, out west to carpenter Matthew Bell's place in St Antoine Ward, and out east to Peter Dago's dye shop in St James.

There was no law against trying to sweet-mouth an ex-slave back into bondage. And you couldn't charge Otts with kidnapping: he

Harrison Stephens's house on Dorchester Street (René Lévesque Blvd) in the 1850s. This is where Osborne Morton was working when an attempt was made to lure him back into slavery.

Romeo H. Stephens, about 1850. He blew the whistle on the plot to return Osborne Morton to Kentucky.

hadn't tried to snatch Morton. But it was an offence to "entice" a servant away from his employer. So Otts was hauled into police court, fined \$4, and jailed for … five minutes. That's all he got, a slap on the wrist – but Morton's eyes had been opened. Otts hung around awhile, thinking he could coax the burnt child back by the fire. Who was he kidding?

Next thing you know, Morton is across the sea, in Scotland. That's one way to shake the bloodhounds and the blues: go far away, cross a stream, and if that stream should be the ocean, all the better. A change of air and occupation works wonders, they say. He works a year or two as a steamboat steward, then as a house servant in Glasgow.

Here's where Scotland comes into the picture for good: he marries over there, a white woman called Catherine. She's a servant in the same house. Catherine T is all we know of her name. It happened. Married slaves often remarried after they fled. They'd run off, leaving wives and children behind because they couldn't get off together, but once they reached freedom, more often than not the gates shut behind them, the lights went out, and out went all hope of reunion. Look at Morton: his wife and his child had been shipped like lost luggage God knows where. No use aching, best to forget. Go away, cross an ocean, make a fresh start.

So now it's Osborne and Catherine, till death do them part. Whose idea was it to take ship for Montreal? He was back in town by the early spring of 1858, and this time he wasn't running from anything. But running was in his blood and Scotland was still on his mind, so on September 9, 1859, he turned out for the 4th Annual Gathering of the Caledonian Society. Och aye, the Highland Games. He ran in the hurdles (came second, won 12s 6d), the sack race (came second there too, but no prize for that), and the wheelbarrow race (came first, won 15s).

Watch a centaur at play and you learn something. Take that wheelbarrow race. All seven runners were lined up blindfolded, the object being to push your barrow straight across to the finish line on the far side of the ring. Well, the signal was no sooner given than Morton shot like an arrow, straight through the rope barrier on the other side, "causing many a damsel to give a little scream," said one who was there. MacThis and MacThat ran this way and that way, crashing into the sidelines and into each other. The first race was such a hoot, they ran it again. And again Morton, "the gentleman in black," was the only one to go straight, as if a centaur didn't need eyes to see.

The crowds cheered and clapped like crazy, and hoisted Morton on their shoulders, would you believe! You wouldn't see the like for a hundred years, till Jackie Robinson played ball for the Royals. Morton ran other races over the years – mile races, hurdles, sack races, potato races – and won some of them too, but none could compare with the kick of that barrow race in '59.

The next year, 1860, was filled with preparations for the visit of Albert Edward, Prince of Wales, Queen Victoria's son and heir, the future King Edward VII. He was coming to officially open the Victoria Bridge on August 25, among other things. It was some deal – the first official visit to North America by a member of the royal family, and the first bridge anywhere across the St Lawrence. There were street decorations to put up, fireworks, parades, one monster trade fair, balls, receptions, hullaballoo, and lots of speeches, what they called congratulatory addresses.

The black men of Montreal met at Clarence Selden's on Notre Dame to cook up their own address to the prince. They made Isaac Turner chairman, and Edmond, his younger brother, secretary. The Turners had been slaves of a woman in Petersburgh, Virginia; she'd planned to sell them on January 1, 1858, but not caring to

Fireworks were part of the hoopla when the Prince of Wales came to open the Victoria Bridge in August 1860. This print appeared in the American magazine *Harper's Weekly* of September 1, 1860.

be anyone's New Year's present, they'd run out on her a few days before and wound up in Montreal.

John Scott was another Virginia fugitive, from Richmond, in his late thirties, a bit older than the Turners. The meeting named him and Selden and Thomas Cook to set the words down on paper. All agreed it was a good speech they wrote, but the prince never got to hear it. His handlers didn't want him getting sucked into the race question, especially as he'd be heading for the States a few days later.

Soon afterwards Morton opened his livery business – the Prince of Wales' Livery Stables, he called it. At first it was on Victoria Square, then from 1862 in a rundown stable on the south side of Craig Street, east of St Pierre. In '67, he moved to a bigger, better place on Bonaventure Street (St Jacques, west of McGill). Bigger and better means more expensive. His rent was $500 a year compared with $120 before, and his taxes went up too.

PRINCE OF WALES' LIVERY STABLE,
Craig Street, near Bleury Street,
OSBORNE MORTON, PROPRIETOR.

Proper attention is paid to Grooming and Feeding Horses. Horses bought, sold or exchanged.
July 9.   6m-163

In choosing the name of his business, Osborne Morton capitalized on the excitement generated by the visit of the Prince of Wales.

Catherine helped to keep the books and pretty soon it was obvious he was in over his head. In the spring of 1869 he went bust. He had racked up $1,740 in debts, $950 of that to his landlord, Senator Charles Wilson. He had to sign over everything at the Prince of Wales' to a trustee. But he cut a deal with Wilson and managed to keep going another year before he threw in the towel.

By the spring of '71, Morton and Catherine had moved out to the parish of Lachine, where Blue Bonnets racecourse was at the time. It was around then that he ran Orchard Banks, John Shedden's riverside horse-breeding farm at Lower Lachine. Morton eventually got back on his feet, starting his own stud farm, with his horses Quito and Tantrum and Sir George and the like, and training and racing horses. He was rated "a very fearless and competent rider, standing high in the opinion of his many friends and acquaintances and one of the best judges of horseflesh in the province."

Nearly 60 years old in 1887, he was still racing, a bit banged up from the tumbles he'd taken. He was booked to ride August 4 in the flat mile at Blue Bonnets. The last twelve days he'd spent training Ely, his ride. Catherine didn't like it. His arm was still swollen from a fall, and she didn't like the thought of him racing just yet. Ely's owner told him, "Say the word, Osborne. It's all right. If you don't feel up to it, we'll find another jockey." But Morton was driven. He felt fine, he felt fit to ride, he said.

The race started around 4 o'clock. Morton had it all figured out. Before the first turn, he fell back into second and hung there and hung there as they went round. On the last turn, he pounced.

But fate seized the reins, and look out! Morton was thrown and Ely rolled over him. And the horse named Young Kelso, hard on his heels, stomped all over his body before crashing down on him hard.

Whoa! Whoa!

Whoa!

"The life of every turf meeting," as Morton was known, had little life left in him now. His back was broken, his ribs, his collar bone. Blood poured from his nose and mouth.

They had a phone at the track, and someone called for the ambulance to take him to the Montreal General, way down on Dorchester Street. In a horse-drawn ambulance, it was a long ride. Ely's owner, Meloche, rode with Morton and stayed by his side at the hospital. About half past six, Meloche asked should he fetch Catherine, and Morton said he'd better.

So off went Meloche.

So now, no one was looking.

So …

In the quiet of the evening, he was a boy again in Lexington, waiting – he knew he'd catch hell for it, but hey! – waiting for that moment when no one was looking so he could slip out in the darkness and steal a ride, streaking like lightning over the blue grass.

26

TRIAL
of the
CENTURY

☞

ALL RIGHT, IT WAS NO BIG DEAL, no big bloody crime. No big names. No high-powered lawyers, no fireworks, no landmark ruling. No media mob on the courthouse steps. None of that. It was a short, open-and-shut case. Routine.

A rough rolly-polly Irishwoman named Eliza Molloy, already a widow at 22, was caught red-handed picking a pocket at St Ann's Market at 9 o'clock on a Saturday night. It was July 30, 1859. She sidled up to Margaret Scott at a butcher's stall, and pretending to be deep in thought over a veal chop, she dipped her hand into Scott's pocket and pinched her purse with four shillings in it. Scott never felt a thing.

Eliza Molloy might have got away with it if hadn't been for the market boss, John Abbott. Pickpockets had plagued the place lately, and that night he'd been warned that this low-looking woman was hanging around. So he watched. He saw her reach under Scott's shawl, and he grabbed her wrist as she walked off

148

holding the bag with the four shillings in it. He called for the cops, and Eliza M. went to jail.

At her trial on August 5, they picked twelve men for the jury. Scott, Abbott, and Fitzgerald the cop told their side. Her turn next. She had no witnesses, no alibi. The best she could do was claim she's clean, that she's been in Canada only a month and done no wrong. She found the purse on the ground, honest! Oh sure. "Guilty," the jury says after hashing it out for all of a minute. Open and shut.

Saturday, August 13. Sentencing time before C.J. Coursol. Just ahead of her, Agnes Smith, another pickpocket, gets three years. She'd worked Bonsecours Market. One thing C.J. held against her was that she looked "respectable," which made her not just a thief but a fraud. People had a right to be suspicious of crooks, and she'd cheated them of that right. How could they suspect her if she didn't look the part? She cried and howled when he sent her away. Not a pretty sight.

Eliza Molloy didn't look respectable – you couldn't hold that against her. And she didn't go to pieces or scream blue murder when C.J. gave her two years in the pen. She curtsied and said, "Thank you, my Lord and gentlemen of the jury, for that short space of time." So polite it hurt.

Will you listen to her! What gave her the right to be so polite? She realize who she was talking to? Because Charles Williams on that jury could count on one finger the times he'd been called a gentleman. The closest he'd come was "colored gentleman," and that was something else.

He lived on St Charles Borromée Street, no. 36, a fugitive slave from Washington with an Irish wife, earning his living washing clothes. Being called a gentleman, pure and simple, even by a thief, was as good as a holiday.

He wasn't the first black man in town to be dealing out justice. It had been going on for several years. Charles Meads, who owned a couple of houses on Versailles Street, had served on juries in the Court of Queen's Bench. William Jackson, who had a restaurant on Wolfe Street, and carpenter Mathew Bell had been jury foremen in the Court of Quarter Sessions. And William Thomas and William Jones had been summoned for jury duty but they begged off, Thomas because he was an American, and Jones the barber because he was sick.

"Economy Is Honour," Charles Williams proclaimed in an advertisement in 1858. How is that for a catchy slogan?

Charles Williams

So, really, what was special about this trial was that it was nothing special at all. Charles Williams just took his rightful place, and in that sense, the century that went on trial with Eliza Molloy – as it did with every accused then, just as ours does with every accused today – was off the hook.

27

MR WOOD
as a Matter of Fact

☞

AT THE END OF *UNCLE TOM'S CABIN*, you may recall, fugitive slaves George and Eliza Harris, with their young son Harry, reunited in Montreal with George's sister and Eliza's mother, had gone to live in Liberia on the west coast of Africa.

The novel doesn't say so, but in Liberia, George and Eliza joined the congregation of the Rev. Alfred Thomas Wood. And Eliza's mother Cassy, she died there before 1852, when the book was published. Wood, who had left Liberia for England in June 1851, reported that he had attended her and "she died a very happy death."

Got a problem with that? Some people in England did in the fall of 1852. They couldn't see how Wood could have ministered to characters in a best-selling novel when he wasn't in the novel and they weren't for real.

That was in Hull, Yorkshire, on the North Sea coast, where the Rev. A.T. Wood, DD, was raising funds for his church in Liberia and spinning his tale. He'd been around Ireland, collecting in Dublin and Cork and Belfast. In England, he'd visited Liverpool and Lancaster and Carlisle, among other places.

In Hull, birthplace of William Wilberforce, he hit on three clergymen. The Rev. John King of Christ Church took Wood at his word and gave him a sovereign. The Rev. Joseph Hargreaves, a Wesleyan minister, had his guard up as soon as Wood mentioned his connection to George and Eliza. He found so many holes and contradictions in Wood's story that he refused to have anything to do with him.

The Rev. Christopher Newman Hall, an independent minister, was friendly and even had Wood over for dinner. But his doubts grew. Here was a man who claimed that his church back in Monrovia counted 2,000 members who had sent him all the way to England to raise just £200 – and he still hadn't managed to do so after a year and a half. Hall made a few inquiries and turned Wood down.

After hearing from the three clergymen and from the former British consul in Monrovia who'd known Wood there and said that his Liberian papers were fake, the authorities in Hull clapped him in jail for obtaining money by false pretences. It may be that they just didn't "collusitate the great principles of action," as old Sam, who'd helped Eliza escape from slavery, said of his fellow slaves in Harriet Beecher Stowe's novel. Or maybe they collusitated only too well.

A strange case, Mr Wood. As though real life couldn't hold him, so his life had to be a novel – not a novel written on paper, but a lived one.

Now, if this story were a novel, we'd know exactly what happened from cover to cover, particularly in the six years or so between the day Wood entered that English lockup and the time he surfaced in Montreal. Because all we'd have to do is make it up, imagining things like: "Behind bars, Wood turned his thoughts to Canada and he saw that the place needed a good novel."

It was A.T. Wood who showed up in Montreal in the spring of 1859 – no Rev. before his name, no DD after it. You might think he was plain Alfred Thomas Wood, but that would be too close to reality for someone whose life was a novel. He was Mr A.T. Wood, civil engineer, architect, and builder, ten years superintendent of public works in Sierra Leone, next to Liberia. You've got to admit: Wood was no cheap paperback as novels go.

The black cook seeking work in April 1852 could not have asked for a better attention getter for his advertisement than to have it right under an ad for *Uncle Tom's Cabin*, the huge best-seller hot off the press.

Soon after his arrival, he gave a lecture at the Mechanics' Hall. If you'd paid your 25 cents, you would have learned a lot about the people living between Cape Palmas and the Rio Pongo, the practice of slavery, and the progress of Christian missions there. In that speech on June 13, "much important information was communicated," reported the *Witness* newspaper, promising to publish a detailed report in its next issue. It didn't. At least Mr Wood delivered.

Or maybe not. To make speeches about far-off Africa was one thing, but to play the civil engineer, architect and builder ... Would you cross a bridge designed by A.T. Wood? Would you sleep under the roof he built? "Great discount allowed on Plans and Specifications," he promised.

Alfred Thomas Wood advertised as an architect and builder
in the summer of 1859.

For his business address that summer he used Mathew Bell's shop on St Antoine Street. Bell, a South Carolina man, was an honest-to-goodness carpenter and contractor. Being a savvy man – and with a short fuse besides – he would have cottoned on to Wood pretty quickly. But suppose he did have his doubts. Do you think Wood, writing the novel of his life as he went, wasn't up to thinking on his feet, coming up with a convincing plot twist, or maybe ending that chapter right there, with the mystery uncollusitated?

Turn the page and hear the Rev. A.T. Wood thunder: "Know ye not that there is a prince, and a great man fallen this day in Israel?" That's more like him. That was in December. He was talking about John Brown. It was Friday, December 2, 1859, the day they hanged John Brown at Charlestown, Virginia, for leading seventeen men in a raid on the U.S. armoury at Harper's Ferry in mid-October and trying to get up a slave revolt. Harriet Beecher Stowe had taken an axe to slavery with the publication of *Uncle Tom's Cabin* in 1852; now John Brown had given it another mighty whack where it hurt and never would heal.

The Rev. Wood understood that. Back to being a man of the cloth, he took a leading hand in the John Brown meetings in Montreal. When the black community met on the evening of November 24 to discuss how to respond to Brown's coming execution, he was the master of ceremonies.

They decided that December 2 would be a day of prayer and fasting by "the friends of the slave." They would hold a public prayer meeting at Bonaventure Hall on Victoria Square at 9:00 AM; at 10:30, Wood would speak; and that night at 7:00 PM there would be another public meeting, with speeches by ministers and others on the subject of slavery. And a collection was to be taken up for Brown's family. Mathew Bell, Thomas Cook, and Clarence Selden, all straight arrows, were elected to be the committee overseeing the arrangements.

There was a good crowd at the prayer meeting. You had to hand it to Wood – he held his audience. Whites and blacks, listened for more than an hour, the press reported:

He glanced briefly at the life of John Brown, and showed that for upwards of twenty years, the project which had cost Brown his life, had occupied his thoughts; and that although the attempt had proved abortive, yet its influence was such that the ball he had set in motion would continue to move, until the doom of slavery was sealed. It was but the beginning; and although with the passing hours of to-day the life of John Brown would return to the God who gave it, yet his death would call upon the scene of action many others of the same stamp. He concluded by urging the colored portion of his audience to make good use of the liberty which was theirs, and to show by their conduct through life that they knew how to prize so dear a boon.

At the evening meeting, where other clergymen took the floor, the Rev. Wood led the crowd in an opening hymn. "O! for a thousand tongues to sing," they sang. After the speeches, at his suggestion, the meeting passed a vote of sympathy to John Brown's family, resolving to help them "by collections and subscriptions so far as it may be in our power to do, together with our humble prayers to Almighty God for their spiritual comfort, and for the downfall of slavery." Another of Wood's proposals, unanimously adopted, was that "an Anti-Slavery Society be established as soon as convenient in the city of Montreal." He closed with a prayer.

They collected \$65.86 for Brown's widow and children that night. More contributions came in during the next couple of weeks. It was all on the up and up, real money (and none of it slipped between the pages of A.T. Wood, the novel).

One of the strongest antislavery speeches at that December 2 meeting had come from the Rev. John Cordner. A true believer, Cordner went on to give two more antislavery talks at his Unitarian Church of the Messiah later that month, on successive Sunday evenings. The only black members of his church were William Henry Paine and his son. James Thomas Nurse, a light-skinned mulatto from Barbados, sometimes showed up; he wasn't a Unitarian, but his wife, a white woman, was. So when the pews were packed with blacks on New Year's Day, the regular congregation wondered what was up.

The explanation came as the service ended. The Rev. A.T. Wood stood to present Cordner with a beautifully bound copy of the Bible inscribed: "Presented to The Rev. John Cordner, By the Colored People of Montreal, as a sincere testimonial of their esteem for his efforts and sympathies in the Cause of Human Freedom. January 1, 1860."

It does seem that Wood had some calling. There was no end of good practical ideas pouring from him. No more was said about that chapter in his life when he'd been superintendent of public works in Sierra Leone. Now he was the Rev. Wood, "recently from Sierra Leone, a recognized minister of the Wesleyan Church." Never mind Liberia or that he'd been associated with the Providence Baptist Church there. This was a new chapter.

Within a couple of months of his presentation at the Unitarian Church, he was leading an effort to set up a library and night classes for black Montrealers. Fellow ministers backed him. Listen to the Rev. Henry Wilkes, DD, pastor of Zion Congregational:

The contemplated movement is eminently desirable, seeing there are somewhere near 200 colored inhabitants in our city. The Rev. Mr Wood, a recognized Minister of the Wesleyan Church, of whom I have a very favorable impression, seems admirably qualified to superintend it ... Surely our brethren of African descent, who, as a race, have suffered so much, ought to have our help.

The equally respected pastor of United Presbyterian Church, the Rev. William Taylor, DD, not only offered his support but raised an interesting point:

In the cities of Canada West the colored inhabitants are provided with schools and churches, but in this city they have nothing of the kind. Why is it so? As there is likely to be a rapid increase of this class of our population for some years to come, it seems the more necessary that something should be done.

But could the Rev. Wood deliver? Nothing ever came of his proposal for an antislavery society. Of the reading room and night classes, no sign. Of the Rev. Wood himself, not a word, not a sign after that. He vanished. For just under a year, he'd had a hand in everything going. Then nothing.

This is no way to end a novel.

28

COOK'S
PLACE

THOMAS COOK HAD THIS QUIET STRENGTH, something that told you loud and clear you could count on him. That may be why, in his early thirties and newly come from Pennsylvania, he was hired as custodian of the McGill Medical Faculty. That was in 1854, before he got into the restaurant business, with a house-painting and laundry business on the side.

You counted wrong if you took him for a push-over, more quiet than strong. Like those four young whites did in '58 when they ordered up steaks at his St Urbain Coffee House and tried to skip without paying. He cornered one, held him till the police came, and hit him with the bill – hit him with an assault charge too. Or there was the time in '59 – after he'd closed the coffee house at 2 St Urbain and moved up the street – this guy came by to pick up his shirts and thought he'd palm Cook's silver watch in the bargain. Wound up doing his thinking in jail for three months.

As a matter of fact, there was a lot more than laundry doing at Cook's. The place was a regular beehive. There was not a black soul

St Urbain Street, St Lawrence Suburb, 1860. Thomas Cook was not the only American-born black who lived here in the 1850s and 1860s. Marylander George Anderson, for instance, had a restaurant and whitewashing business at no. 6 from 1856 to 1862. And after Cook moved from no. 2 to no. 13 in 1859, Francis Thomas of Florida took over at no. 2, operating a tavern and whitewashing business there until 1862, when he moved to no. 6.

in town right through the 1860s who didn't know that two-storey house at 13 St Urbain (renumbered 33 in 1865). For a while, Cook ran a home-cleaning and painting business there, as well as the laundry and dying works. And he and Anna Owens, his wife, took in boarders.

You had all kinds of people living there – some whites, but mostly blacks. Jacob Lattimore, for instance, lived at the Cooks' in 1860–61, at least, before getting a place of his own. He was about fifty then. Looks like he'd come up the sea route in the late fifties, by way of Boston and Saint John, from Norfolk, Virginia, where some of his friends and relations were still slaves. He held the kinds of jobs blacks did – tobacconist, whitewasher and launderer, hairdresser and barber. But on the side, starting in 1860, he lent money on mortgage to middle-class whites: $600, $1,000, $1,200 …

NOTICE TO HOUSEKEEPERS

THE Subscriber beg leave to inform his Customers and the Public generally, that he is now prepared to receive and promptly execute all ORDERS for

WHITE WASHING AND COLORING,

With which he may be favored

Residence No. 2, St. Urbain Street.

JOS. COOK

October 9   am-291

THOMAS COOKE'S ST URBAIN COFFEE HOUSE

2 St. Urbain Street 2.

JUST RECEIVED at the above Establishment a FRESH SUPPLY of

NEW YORK OYSTERS

AND

LOBSTERS

Which can be prepared as well as SOUPS STEAKS, CHOPS and every other article requisite in the Restaurant Line, on the shortest notice, and in a Style not to be surpassed in this city.

Mr. Cooke will also be prepared to execute all orders for Breakfasts, Luncheons, Dinners and Suppers to be served without delay either at his Coffee House or at Private Dwellings in any part of the city, the whole of which will be on the most reasonable terms.

Sept 10   265

ST. URBAIN COFFEE HOUSE.

THE Subscriber, in returning his sincere thanks for the liberal patronage he has heretofore received, begs to give notice that he has

REFITTED HIS SALOON,

where wines and Liquors of the Best Brands and Choicest Descriptions can always be had.

—ALSO,—

LUNCHEON

Served up from 11 till 2 o'clock, on the shortest notice.

T. COOK,
No. 2 St. Urbain Street.

Montreal, June 21.   am-193

NOTICE.

WHITEWASHING, COLOURING, PAINTING and HOUSE CLEANING, &c, done on the shortest notice and on moderate terms, by
THOMAS COOK & CO.,
13 St. Urbain Street.

February 29.   T 259

WHITEWASHING.

THOMAS COOK,

GRATEFUL for the liberal patronage hitherto extended to him by the citizens of Montreal, begs leave respectfully to thank them for the same, and intimate that he is prepared to execute all orders in the

WHITEWASHING & COLORING LINE,

warranted to give the most entire satisfaction.

Application to be made till 1st May, at No. 2, St. Urbain Street; after that date at No. 13, same Street.

N.B.—All orders promptly attended to.

Montreal, April 26, 1859.   303

You get an idea of Thomas Cook's enterprise and addresses between 1857 and 1860 from advertisements he placed in the newspapers.

Then you had Pauline Williams, another Virginian. For her, Cook's place was more like a refuge. In June 1860 she'd married Henry Smith, a Marylander who'd spent some years in Montreal working as a hairdresser. Five months they were married, then he died. She went to Cook's.

Besides offering jobs, shelter, food, and other things, Cook probably doctored people's souls. He had that in him. Sometime after the spring of 1863, when Caroline Augusta, their one child, died at 13, he and his wife left the Baptists for the Plymouth Brethren. No smoking, no drinking, no dancing; they were a sober set. Didn't believe in building churches; they rented a room on Fortification Lane. Didn't believe in ordained ministers either; every member was his own priest. That suited Cook. That solid self-reliance of his, with Anna Owens's TLC, might be why Jacob Lattimore moved back in with them for his dying days in 1876.

The faded inscription on Jacob Lattimore's grave in Mount Royal Cemetery reads: "In Memory of Jacob Lattemore, Died 5 June 1876, Aged 66 years – Erected by his Friends." He died at the Cooks' home at 99 Vitré Street (now Viger).

You could count on Cook and his wife. No wonder, then, that in '61 Lavina Wormeny, the widow of Henry Bell of Texas, was brought to them that winter night she came in on the train. You'd have needed a quiet strength to help her. You need it now to read her story through, or it'll give you nightmares and make you want to kill, over and over in your head, a lot of devils long dead and buried.

This is how it ran in the *Gazette*:

Narrative of the Escape
of a Poor Negro Woman from Slavery

When some years ago Mrs Stowe wrote "Uncle Tom's Cabin," and the whole world read the story of the wrongs of the black man, some there were who did not hesitate to say that though such things might exist in the brain of the novelist, they could nowhere else be found. We lay before our readers to-day a brief account of the sufferings of a poor negro woman, caused by the brutality of a master, which for hideous malignity and fiendish cruelty were beyond the imagination even of a Legree, and a recital of her escape from bondage, which for romantic interest is far beyond anything we have ever heard of, and another proof that truth is stranger than fiction. We have the account from the lips of the woman herself, who arrived in this city on Monday last, and we have also the statement, over his own signature, of Dr Reddy, under whose treatment she now is, which fully bears out every word of hers regarding the cruelty to which she had been subjected. Her history in brief is as follows: -

Born in Washington of free parents, she was while yet an infant stolen from there, with two or three colored men and thirty or forty other "cattle" by a man named Tom Watson, now expiating the theft by imprisonment for life in Richmond Penitentiary. She was taken down to the neighbourhood of Galveston, Texas, as the property of Wm. Whirl, and whose wife, Polly, performed to her the part of a mother. It was from Polly Whirl she learned all these particulars, she being of course too young to know anything. Until she was thirteen or fourteen she was brought up as a "show girl," taught to dance, sing, cackle like a hen, or crow like a rooster, so that you could not tell the difference, and perform in various other ways; Whirl always being able to attract a crowd from the country round to see her perform. After that time she was sent into the cotton field with the other field hands, where the treatment was cruelly severe. No clothes whatever were allowed them, their hair was cut off close to their head, and thus were exposed to the glare of a southern sun from early morn until late at night. Scarcely a day passed without their receiving fifty lashes, whether they worked or whether they did not. They were also compelled to go down on their knees, and harnessed to a plough, to plough up the land, with boys for riders, to whip them when they flagged in their work. At other times, they were compelled to walk on hackles, used for hackling flax. Her feet are now dotted over with scars, caused by this brutality. She often, over and over again, attempted to escape, but having no knowledge of the way, was easily overtaken and brought back. On one occasion, she and her husband, (if he could be called so) made an unsuccessful attempt to fly. The poor man had had on his legs for two years irons which had grown into the flesh; these impeded him in his flight and caused their capture. He was then shockingly beaten, and otherwise cruelly ill used, so that he died under the treatment, and she was brought back. Her Mistress, Polly Whirl, a Dutch woman, and a woman, had always been a friend to the poor negress, who went by the name of "Captain Bull," and at last told her of Canada, that refuge for the hunted fugitive and pointed out to her the North Star as her guide by night. This of course was done without the knowledge of the brute Whirl. She again started, and travelled on foot without a vestige of clothing, subsisting on herbs and nuts, sometimes parched with thirst, until she actually reached a place in the state of Mississippi called the "Shades of Death." Here she gave birth to twin children, one of them dead. The other she gave in charge to a woman there. While at the "Shades of Death" she was arrested as a fugitive, put in jail, and claimed by Whirl who had come in quest of her, and taken back by him to Galveston. This first regular flight was commenced in March 1858. On her return to Texas, her master having had some difficulty in proving her identity swore that he would mark her in such a manner that hereafter there would be no such trouble. He slit both her ears, then branded her on the back of her left hand with a hot iron, cut off with an axe the little finger and bone connecting therewith of her right hand, searing the wound with a hot iron, and also branded her on the stomach with a letter.

He heard she had tried to incite more of the slaves to escape to Canada, and tried to force her to tell who had told her anything about Canada, promising not to whip her if she did so. She with the spirit of a martyr refused to give any information, whereupon he had her fixed in what is there technically called a "buck." This was doubling her in two, until her legs were passed over her head, where they were kept by a stick passed across the back of her neck. This violence was the cause of the distortion mentioned in the doctor's statement. While in this position, several panels of a board fence were raised, a notch cut in the boards and her neck placed in the notch. She was then whipped to such a degree that the overseer, more humane than the master, interfered to prevent a murder. The wounds caused by the lash were rubbed with salt and water, and pepper, to keep away the green flies. After this, on one occasion, Whirl struck her on the head with a hoe-handle a number of times, and actually broke her skull. She says herself that a silver plate had to be put in, and that her master afterwards told her, cursing her, that she had "a dollar in her head to pay her way to purgatory." At another time she was left for a number of days without anything to eat or drink. She says she tried to tear her eyes out to eat them, she was so hungry. Still later, for some disobedience on her part, they hoisted her into a tree, locked a chain around her neck, and handcuffed her wrists, the marks being yet visible. There she was left for two days and nights, without a morsel to eat, being taunted with such questions as to whether she was hungry, and would like something to eat, &c., &c., she never giving the satisfaction of answering a word. She succeeded at length, by spitting on her hands, in slipping off the cuffs, with which she wrenched asunder the locks of the chains around her neck, and then fell exhausted to the ground. At another time several of her teeth were knocked out by a hammer, she having bitten off a part of her master's nose, and at another time she was knocked down with a whip, leaving a scar of more than three inches in length on her cheek.

For more than another year, she remained in Texas, when she again escaped. She crossed to the gulf in a steamer, hiding among some barrels, and when the Captain discovered her and interrogated her as to who she was, she answered him in unintelligible gibberish, so that he could make nothing of it. She was quite naked, and one of the passengers gave her a blanket to throw around her. When they arrived in Louisiana, she went ashore, and commenced her course Northward. She was recognized, however, before long, and pursued. She escaped, she says, by plunging into a river and swimming across – her master having taught her how to swim like an eel. The river was full of alligators, but they never touched her. She then went through hardships similar to what she had endured the previous year, made her way to the "Shades of Death," got her child, started again, and, travelling by the aid of her heavenly beacon, reached Warren County, Illinois.

She was now on free soil, but she was doomed to still further sufferings. A negro there, by artful means, entrapped her and sold her for $350 to a resident of Natchez, where she was taken. From Natchez she contrived to escape, and wandered into Virginia to New Richmond, where she was arrested as a runaway, and put in jail. She again contrived to escape, and got as far as Cumberland, where she was taken up. There she received some assistance which enabled her to break out of jail and she again went on her journeyings towards a place of freedom. After various vicissitudes, being arrested and again escaping, she came to Louisville, Kentucky, was arrested, broke jail and came to Boydstown, where she was again taken up. At Boydstown, they took the child from her, which hitherto she had carried with her, and she was hired out to a man until some one should claim her. She was once more successful in getting away, was put across the Ohio river in a boat, and got as far as Zanesville, Ohio. There she was again stopped and carried back to Boydstown, under the Fugitive Slave Law, once more a slave. Again she got away, travelled, through Ohio, to New York State, mentioning Watertown and Whitehall as places through which she passed, always on foot.

Finally when near Rouse's Point, she was taken to that place in a freight train; there some man performed the Christian act of paying her way to Montreal by railroad, and on Monday evening last she arrived here, was brought to the house of a man of her own race, Mr. Cook, No. 13 St Urbain Street, where she now is in a state of perfect destitution, covered with a patchwork of rags, suffering from the severe injuries she received from the brutal Whirl.

Her object now is, if possible, to earn money to support herself, and to raise enough to purchase the freedom of her child, the property of Ann Choil, Boydstown, Kentucky. $250 is the amount necessary to restore the child to his mother. Need we commend the poor woman to the citizens of Montreal for their practical aid, after the history we have given of her? We feel that there will be an immediate response from all.

The following is the statement kindly furnished to us by Dr Reddy, he having been called in to see her by Cooke the man who has so humanely sheltered her: –

Montreal, January 28, 1861.

I was requested by Mr Cook to call and see a negro woman who had arrived the previous day in Montreal, he telling me she was very ill from injuries she had received while a slave. On visiting the woman, she complained of severe pain in her right side, caused as she said, by a violent wrench which she received at the hands of her owners. On making examination I found her body very much distorted, her spine curved towards the right side, and the ribs forced completely in the same direction, having a very bulged appearance. I also found the following marks of ill treatment on her person. A V shaped piece has been slit out of each ear; there is a depression on the right parietal bone where it had been fractured and is now very tender to the touch; the corresponding spot, on the opposite side, has a large scar uncovered by hair; there is a large deep scar, 3½ inches long, on the left side of the lower jaw; several of her teeth are broken out; the back of her left hand has been branded with a heated flat-iron; the little finger of her right hand with a portion of the bone that it connected with, has been cut off; the abdomen bears the mark of a large letter 4 inches long in one way and 2½ inches in another, also branded in with a hot iron; her ankles are scarred and the soles of her feet are all covered with little round marks apparently inflicted by some sharp instrument which she accounts for by her stating that she was obliged to walk over hackles used for hackling flax; her back and person are literally covered over with scars and marks, now healed, evidently produced by the lash. Altogether, she presents a most pitiable appearance.

John Reddy, M.D.

The poor woman, who has, since she left Texas travelled under the name of Lavina Bell, (the name then given her by Polly Whirl) is still very ill, but is receiving every medical attention from Dr Reddy, who will continue his attendance as long as necessary.

In the foregoing account we have omitted many particulars communicated to us by the woman, the many *ruses* she practiced, counterfeiting madness, inability to walk &c., &c., in order to throw off suspicion; but we have given the recital in as tangible a form as we could from her account, which coming from a poor ignorant negress, – unable to read or write – was necessarily disconnected, but in which nevertheless after a thorough cross-examination, no contradiction could be discovered ...

Thomas Cook

———

29

SAME OLD SONG

☞

LUCKY FOR THOMAS O'BRIEN that one of his tenants was a medical man because, being a grocer, he really had no idea what a threat blacks were to public health. See, all he asked was that his tenants play by the rules – pay the rent, furnish the place, keep it in order, don't sublet without his say-so, etc., etc. But when Dr William D'Eschambault and a friend rented a ground-floor flat from him on east-end Lagauchetière in 1853, they wanted a clause in their lease that said O'Brien "will not have the right to rent the upper part of said tenement to any colored man and will be obliged to put [a] decent and respectable family so as the said Lessees will not be troubled."

Without the doctor and his friend, O'Brien might have rented that upper flat to a black family, and that could have spelled disaster. Because it's a well-known fact that a lot of blacks in Montreal at this time, especially the ones from the States, were carriers. You never knew which ones exactly, and you never knew when they might break out.

It was very, very catching, and the results could be too terrible for words. Take the case of Jones's barbershop in the west end, where one of the most potentially devastating outbreaks occurred in 1860.

Dr Duncan McCallum, despite all his Scottish medical training and his teaching position at McGill, obviously wasn't clued in like D'Eschambault about the black peril. He actually leased the ground-floor shop in his building at 17 St Joseph Street (north side of Notre Dame, just west of McGill Street) to Marylander William Francis Jones and his 20-year-old son, George Edward.

The Joneses moved in on May 1 and it didn't take a month of Sundays for McCallum, who lived over the shop with his wife and eight-year-old daughter, to diagnose an outbreak. On May 15 he complained that the Joneses "do not occupy the said shop in a proper manner and in a way as a shop of this nature ought to be used, the said Lessees making great noise by playing fiddle, serenading, dancing, jumping, and calling in and inviting in the passers by, Keeping their shop open on the Sabbath day for the purpose of labor and allowing therein the constant attendance of a band of loafers."

To McCallum, a good man at heart but one serious Methodist and as uptight as they come, this was a clear clinical case of hellraising – before the eyes and within earshot of his innocent daughter! She might never recover.

Well, the Joneses took a pill, and William Jones kept his shop there for two years – the second year in partnership with his son-in-law John Watkins – right through to the end of April 1862. You heard no more fiddling from Jones' barbershop and saw no more dancing and jumping, and no band of loafers hanging around on the Lord's day.

One source of contagion down. How many more to go?

Henry Harris had a bad attack of it. He was picked up on Notre Dame Street one day in April 1860. He'd started singing at the top of his voice for no reason. When a constable told him it wasn't singing, it was "roaring" and he'd better stop, he went right on, claimed it was a free country and he had every right to sing. The court gave him a fine of ten shillings (or fifteen days in jail) and that seemed to work.

Henry Lewis from Richmond, Virginia, by way of St Thomas on Lake Erie, might have been a carrier, but he never came down

Dapper George Edward Jones in 1863. He and his brother James Henry were partners in a "shaving and hair cutting emporium" at 133 McGill Street, which they ran together for a decade.

William Jones

John Watkins

George E Jones

with a full case. That was probably thanks to the preventive medicine in the lease he signed in 1865 for part of a cellar in the Delvecchio building on Jacques Cartier Square. The cellar was to be used for storing and selling fruit and provisions, and nothing else, and the lease said that "any Singing or meetings held on said leased premises at any time so as to annoy" his landlord would get Lewis kicked out.

This was strong medicine, but it was necessary because even a mild case was hazardous. Look at Lizzie Harris. She wasn't caught in time. She came up from Boston and married Charles Van Schaick the year of Confederation, 1867, when she was about 19 or 20. He was a barber from Troy, New York, who bounced back and forth between Montreal and Quebec City through the sixties. He'd married in Montreal in 1859, but his wife had died, so he was a widower, living in Quebec, when he married Lizzie Harris in Montreal, where they settled down. He did his barbering and she was a music teacher. Well, mild case or not, you can imagine how many people she infected, giving piano lessons at her home. Some of her pupils probably spread it to their families and friends, who may have passed it on from generation to generation, down to this very day.

As you can see, these things are hard to keep under control. Some people managed, though.

Elizabeth Taylor Greenfield, born a slave in Natchez, Mississippi, raised free in Philadelphia, was a perfect example. She never lived in Montreal, just came up a few times to sing. She sang opera pieces and traditional ballads, sang for Queen Victoria at Buckingham Palace in 1854. They called her the Black Swan.

The first time she played Montreal, in early June 1855, one man who heard her at rehearsal was bowled over. Her voice had a wingspan you wouldn't believe! "A most astonishing singer," he said, "not only strangely powerful, but sweetly melodious beyond belief."

She packed Mechanics' Hall three nights running and left her audiences begging for more. So after performing in Quebec City, she returned to Montreal in mid-June to give three more concerts, again to full houses. One night she sang "Annie Laurie" and "Charley Is My darling" and other Scottish songs. "It must have astonished the Scotchmen present, to hear their national songs so charmingly

Elizabeth Taylor Greenfield, the Black Swan, charmed everyone with her exquisite voice.

sung, and their native idiom and accent so correctly rendered by a colored lady," a member of the audience said later.

She was supposed to come back for more in 1856, but she cancelled; then made up for it in 1857 by coming twice – once in the spring and again at the end of September, when she was supposed to give one concert but gave two, then returned, after performing in Quebec City, to take part in a benefit evening at Bonaventure Market on September 30. It was a Grand Promenade Concert by the Montreal Field Battery of Artillery, with band music, singing, and dancing into the wee hours. "The singing of Miss Greenfield was excellent, she filled that immense Hall, so that her voice could be distinctly heard in every part," a reviewer said.

In February 1862, in her forties, with retirement in mind, she was persuaded to come and sing one last time in Montreal. Here as elsewhere, as the newspaper put it, she "appeared before a prejudiced public, and carried their hearts by storm."

It's not everybody who could be the Black Swan and make whites sit still and face the music. So the search for a cure went on. Still does.

30

THE PERFECT
CRIME

THERE'S NOTHING WRONG WITH BEING GOOD. Better might be better, but good will do fine. Shooting for perfect, though, you're asking for trouble, with a capital T.

Perfect is all or nothing, like going for control in a game of Hearts. Pick up no points and you win; get stuck with a few, you might lose – and the only way to snatch victory from the jaws of defeat is to go for broke and try to scoop up every single point. That's perfect.

Still, Hearts is just a game. Charles Albert Smith was impressive in real life. He was a bit on the short side and skinny, but good looking and sharp at 24. He'd come up from the States and worked as a Pullman porter before landing a job as a bellhop at the Windsor Hotel in December 1881. It was the classiest hotel in town. Within two months, he had been promoted to night bell captain, over the heads of others who had worked there much longer.

To the brass and the gents who frequented the hotel, Charles Smith was as close to perfect as they come. "Perfectly sober and

CHARLES ALBERT SMITH,

Charles Albert Smith was always neatly attired.

upright, most reliable," George Swett, the manager, said. To Senator Peter Mitchell, Smith was one of the "most efficient, active and courteous young men" at the Windsor. "Honest, capable, sober and industrious" were the words that Captain Robert Kane, who lived at the hotel, used to describe him.

Of course, in a perfect world, a comer like Charles Albert Smith would have enjoyed more career choices than railway porter or bellhop. And he would have been judged on more than how he jumped through hoops for train travellers and hotel guests. It wasn't a perfect world, not by any stretch, but Smith was determined to make the best – the very best – of a bad hand.

He was always well spoken, neatly dressed, with his high collar starched and stiff, and clean shaven, his moustache clipped just so. Behind his back, it's true, some bellhops said he was uptight, the type to lord it over you, but that may have been green envy talking.

He wasn't standoffish, just played his cards close to his chest. Once a week or twice, he'd drop by the Sea Shell on Notre Dame

Street, have a drink or a cigar, chit-chat, play a hand of cards. David Jones's saloon, below street level, corner of McGill Street under the Ambrose pharmacy, was a favourite spot with blacks. You'd go down the steep stairway and take the door on the left into the bar that ran along the McGill Street side; the door on the right led to the eating room. If you happened to saunter by of a Sunday around noon, you'd hear spirituals rising from the Sea Shell like the sound of the sea or like summer come to February.

Jones was a burly black man. Esau was his middle name, like Easy, and it might as well have been Easy because that was his way. If you'd asked him whether he'd ever seen Smith drunk (like some of the other porters, past or present, who hung out at his place – like Billy Barnes, for instance), he would have laughed. Smith drunk? Ha ha ha! Might as well have asked him if men could fly.

It is surprising, then, that he allowed himself, even for a minute, to suspect Smith of filching a dollar. That's what started it.

That was on Saturday, February 18. Smith was at the bar with Benny Matthews, his pal from the Windsor. Jones at the counter counts his takings – three dollar bills and some silver. He leaves the room to fetch a towel to wipe the counter, and when he returns there are only two bills and change in the till – and Smith and Matthews are standing right there.

Jones is easy, but he's not the soul of discretion at the best of times. "Smith," he says, "you or Benny have taken a dollar out of my till and I think it was you."

"I did not take your dollar but if you want a dollar I'll give it to you," Smith says, reaching into his pocket, the perfect gentleman.

Jones turns to Matthews. But no, he didn't take the bill, either. Jones is miffed, but he's not about to let it spoil his evening and ruin his life. "Never mind, let the dollar go," he says.

Smith can't let it go. His face won't show it but he's stung. Billy Barnes rubs it in, in that slow Virginia voice of his: "Ain't you afraid to go out for fear the police will take you?" he cracks as Smith is leaving. Ha ha. Smith just heads on out the door, smiling and all.

Jones and Barnes have no idea that all that week it's eating Smith. He hears things, reads things in the looks of people at work, and he gets it into his head that Jones and Barnes are spreading the word that he's a dollar stealer. Barnes, especially. Barnes, who boards with Jones's family on St Maurice Street. Barnes who knows the Windsor crowd: he'd worked there as a bellhop for two months

The palatial Windsor Hotel, where Charles Albert Smith was the night bell captain. The Windsor, on Dominion Square (Dorchester Square) at the northwest corner of Peel and Dorchester streets, was opened in 1878.

after losing his job on the cars last fall. Barnes, 28, married, and out of a job, is after his, he just knows it.

It's near closing time on Friday night before Smith returns to the Sea Shell, ready to lay his cards on the table. Barnes is there, slouched in a chair by the stove. Smith makes for him.

"I heard you have been talking about me," he says.

No response.

"Barnes, I can lick you," and he pulls out this Robin Hood, pointing it at Barnes. It's no use. Barnes is passed out, sleeping it off.

"Closing time," Jones calls out, ready to wake Barnes enough to walk him the couple of blocks home.

Smith turns on him. "I can lick you too."

"Here, I won't have any racket," Jones replies. "It's near twelve o'clock. Let's close up."

Smith stalks around the bar and faces him. "You have been talking about me, and I can lick you too, Jones," he says.

"Oh don't talk nonsense," says Jones. "Go away, you can see me tomorrow."

That's the bother with setting yourself up as perfect. Threatening people is so not *you* that some people won't recognize it. And his gun, that five-shot Robin Hood No. 2 – wouldn't you know it – the standard nickle-plated model couldn't do for Smith. It had to be a silver-plated job. Ha ha.

Still, it was a gun. You might question the wisdom of Jones telling Barnes what had happened in the Sea Shell the night before while he was smack at the heart of the action, out cold. But Barnes needed warning, in case. Jones told him over breakfast, and it spooked him: "I don't know what he is going to shoot me for. I've done nothing to him."

Smith dropped by the Sea Shell that morning. J.J. Hayes, an Irishman and a regular, was the only one there with Jones at the time. A sad case, Hayes. Not yet 30 and dying of TB, with a young wife and two kids. He'd had to give up his grocery store. Did the odd bit of bookkeeping and trading; that was all he was up to now. Lived with his in-laws, the Brennans, on Duke Street. He and Jones were off in a little side room, playing a game of Forty-five when Smith walked in.

He sat with them. He was his usual polite and proper self. No sign of the anger that had troubled him the night before.

"You want to fight now?" Jones finally asked him. "What was the matter with you last night?"

"I heard that you have been talking about me, telling things at the Windsor Hotel."

Out it comes.

"Smith, what you have heard, you should never go on what you hear," Jones lectured him. "You should go to the man first and ask him if he said that, and if he did say those things, you demand satisfaction then, but if he denies it, then it's all right."

"I have no more against you," Smith waved him off. "It's all right."

Two men came in together off the street. Tom MacDonald, 22, new in town from Halifax, had caught sight of Smith for the first time that morning when he'd gone to see about a job at the Windsor. And William Henry Duport, he'd never met Smith. A porter, Halifax-born and a year up on his friend Macdonald, he worked the trains going east.

176

Smith went next door to the eating room, and when he came back he found them standing up to the bar. All but Hayes, who was sitting.

"Smith, won't you have a drink?" MacDonald asked.

"No, but I'll take a cigar."

"Hayes, take a drink?"

But Hayes wasn't drinking either. On medication.

Jones had a good laugh over MacDonald's name. "I've never seen a MacDonald a black man," he chortled. They were all chatting away at the bar when Barnes blew in a little after noon and made a beeline for Smith.

"What were you shooting off your lemon at me last night for?" he demands.

"You've been talking about me," Smith shoots back.

"Well, what have I said about you?"

"It makes no difference what you've said about me."

"Then it makes no difference – whoever told you told you a lie."

"You tell me I lie, you son of a bitch?"

MacDonald sets his beer down gingerly, and Duport his lemonade. End of happy hour. Good time to go sight-seeing. They get their coats and make for the door.

"You must be a hell of a fellow," says Barnes. "I hear you are carrying a revolver for me. You got the youngster with you now?

"Yes."

"You ain't game to use it!"

"I'm a son of a bitch if I ain't game to use it," Smith replies, whipping his shooter out of his coat pocket.

"Hold on boys," Jones cries, "I don't want any muss here!"

But Smith has stepped back and is cocking his gun, and Barnes jumps him, pinning his arms from behind, yelling, "Jones, get his gun! Get his gun!"

MacDonald and Duport are just hitting the street, and Hayes, poor Hayes, is rising from his seat to get clear when the shot rings out.

Jones dashes around the counter to grab Smith, fighting him for the gun. They're clinching and grunting. Jones catches sight of Hayes lying by the stairs.

"There!" he shouts, "You've killed that man. Give me up that revolver."

"I won't," Smith shouts back, but just then Jones manages to wrench it out of his hand, breaking it.

Judge Thomas Kennedy Ramsay

Barnes runs for cover in a back room, because Smith's not through. He pulls a straight razor out of his right pocket and takes a slash at Jones, barking, "Give me my revolver!"

Jones, who just missed being cut, is leaning back to grab a bottle to beat off Smith as the policeman comes in. Relieved, Jones tosses the gun on the counter. Smith grabs it and runs to the water closet.

"Here he is!" Jones shouts to the cop. "Come and take him!"

They took him. They later found the razor in the toilet, and the gun – one chamber empty, four loaded. In his coat, they found forty-five more bullets. No question, he was going for control.

When they led him out, the crowd gathered on the street. Those who had not seen his fury could see only his perfect side. They took his side. "Don't let them search you!" they cried. Too late.

John Joseph Hayes was buried on the following Tuesday, the last day of February. The Irish turned out in force. He was well connected. His wife's uncle was M.P. Ryan, the member of parliament, for whom he had once worked. St Ann's Church in Griffintown was no cathedral, but 500 people packed it for the service. About 300 of them walked behind the coffin up to Côte-des-Neiges. They moved out along Wellington, then up McGill … Passing the Sea Shell, some of them flashed dark looks at the place. It was closed, out of respect, and that they saw as a good thing. Jones himself was walking with them. That they saw as better.

At Smith's trial, the prosecution called it murder. Judge Thomas K. Ramsay, you could tell, agreed. "I have heard a good deal said here about sympathy," he summed up, "and I may say I consider that sentiment most natural where there is concerned a young man of good character and evidently some qualities of fidelity and worth." But if Smith meant to kill Barnes, missed, and killed somebody else, it was murder because murder was his plan. Still, he told the jury, if you really don't think he meant to kill Barnes, you nail him for manslaughter because he shot Hayes dead, no doubt about that.

The jury didn't see it that way. To ramrod Ramsay, it might be guilty of this, guilty of that, but some of them held out for guilty of nothing at all. Smith was a perfect gent, some thought. The gun had gone off as he'd scuffled with Barnes – who knew who had pulled the trigger? Nobody was gunning for Hayes.

After haggling all day over it, they reported at 9 o'clock at night that they couldn't agree. Judge Ramsay wouldn't hear it. Get back in there, he told them, and come up with a verdict. It's murder or it's manslaughter. Period.

It took them another hour or so. In the end, they settled for manslaughter, and Smith got twenty years. "Had it not been for your previous good character," Judge Ramsay told him, "I might have sentenced you to a much heavier penalty, and one that might have been as hard as death."

Smith went to St Vincent de Paul. Everyone at the pen, from the warden down, considered him the perfect prisoner.

THE END FOR NOW

WHY AREN'T THE PEOPLE IN THESE STORIES, their friends and their world, better known? There are many reasons. "It is only after 1897 that the Negro became a factor in the city and its development," claimed Wilfred Emmerson Israel in "The Montreal Negro Community," his 1928 master's thesis in sociology at McGill University. The period from the end of slavery to the late 1920s was "obscure," he wrote: "Little is known of [the Negro's] occupation in this city prior to the building of the Canadian railroads. He had nothing to offer a prospective employer except a strong and untrained body."

Tell that to Alexander Grant and all the others!

Writers on the black presence in Canada have mostly followed Israel's lead and ignored Montreal throughout this period. After dwelling on slavery in early Quebec, they have turned away for the better part of a century to train their gaze elsewhere, especially on the colonies of refugee American blacks in southwestern Ontario.

The few who have commented on the condition of blacks in Quebec have done so on the basis of what they found next door – as if the Ontario and Quebec of those days were essentially the same, regardless of differences in origin, population, language, culture, religion, law, institutions, politics, social dynamics, etc. It does not seem to have occurred to them that some blacks may have *chosen* one place over the other precisely because of one or several of those differences.

The neglect of Montreal is particularly dismaying, because in these years the city quickly grew to be the metropolis of Canada (the population rose from less than 10,000 to more than 100,000). It was the unrivalled hub of commerce, finance, industry, transportation, and communications, not to mention being the capital of the united Province of Canada from 1844 to 1849. Could a historian of blacks in the United States skip over New York City through most of the nineteenth century?

Where were the black Montrealers in the days of the city's rise to prominence? Invisible, you might say – if you didn't look. Looking and seeing involve more than scanning the census records in search of an important statistic. You need to dig into the records of the nineteenth century as thoroughly as historian Marcel Trudel did when searching the seventeenth and eighteenth centuries in his search for slaves. No single source holds the answers. Government, church, cemetery, court, and prison records, census returns, notaries' deeds, newspapers of the period, city directories and tax rolls, books and pamphlets, – all must be probed, and the results from one source compared and combined with the information in the others.

Rooting through these sources – some in French, others in English, some in such bad handwriting or so damaged that they are barely legible – poses its problems. One of the trickiest is the name game. A few of the stories here hint at it.

When slavery ruled, many slaves went by the same single name. So it can be hard for us today to tell Caesar from Caesar, Rose from Rose. Once free, if not before, they generally took on family names, but this doesn't necessarily make things easier for us. Variations in the written forms of a name can lead us to think we are dealing with several different people when in fact we are dealing with one person. The man here called Manuel Allen, for example, turns up

as Emanuelle, Manuel, Emmanuel Alenne (and Aleinne), Mandaville Allen, Mandaville Turner, and Montreal Allan (and Allen). If
you were to hunt up Isaac Wily's baptism record, you would find
that he was christened Isaac Newton Waylay. (Weelly, Wiely, Wily,
and Wyley were other forms of his name.)

Record keepers wrote the names of illiterate persons by ear,
just as they often estimated age by sight. They heard the names
differently, depending on whether they were French- or English-
speaking. The confusion affected whites as well as blacks, but variations in black names seem wider, perhaps because the names or
the accents of their bearers were less familiar. Some scribes may
also have been only too ready to bestow fanciful names on people
of African origin. So we get Montreal Allen. We also get plain
Montreal, otherwise known as Murry Hall. And we get names like
Scischahungken.

"What's the name again?"

"Scishahungken."

"Can you spell it, please?"

"No, I can't."

"O.K., run it by me again."

"Scishahungken."

"Um, sounds like an Indian name."

"Do I look like an Indian? It's Sci-sha-hung-ken."

"When you say it slowly like that, it sounds like Caesar Hunkin."

"That's what I said."

"Or maybe Caesar Hernking."

"You got it."

"Caesar Hernking is your name? Or Caesar Hunkin?"

"Yes, I told you: César Angune."

The conversation is made up, but the confusion was real.
Scishahungken was the name of a black man, 60 years old, as written in the French-language record of his Catholic burial in September 1807. Play with it, roll it around on your tongue, say it out
loud, slowly, quickly: you will see that it is a variation of Caesar
Hunkin, the name, as recorded in English, of a man charged with
grand larceny in the Court of General Quarter Sessions of the
Peace in April 1796.

In the English-language record of the Protestant burial of the
slave Nancy Buckley in 1801, the name was written Cesar Hernking.
At his wedding in June 1802, the (English) record made it Cesar

Hunkins, identifying him as a labourer and his wife as the French Canadian widow Mary Margaret Lapron. They had a daughter, Marie-Françoise, in April 1804. In the (French) record of her baptism, he was identified simply as César, *nègre journalier* (negro day labourer), and his wife as Marguerite Colleret. At the girl's death, she was called (in French) M. Françoise César Angune, and her father was called César Angune. (Say it out loud, with an English twist.)

In one form or another, the name game persisted beyond the days of transition from slavery to freedom, well into the second half of the nineteenth century. And it affected some people who could write their names as well as those who couldn't. Caesar Johonnot, as we saw, used different spellings for his own name, though he never altered it beyond recognition. Others tended to Canadianize it into something more familiar (and less recognizable) like Jeannot or Joannot. And when his daughter married in 1832, the church record gave her name as Catherine Johnson!

John Pruyn always wrote his name Pruyn (a New York Dutch name pronounced Prine), even though his signature is sometimes hard to make out. Almost invariably, other English speakers wrote it Prime; in French records, variations include Bram and Praime.

John Pruyn's signature was not always easy to make out.

Jacob Abdella's family name was written every which way, including Abadillard, Bissernet Abdeloy, Dabdala, and Obdelay. Variations on Peter Dago's included Dagau, Deggo, Dogo, and, at his death, Vago; and his first name alternated between Peter and Pierre. Clarence Francis Selden, a leading black figure in Montreal from the 1850s till his death in 1884, had a clear, practised signature, but that didn't prevent someone from recording his name as Sheldon O. Francis.

The record keepers have much to answer for, but they were not the only ones responsible for the confusion. Look at John Pruyn's brother-in-law. At 14, when he was a slave of Benoite Gaetan, widow of the painter François Malepart de Beaucour, he was baptised Jean-Baptiste François in April 1796. By September 1801, he was a free man when at the age of 20, under the name Jean Beaucour, dit l'Africain, he married Charlotte Bonga. The taking of his former master's name seems to have been a passing thing; thereafter, until his death in 1815, he went by the name Jean-Baptiste L'Africain. Consequently, it is easy for researchers to confuse him with his contemporary, the carpenter Jean-Baptiste L'Africain, (also known as Jean-Baptiste Tribot, dit L'Africain), who was white. Indeed, despite their name, all the L'Africains of the time were white, except for Jean-Baptiste, husband of Charlotte Bonga, and their children: François-Xavier (1804–6), Marie Jeanne (1805–6), Étienne (1807–8), Marie Rosalie (1809–11), and Charlotte (1814–23).

With women, of course, there was the added wrinkle of maiden name/married name, even if the maiden name remained the only legal one. So Julia or July or Juliet is sometimes Julia Johnson, sometimes Julia Jackson, and as John Flemming's wife she is Julia Flemming. Another example is Catharine Crowell, who became known as Catharine Fortune when she married the labourer Titus Fortune in March 1819. She was said to be 22. Their son William was born that same month. Titus Fortune died the following January.

No further vital records have been found in Montreal for Catharine Crowell or Catharine Fortune. If you were to rely only on such records, you would miss the connection between Catharine Crowell and Catherine Moss, who died on August 2, 1834, at the age of 37. Fortunately for us, Catherine Moss, widow of Jonathan Moss, went to court a few weeks before her death to have herself appointed legal guardian to William Fortune, who was identified as her 16-year-old son (he was really 15) by her first marriage to Titus Fortune. In the absence of a record of her marriage to Jonathan Moss, Catharine Crowell would have been just one more figure who vanished into thin air if it hadn't been for that court record.

Along with other factors, the name game makes it difficult to follow the thread of people's lives and to count heads. But you must play it if you ever hope to get a halfway clear picture of things as they were. In the end (does it ever end?) research will yield a skeletal record: names, more or less sure vital statistics, some home and business addresses, a few leases, indications of what jobs the people had – and, with luck, a telling detail or two.

Only by juggling with these bits and pieces, letting them roll against each other in your mind, sleeping on them, and playing the name game under your breath or out loud, will you find some of the pieces falling into place, so that life creeps back into those long-sleeping forms. Once awakened, they will begin to tell you their stories, some of which are passed on here.

DOCUMENTS

A Petition from sundry persons inhabitants of the city of *Montreal*, whose names are thereunto subscribed, was presented to the House by Mr [Joseph] *Papineau*: and the same was received and read:

SETTING FORTH – That by an Ordinance of *Jacques Raudot*, Intendant of Canada, bearing date the thirteenth day of April, which was in the year of our Lord one thousand seven hundred and nine, registered and published according to law, It is Ordained, under the good pleasure of his Most Christian Majesty, that all Panis and Negroes which, before then were, and which thereafter should be purchased in *Canada*, should appertain, in full property, to the purchasers thereof, as their proper Slaves; and the said Panis and Negroes are thereby enjoined not to leave the service of their Masters, and all persons not to encourage them to desert, or harbour them, under a penalty of fifty livres.

That His Most Christian Majesty did never signify his displeasure or disapprobation of the said Ordinance, whereby the same was in force at the definitive Treaty of Peace and Cession of this Province to His Majesty, and therefore by the Statute of the 14th *George* III. Chapter 83d, commonly called the *Quebec Act*, makes now part of the Laws, Usages and Customs of *Canada*.

That the Importation of Negroes from *Africa* to the *West India*

Islands and British Plantations, has, from the first establishment of an *African* Company, and since the Trade has been set free to all His Majesty's subjects, under Parliamentary Regulations, been deemed lawful, and the owners of such Negroes vested with the right and power of selling them and their children, whereby Slavery was effectually established in the said Islands and Plantations.

That by the Statute of the 5th *Geo.* II. Chap. 7. Section 4, intituled, "An Act for the more easy recovery of debts in His Majesty's Plantations and Colonies in America," It is enacted, "That from and after the twenty ninth day of September, one thousand seven hundred and thirty-two, the Houses, Lands, Negroes and other hereditaments and real estates, situate or being within any of the said Plantations, belonging to any person indebted, shall be liable to, and chargeable with, all just debts, duties and demands of what nature or kind soever, owing by any such person to His Majesty, or any of His Subjects, and shall and may be assets for the satisfaction thereof, in like manner as real estates are by the laws of *England* liable to the satisfaction of debts due by Bond or other specialty, and shall be subject to the like remedies, proceedings and process in any court of Law or Equity, in any of the said Plantations respectively, for seizing, extending, selling or disposing of any such Houses, Lands, Negroes, and other hereditaments and real estates, towards the satisfaction of such debts, duties and demands, and in like manner as personal estates in any of the said Plantations respectively, are seized, extended, sold or disposed of for the satisfaction of debts." – Which Statute forms a part of the Laws of the Province under the *Quebec Act*, whereby all Acts of Parliament before them made, concerning or respecting the said Colonies and Plantations, are declared to be in force within the said Province of *Quebec,* and every part thereof.

That by the Statute 30. *Geo.* III. Chap. 27th, intituled, "An Act for encouraging new settlers in His Majesty's Colonies and Plantations in *America,*" It is enacted, "That from and after the first day of August, one thousand seven hundred and ninety, if any person or persons, being a subject or subjects of the territories or countries belonging to the United States of America, shall come from thence, together with his or their family or families, to any of the *Bahama* or *Bermuda* or *Somers* Islands, or to any part of the Province of Quebec, or *Nova-Scotia,* or any of the territories belonging to His Majesty in *North America,* for the purpose of residing and settling

188

there, it shall be lawful for any such person or persons, having first obtained a Licence for that purpose from the Governor, or, in his absence, from the Lieutenant Governor, of the said Islands, Colonies or Provinces respectively, to import into the same, in British ships, owned by His Majesty's subjects, and navigated according to Law, any Negroes, Household Furniture, Utensils of Husbandry, or Cloathing free of duty." And it is also enacted by the said Act, "That all sales or Bargains for the sale of any Negro, Household Furniture, Utensils of Husbandry, or Cloathing so imported, which shall be made within Twelve Calendar Months after the Importion of the same, (except in cases of the Bankruptcy or death of the owner thereof) shall be null and void to all intents and purposes whatsoever."

That upon the faith of His Majesty's Government, solemnly pledged by the above mentioned laws, the inhabitants of this Province in General and the inhabitants of the City and District of *Montreal* in particular, have purchased for a valuable consideration, a considerable number of Panis and Negro Slaves; and divers persons, formerly subjects of the United States of *America*, have, upon the faith of the above in part recited Statute of 30th *George* III. Chapter 27th imported into this Province, according to Law, a number of Negroes Slaves belonging to them; and which Panis and Negro Slaves have always demeaned themselves in a becoming manner until lately, that they have imbibed a refractory & disobedient spirit, under pretext that no slavery exists in the Province. – In February 1798, one *Charlotte*, a Negro woman, belonging to a Miss *Jane Cook*, absconded from the service of her mistress, and having refused to return, was, upon a complaint on oath, apprehended in virtue of a warrant from a Magistrate, and having still persisted in refusing to return to her duty, was, upon legal conviction, committed to the prison of the District (for want of a House of Correction,) but having applied for, and obtained a Writ of *Habeas Corpus*, she was, in vacation, discharged by his Honor the Chief Justice of this District, without being obliged to give security for her appearance in the Court of King's Bench. Upon this enlargement, the Negroes in the city and district of *Montreal* threatenend a general revolt; and one Jude, a Negro woman belonging to *Elias Smith*, of *Montreal*, Merchant, purchased by him at *Albany*, on the 27th day of January, 1795, in consideration of eighty pounds, *New York* currency, absconded, and refusing to return, was upon conviction, committed to prison; but upon a petition presented by her to the Court of King's Bench for this district, holding criminal pleas, she was on the eighth day of March, 1798, without deciding upon the question of Slavery, discharged; the Chief Justice, declaring at the same time, in open Court, that he would, upon *Habeas Corpus*, discharge every Negro, indented Apprentice, and Servant, who should be committed to Gaol under the Magistrates Warrant in the like cases.

That His Majesty's Justices of the Peace having thus no power to compel absconding Slaves to return to their owner's service, nor the owners any power to enforce obedience, or detain their Slaves, in their service, Your Memorialists forsee that alarming consequences to this Province may ensue therefrom, independent of the great loss which his Majesty's Subjects of this Province, owners of Negro Slaves, and the Creditors of such owners, may sustain by the disability such owners now labour under of preserving their property in their Slaves.

That it may therefore please this House to frame an Act to be passed into a law, ordaining and enacting, That until provision shall be made by Law for establishing a House of Correction, whenever any Panis or Negro Slave shall desert from his owner's service in this Province: it shall be lawful to proceed against him or her in the manner directed and provided for against indented Apprentices and Servants in *England* in *Great Britain*, and to commit him or her to the common Gaol of the district where he or she may be apprehended, there to be detained as effectually as if the same was such House of Correction, as by the Laws respecting indented Apprentices and Servants in *England* is intended; and that the Keeper of the Gaol shall be as compellable to receive and detain such Slave or Slaves, under the Penalties to which a Keeper of a House of Correction may be liable on a commitment of indented Apprentices and Servants in England, until such Slave shall return to his or her owner's service, or until such Slave shall be delivered by the due course of Law. And farther, that no person shall knowingly aid, countenance, harbour or conceal, any such deserting Slave; or, that a Law may be made declaring that there is no Slavery in the Province; or such other provision, respecting Slaves as this House in its wisdom, shall think proper.

Montreal, 1st April 1799[1]

---

1 *Journals of the Legislative Assembly of Lower Canada,* 19 April 1799

A Petition of divers inhabitants of the District of Montreal, whose names are thereunto subscribed, was presented to the House by Mr *Papineau*, and the same was brought up and read -

SETTING FORTH – That doubts have lately been entertained how far by the laws and statutes in force in this Province there can be any property in Negroes and Panis. From such doubts having effected the interests of many of the Petitioners, they feel themselves deeply impressed with the necessity of having it determined by an Act of the Legislature that slavery under certain modificiations exists in this Province, and at the same time of vesting in a more effectual manner the property in slaves in their masters, and of providing laws for the proper regulation and government of such a class of men as come within the description of slaves. That the Petitioners humbly conceive that such an Act would be of great and general advantage to the Province.

That the Petitioners beg leave to submit that an Ordinance of Mr *Raudot*, Intendant of *Canada*, dated 13th of April, 1709, Enacts under the pleasure of His Most Christian Majesty, *"Que tous les Panis et Nègres qui ont été achetés ou qui le seront par la suite, apartiendront en pleine propriété à ceux qui en ont fait ou qui en feront l'acquisition en qualité d'Esclaves."* That this law which was duly enregistred and published, and was never altered or repealed, the Petitioners humbly conceive, was in full force at the Definitive Treaty of Peace, and under the 14th of His present Majesty, makes a part of the laws of this Province.

That it appears in the opinion of the Petitioners, that since the Establishment of the African Company, in the year 1661, the existence of slavery so far as it respects Negroes, has been established and confirmed in all His Majesty's Dominions in *America*. Free liberty was given by a variety of statutes from that time to the present day, to purchase slaves on the Coasts of *Africa*, and they, their children and posterity, were declared the property of the purchasers, and of those to whom they were afterwards sold. That by the statute 30. Geo. 3. c. 27. made after the close of the late unhappy war, it is enacted, "That from and after the 1st day of August, 1790, if any person or persons, being subjects of the Territories or Countries belonging to the United States of *America*, shall come from thence, together with his or their family or families, to any of the *Bahama* or

Bermuda or *Somers* Islands or to any part of the Province of *Quebec*, or *Nova-Scotia*, or any of the Territories belonging to His Majesty in *North-America*, for the purpose of residing and settling there, it shall be lawful for any such person or persons, having first obtained a licence for that purpose from the Governor, or in his absence from the Lieutenant Governor of the said Islands, Colonies, or Plantations respectively to import into the same in British ships, owned by His Majesty's subjects, and navigated according to Law, any negroes, household furniture, utensils of husbandry, or cloathing free of duty." And it is also enacted by the said statute "that all sales or bargains for the sale of any negro, household furniture, utensils of husbandry or cloathing so imported which shall be made within twelve calendar months after the importation of the same (except in case of the Bankruptcy or death of the owner thereof) shall be null and void to all intents and purposes whatsoever."

That if any doubts remained before the passing of this Act whether slavery really, under any modification, existed in this Province, the Petitioners flatter themselves this statute expressly recognizes its existence in the same manner as it prevailed in all His Majesty's Plantations in *America* before the late war.

That the Petitioners can assure this House with confidence, that many faithful and loyal subjects of His Majesty, after exposing their lives in his service, and sacrificing almost the whole property they were possessed of in the late calamitous war, came into this Province with their slaves under the sacred promise held out to them in the last mentioned statute, and from an idea lately gone abroad, that slavery does not exist in this country, have found that their slaves on whom was all their dependance for support, have deserted them, and held them at defiance. That as the Petitioners most ardently desire to put the House in possession of all the facts which belong to their case, they beg leave to inform the House that a Mr *Fraser* of their district, obtained lately a warrant from three Justices of the Peace to commit to the House of correction his slave who had deserted his service, (and who was one of three, the only property he had saved from the ravages of the late war, and his chief dependance for support in his old age); and that on a writ of *Habeas Corpus* being sued out, the slave was discharged by the Court of King's Bench, under an opinion that the property was not sufficiently proved by Mr *Fraser*. The petitioners tho' they entertain a high opinion for the authority of that Honorable Court, cannot but remark that the evidence produced on that occasion was, in their apprehension, the best which it was possible in any case to produce, and that the Court in desiring more, have asked what it would be impossible almost ever to obtain, and in this manner have divested all the owners of slaves of any property in them.

That it was stated in the course of the judgment of the court that the Act of the 37th of His present Majesty, C. 119 had repealed all the laws respectng slavery: but this statute in the humble opinion of the petitioners only goes the length to declare, that slaves shall not in future be assessed for the payment of debts due by their owners; it does not go so far as to divest such owners of their property in their slaves, nor can it be considered as tending to emancipate the slaves in His Majesty's plantations. That so far from this, subsequent Acts still further recognize slavery to exist, and encourage the importation of Negroes from the coast of Africa.

That the petitioners are extremely sorry to detain the House so long on this occasion, so interesting to them, as many of the petitioners have paid considerable sums for slaves who have deserted their service, and all of them are deeply sensible that this class of men who are now let loose on society, and live an idle and profligate life, may be tempted to commit crimes, which it is the duty of every citizen to endeavor to prevent.

That the petitioners under all the circumstances which they have taken the liberty to state, cannot but entertain a well grounded hope, that the House will take this subject into their serious consideration, and that they will pass such a Declaratory Act as will give force and efficacy to the Laws and Statutes which relate to this subject, and at the same time that the House will by such means as they think fit, secure to the owners a property in their slaves, and make such further regulations for the proper government of slaves as in their wisdom may be thought expedient.

And that it may therefore please this House to frame such an Act as will declare that slavery exists under certain conditions in this Province, and will completely vest the property in Panis and Negroes in the owners thereof; and further, that this House will provide such Laws and regulations for the government of slaves as in the wisdom of the House may be thought expedient.[2]

---

2 *Journals of the Legislative Assembly of Lower Canada*, 18 April 1800

CIRCULAR ADDRESS TO THE FREE PEOPLE OF COLOR
THROUGHOUT THE UNITED STATES
BY PAOLA BROWN (1832)

Countrymen, Friends, Brethren. – You are all, no doubt, aware of the oppressive and despotic measures which took place some years ago in the States of Ohio, and Illinois, and in several other States, by which all the colored inhabitants were driven from their houses, and thrust forth as wanderers upon the face of the earth. I am connected by ties of blood and otherwise, with those then unfortunate people. They relied, however, on the goodness of Almighty God, and were animated by the most ardent desire of redeeming themselves from bondage, for those who are in the legal condition of slaves in the States, are not the only slaves, but the free people of color, so called as it were in mockery, are slaves perhaps in a worse sense, from their legal disabilities, their rejection from society, and the utter contempt in which they are held by the whites. Animated by that desire, and that of procuring for themselves some security for the enjoyment of property, freedom, and religious rights, and perhaps by that of shewing to their oppressors, that being trampled upon only roused their energies; after making the necessary preliminary inquiries, a large body of them emigrated to Upper Canada. They were cordially received, protected, and admitted at once to all the rights of citizenship. Here they found the theoretical maxim of the American Constitution, that "All men are born *equal,* and endowed by their Creator with certain inalienable rights," practically in existence – here no distinction of color, race, language, or religion, prevails to deprive a single individual of his civil and religious rights in the amplest sense. When they resided in the States they were taught to believe that theirs was the only free Government, the only country where republican principles were fostered. They were awakened from that dream, by the persecutions they suffered. We find, however, that under this limited Monarchy more real freedom and real republicanism exist than in a professed Republic. We are here, my Brethren, in all respects, upon an equality with the whites – we are as much entitled to our elective franchise as they are, and in a Court of Justice it is not inquired of what color a witness is, but whether he is worthy of credit.

Most of you, my countrymen, have been educated in the principles of liberty and equality. Do you find them exemplified around you? It is far from my wish, wherever you are not persecuted and oppressed, *on account of your color*, to estrange you from your native country; but if you are so persecuted and oppressed, here is an asylum, here is a refuge, where persecution and oppression, by reason of a different colored skin are wholly unknown. So far as the civil and religious advantages we possess.

Now, as to the temporal: We are admitted to purchase lands in free and common soccage, without the slightest quitrent, and but a very moderate tax for highways, which may be paid by personal labor, and we are subjected to no other tax whatever. We have two extensive settlements, one named Wilberforce, and the other Colbornesburgh, (the latter was named, by special permission, after the Lieutenant Governor of Upper Canada, Sir John Colborne, who has been a good friend to us). There are tens of thousands of acres around, that may be procured at moderate rates and easy terms of payment; and we are daily receiving accessions to our number from various States of the Union by way of Buffalo and Amherstburgh, &c. I belong to the settlement of Colbornesburgh, and have had the honor of filling situations of trust and repute amongst my colored brethren. I was lately deputed by them as their Agent and Trustee to solicit subscriptions for the erection of a place of Divine Worship, and a School in Colbornesburgh, in which, through the blessing of God, I have been very successful, in both the Canadas, so that whoever hereafter joins us may depend upon enjoying the inestimable benefits of public worship, and of education for their children. In Quebec, I received much encouragement from Lord Aylmer, the Governor in Chief, from the Reverend the Clergy of all denominations, and from the influential inhabitants. You will find, in the same paper in which this Address is inserted a copy of my petition to Lord Aylmer on that occasion; and such was the lively interest excited in Quebec that copies of that document were distributed from the pulpit by ministers of all persuasions, to their congregations.

Our settlement of Colbornesburgh is situated only 12 miles from the Guelph settlement of the Canada Land Company, a place which is rapidly rising to the rank of a city; Colbornesburgh is only 25 miles from the head of Lake Ontario, whence a navigable communication by the Great River St Lawrence, and its tributary Canals, extends to the Atlantic Ocean, with innumerable and profitable markets between, for the disposal of the produce of these regions.

Industry and enterprise will do wonders, and so there is no check upon them in this country to one set of men more than another, we, of African origin, have the path opened to us, as freely as it is to our white neighbors. Colbornesburgh is about 55 miles from York [Toronto], the capital city and seat of government of Upper Canada, and 145 miles from the other colored settlement of Wilberforce. Though our two settlements are [at] present separate, I believe there is a great likelihood, from my having lately met with Mr Nathan [Israel] Lewis, the Agent for Wilberforce Settlement, of both being united, which will form a bond of harmony and strength, that cannot fail to be of benefit to both.

Generally speaking, the country of Upper Canada, consists of excellent good land, with, of course, those exceptions that always occur, of occasional barren tracts, rocks and mountains, and swamps, but it will, on the whole, amply repay the toils of the husbandman, and enable him soon to lay up a store for the infirmities of age, the education of his children, and for providing them with a future independence.

Countrymen, Friends, Brethren! I have no interested motives for this address. We invite you to settle amongst us, because we ourselves feel happy and contented – if you feel happy and contented where you are, for God's sake remain there – but to those who are oppressed and miserable, on account of their degraded state in the different parts of the Union, we should be wanting in christian charity and humanity, were we not to point out to them the way we have followed ourselves, and invite them to partake of the benefits we ourselves experience.

PAOLA BROWN

Any further informations that any individual may desire shall be willingly given in reply to a letter addressed to Mr P. Brown, Colbornesburgh, Waterloo Post Office, Gore District, U. Canada.

Quebec, 28th September, 1832[3]

ALEXANDER GRANT'S SPEECH AT ST ANN'S MARKET
AUGUST 1, 1834

My dear Friends and Brethren, – It is with feelings of peculiar pleasure that I address you this day – a day on which we are met to cele-

---

3 *Liberator*, Boston, 27 October 1832

brate the birth of real liberty to the long injured and suffering sons of Africa – a day which *England* has decided shall be the auspicious moment which is to give light, life and liberty to 800,000 of our fellow-creatures, namely, to the slaves of the British West India Colonies; this day their bonds are broken and their shackles fall; they tread under their feet, with manly indignation, the chains and the lash; and, standing erect, while the tear of gratitude trembles on their cheek, they breathe a prayer to Heaven for the future happiness of that nation which has thus raised them in the scale of beings, made them feel that they are really men, and has given the death-blow to slavery all over the world. Spain and Portugal cannot long sustain the hellish traffic, and America will then stand alone, the champion of those principles which will receive the curse, the contempt, and the detestation of the civilized world; for slavery and the trade in human blood are violations of the laws of God and the rights of man. In accordance with this principle is the American Declaration of Independence – a declaration which every noble-minded man will naturally accede to; it says, "We hold these truths to be self-evident: – that all men are created equal; that they are endowed by their Creator with certain inalienable rights; that among these are life, liberty, and the pursuit of happiness." In the face of this declaration will America be permitted to stand alone? Will she have the effrontery – will she be so ridiculously absurd as to call herself the "land of liberty," while she holds in slavery 2,000,000 of her fellow-creatures; But will these continue to kiss the lash? Will they continue to be insensible to that liberty which their brethren in almost every other part of the world enjoy? I answer no! They will duly estimate the blessing; they will burst asunder their chains, and awful will be the lesson to those who will have the folly to oppose them. – But I hope the dreadful catastrophe will be prevented by a timely following of the noble example of England, and prove that she is in reality, and not merely in name, "the land of the brave and the home of the free."

And now, my dear friends, that you may have some idea of the infernal traffic to which England this day gives the death-blow, and the blessings which will flow to 800,000 of our brethren in the West Indies, and their posterity for ever, I will read you a short extract from the writings of Abbé Raynal, as quoted in a speech delivered at Boston lately, by your real friend Garrison. (After giving some quotations from the Abbé Raynal, and Garrison's speeches, in relation to the slave trade, Mr Grant proceeded.) No systematic efforts were made to effect its overthrow, till the godlike and philanthropic exertions of the great and good Wilberforce and Clarkson, aided by the mighty minds of Pitt, Fox and others, induced the British Parliament to examine thoroughly this trade of blood. The amazing facts disclosed, horrified the whole nation; the contest was long and arduous; for more than twenty years the demons in human shape continued the combat; but the friends of justice and humanity at last obtained a glorious triumph by the United Parliament making the trade *piracy*! But it is to commemorate a nobler deed that we are met this day; the slave trade has been for some time abolished, but the unhappy thousands who have outlived their captivity were still in bondage, and would have remained so to the end of their existence, had not England's mandate gone forth; and from this day forward, they will rank as men. I am sure I need not call upon you, who enjoy the blessings of liberty, to rejoice at the deed, and to bless the men who have bestowed it. Yes, a Wilberforce and a Clarkson; a Pitt, a Fox, and a Sheridan; a Curran, a Macintosh and a Canning; a Buxton, a Brougham and a Grey; the brightest talent and the noblest characters in Britain, constantly advocated (during a great portion of their valuable lives) the glorious object which we this day commemorate; and, I am sure, your gratitude will be accorded to them, as they will unquestionably receive the praises and the affection of millions yet unborn. I will not shock your feelings by a recital of the horrid barbarities which have always been the consequence of the slave trade; oppression, cruelty and blood have been of every day occurrence; and the only excuse your enemies plead is, that you are not to be considered as belonging to the human species! With such a disgraceful feeling as this in their minds, it is no wonder that they advocate slavery. Mr Clay, late Secretary of the United States, was of this opinion, and Mr President Jefferson says, in his Notes on Virginia, "Whether they were originally a distinct race or not, or made so by time and circumstances, I am of opinion that they are inferior to the whites in mind and body"; but England, which has compelled the world to admire her for her virtue, her talents, and her humanity, has decided otherwise; she considers you as rational beings, and as such has opened the door of the British Constitution to you, with all its enviable privileges. No less than 800,000 persons in the United Kingdom last year petitioned Parliament for the total abolition of slavery; one petition alone contained 150,000 names, presented by Lord Brougham, the Lord Chancellor of England, and another, from ladies only, with the amazing number of 50,000 names affixed to it, was presented by Mr Buxton, the second Wilberforce. Yes, that dearest part of the creation, who have ever been the enemies of oppression, and upon whose bosoms we always find a soft pillow in the hour of agitation and affliction, have nobly sustained their character, and proved themselves worthy of the respect, the admiration and the affection which we freely devote to them.

My dear friends, from what I have now stated to you, I am sure that you will join me heart and hand in giving our warmest acknowledgments to Great Britain for the noble act she has performed; and that you truly congratulate your brethren, that they were placed in a situation to partake of the blessings you enjoy. I am also sure that you will join me in hoping that, under the protection of the British flag, (that flag which has borne the battle and the breeze for a thousand years), our emancipated brethren will so conduct themselves as peaceable and loyal subjects, as will prove to the world that they not only duly estimate their privileges, but are worthy of the glorious boon bestowed upon them. I trust that you will now join me in three hearty cheers for Old England, the true "land of the brave, and the home of the free."[4]

THE LAST DAYS OF MARTHA HYERS, 1841

Martha Hyers. – a Colored Woman about 25 [sic] Years of age has been repeatedly an inmate of this Goal, and has frequently during four or five Years past, been under my Care – mostly for Venereal Complaints. – On the 23 Octr. last She was committed as an Ordinary Vagrant, but in fact to get herself Cured again as She was affected with Chancres, &c. &c. – for which I put her under a Mercurial Course. – about five or six days ago she said that Something was riding up in her Body, and Seemed as if it would choak her. – These Symptoms she has had Several times, and were always considered, and relieved by the Ordinary Medecines, as Hysterical. –

Mr [jailer Thomas] McGinn, came up to Town late in the evening to inform me of her Situation. Knowing her Complaint, I contented myself by sending down the usual Medecines, and saw her early next Morning. No symptoms of unusual discription were

---

4 *Montreal Gazette*, 19 August 1834

present, and I confidently expected her to get better as she had so often done in similar circumstances. – The day before yesterday, she was rather worse and consequently removed to the Hospital [infirmary], where I prescribed for her. –

Towards this Morning an unfavorable change took place and she died very unexpectedly. – She has labored for Many Years past, under a desent of the Womb. – of which she made more than usual Complaint these three or four days past. – Yet upon examination, nothing indicative of extraordinary mischief manifested itself, neither were there any symptoms of Abdominal Inflamation present. – She was a Very debauched Character, and had suffered lately from the inclement weather, previous to her last admission.

Danl Arnoldi
Pr.m.g.
Montreal Goal
Novr 25, 1841[5]

CRISIS IN NORTH AMERICA! BY ISRAEL LEWIS (1846)

A meeting of the Consultation Committee of Coloured People of Montreal, met according to notice for the purpose of Petitioning Her Majesty to allow the organizing of 100,000 Coloured Men from all parts of the world, to assemble at Niagara for the purpose of putting an end to Slavery.

Mr Moses Carter, being appointed Chairman, and Mr P.J. Lee, Secretary.

It was moved by Mr [William] Paul, and seconded by Mr Dego [Peter Dago], that Mr Israel Lewis report his Preamble and Resolutions; adopted.

Mr Lewis then submitted the following.

Whereas, we believe that all the human race that are found on this great globe, are the children of one Almighty Parent, who has declared that, "He of one Blood has made all men." And whereas, He hath said "I am no respector of persons." "The Ethipian cannot change his skin, nor the leopard his spots; and Ethiopia shall stretch out her hands to God."

And Whereas, we believe that black men have souls, to be saved or

5 Archives nationales du Québec à Montréal (ANQM), Coroner's Inquests, 1841, no. 421, Martha Hyers, Report of prison doctor Daniel Arnoldi

lost, as well as white men, and that black men have the same love for liberty as white men, such as the liberty of his body and mind, the right of the franchise, reading of the bible, the observance and keeping the sabbath-day, a proper knowledge of the Saviour and his mission into this world; also to enjoy the company of his wife and children, so he may educate them, that they may acquire true religion, industry and economy, and thereby enjoy the fruits of his labor.

And whereas, there is a state of slavery and degradation on this continent, which is at this moment depriving *four millions* of our race of all the blessings above mentioned, intended for them as part and parcel of the human race; and they are deprived of their rights in various ways, many of which are too shocking to submit to the people of Canada; they part man, wife and child, as the Canadian farmer does his lambs, pigs and calves! And send them to every market in the slave holding regions, to be butchered or used in any other way that their purchasers think most to their profit.

The ungodly slave-holder, seduces the helpless unoffending slave-woman, and she is compelled to act as the lamb who licks the knife of its bloody slaughterer! Many of the slave-holders treat their slaves in the most barbarous manner, they shoot them! They brand them!! They dirk them, and starve them!!! These poor coloured fellow-creatures, move about with their heads bowed down, almost afraid even to look at the sun which the Almighty has created. They know not what moment the overseer may order them to receive forty stripes, save one, for not performing more work than perhaps they are able to, in order that their master may supply the christian markets with sugar, cotton, rice, tobacco, rum, brandy, coffee, hemp, and other articles too numerous to mention.

Four millions of slaves producing one hundred dollars each, annually, would be four hundred millions of dollars yearly. We ask the christian public, if this sum is taken from our race in one year? What has been taken from them in fifty years!!! comment here is unnecessary, – an elightened people will estimate for themselves.

We have often heard it asserted, by the enemies of our enslaved and down trodden race, that they are poor, ignorant, degraded, and unfit for freedom; now we put the question to the civilized world, (slave-holders excepted) suppose the many thousand millions of dollars, which have been *wrongfully kept from them* had been properly laid out on their education and moral improvement, would they not, in all probability, be as well qualified for the various stations in life as these unfeeling slave-holders and task masters? It is the want of philanthropy in the slave-holder that causes our degradation, and not the want of capability in our organization; give the coloured population of the world the same opportunities as the white population, and will they not be equal: it is therefore unjust to charge our race with being unfit to appreciate and enjoy liberty.

Another of the horrifying evils of slavery is amalgamation, and cohabitation between father and daughter! Mother and son!! Sister and brother!!!

These occurrences happen in consequence of the manner in which they are separated, sold when they are young, and sent into various parts of slave-holding countrys, where they grow up without any knowledge of their relationship; and then amalgamate in the way above mentioned. Good God! stop the institution of slavery for the sake of thy Son!

And whereas, the American people have often said that Great Britain was the cause of slavery! – This base and foul libel, we have always denied on the ground that when the United States declared in their Declaration of Independence, "that all men are born FREE and EQUAL," Great Britain agreed to it, and gave *them* their *freedom*, as they call it, but at the same time, did not tell them to hold the African in *bondage*, therefore, Great Britain has a *right* to allow slavery to be abolished, in the way we propose, in order to rid herself of the wicked charge of being the cause of perpetual slavery in the United States.

And whereas, it seems to us, the time has come when Great Britain and her allied friends, should exercise their power and authority to give freedom to the whole of mankind, without distinction of either *kindred* or *color*.

And whereas, there seems to be great questions to be settled, viz: such as Oregon, Calefornia, and Texas, by negociation or otherways; therefore, we beg leave to add to the catalogue, that of *slavery*. In order to settle these matters, great preparation is necessary; therefore be it

Resolved, That we, the Consultation Committee of Coloured People of Montreal, will petition Her Most Gracious Majesty Queen Victoria, to authorize the assembling of 100,000 coloured men, and all others who may feel disposed to join us, at Niagara, Upper Canada, for the purpose of putting an end to slavery.

Resolved, That we hope the christian world will sympathise with us, in this philanthropic move, in order that the holy bible may be freely given to ALL the human race, and thereby promote the Redeemer's kingdom.

Resolved, That we refer our friends to the following passages of Scripture, viz: Jeremiah, chapter 47, concerning the destruction of the Philistines, also the 48th chapter, same book, against Moab; these rules of action, laid down for the correction of evil by the Almighty in bygone years, are intended to be used at any time, when circumstances shall require it, against the wickedness of any nation, when they have filled their cup of iniquity; we would likewise call the attention of our readers to the 5th chapter of the epistle of Saint James.

Resolved, That the Hon. Henry Sherwood, of Toronto, and the Hon. T.C. Aylwin, of Quebec, take charge of the Organization, under the control of Her Majesty's Representive [*sic*].

Resolved, That the proceedings of this meeting be published in all the newspapers friendly to the abolition of slavery.

Resolved, That Mr Israel Lewis take charge of the Petition, and forward it to Her Most Gracious Majesty, with all possible despatch.

MOSES CARTER, Chairman

P.J. Lee, Secretary[6]

SOME MAN-STEALING INCIDENTS, 1794–1855

Diah, Fugitive Slave from Plattsburgh, New York

I Eden Johnson, Do Declare that I am a Native of America, thirty four years old, and by Occupation a farmer, that I resided these six months past at Platsburgh in the State of New York, that I came into this Province by the Way of Lake Champlain, and that I am in quest of a Black Man belonging to Nathaniel Platt Esq. – Given under my hand at St Johns this 23d Day of Sept. 1794

Eden Johnson[7]

---

6 Israel Lewis, *Crisis in North America! Slavery, War, Balance of Power and Oregon* (Montreal: Harrison Printer, 1846), Canadian Institute for Historical Microreproductions, no. 22016.

7 National Archives of Canada, RG4 B45, Declarations of Aliens under the Alien Act, 34 Geo. III, Ch. 5, Lower Canada, 1794–1811, f. 244

Deposition of Eden Johnston
Province of Lower Canada
District of Montreal
Eden Johnston of the State of New York farmer being duly sworn upon the holy Evangelists deposeth and saith that on or about the thirteenth day of September last past one Diah, a Negro at that time a Slave to one Nathaniel Platt of Plattsburgh in the county of Clinton in the State of New York having been sent to work with one George Platt Son of the said Nathaniel Platt, escaped from the said George Platt and fled to the province of Lower Canada that this deponent hath been informed he is now living with one John Cheshire upon the River Duchesne in the said province, and this deponent further maketh oath and saith that Since the Escape of the said Diah he this deponent hath purchased him from the said Nathaniel Platt for the sum of Eighty pounds New York Currency and that the said Diah is now the Slave and property of him the deponent, and that without the benefit of a warrant to apprehend him, he the said deponent will be deprived of his said Slave and further Saith not

Eden Johnson
Sworn the 8th of October 1794
before Thomas McCord J.P.[8]

Warrant to apprehend Diah a Negro
Province of Lower Canada
District of Montreal:
George the Third, by the Grace of God, of Great-Britain, France and Ireland, King, Defender of the Faith, and so forth. To our Sheriff of the District of Montreal aforesaid, and to each and every of his Deputies, to the High Constable, and petty Constables same District, Greetings. Forasmuch as Eden Johnson hath come before Thomas McCord Esquire, one of our Justices assigned to keep our Peace, within the said District, and upon oath hath declared that a Certain Negro lad named Diah being his Property hath absconded and been living and is now concealed in this District and as he believes is now at the river Duchesne – these are therefore to authorize and require you, and every of you, to seize, and appre-

---

8 ANQM, Court of General Quarter Sessions of the Peace, October Term, 1794, deposition of Eden Johnson and warrant to apprehend Diah a Negro, 8 October 1794

hend, the said Dick [sic] a Negro lad and him safely keep, so that you may have his body, before the said Thomas McCord Esquire, or some one of our Justices, assigned to keep the Peace, at our said City of Montreal, forthwith without delay, to answer to such matters and things, as shall then and there, be objected against him on our behalf, and to be further dealt with, according to law, and herein fail not, and have you then there this Warrant. Witness the said Thomas McCord at Montreal this Eighth day of October, in year of our Lord, One Thousand Seven Hundred and Ninety four, and in the thirty fourth year of our Reign.[9]

Eden Johnton
vs
Diah a Negro – His Slave
On an information of the Plaintiff against the defendant for running away from his service

The Bailiff returned the Warrant under which the defendant was apprehended and the defendant being brought before the Court –

Mr [Stephen] Sewell in the behalf of the Plaintiff Shewed Cause why he should be delivered up to the Plaintiff. Mr [John] Antill replied on the part of the defendant –

The Court having heard the parties by their Counsel respectively, it is ordered that the defendant be discharged.[10]

Diah's case reported in a Quebec newspaper:

Montreal, 16th Oct. 1794
A Negro Man came into this Town, a short time ago and went to work at the *River du Chêne*[;] he was followed by a person who brought a power of Attorney from a Mr Platt of Platt's Borough, on Lake Champlain, in the States of America, claiming the Negro man, as Mr Platt's slave. Being informed that he could not take the said Negro out of this Province by a power of Attorney, he returned and obtained a Bill of Sale and a receipt for the value of the Negro

9 ANQM, Court of General Quarter Sessions of the Peace, October Term, 1794, deposition of Eden Johnson and warrant to apprehend Diah a Negro, 8 October 1794
10 ANQM, register of the Court of General Quarter Sessions of the Peace, 14 October 1794

man from the said Platt; the Negro was then apprehended and brought to Montreal when Major Antill opposed the man's taking the negro out of the Province. The matter came before the Court, Major Antill for the Poor Negro and Liberty. Messrs Russell and Ross for the Plaintiff. The Court heard the argument on both sides, and made (much to their Honor, and the Honor of humanity) the following decree. That slavery was not known by the Laws of England and therefore discharged the negro man.[11]

The Case of Paul Vallard

In the year 1829, one Paul Vallard took a mulatto slave in the State of Illinois, secretly from his master and brought him into the Province of Lower Canada; complaint was made to the Administration at Washington, and the Secretary of State made a formal request to the Administrator of the Government of the Province for the delivery up to the Government of the United States of Vallard for this alleged crime ...

The Administrator of the Government, Sir James Kempt, referred the matter to his Executive Council; and the following is a copy of the official record, kept in the Department of Archives of the Dominion of Canada at Ottawa.

Report of a Committee of the whole Council Present The Honble. the Chief Justice in the Chair, Mr Smith, Mr DeLery, Mr Stewart, and Mr Cochran on Your Excellency's Reference of a Letter from the American Secretary of State requesting that Paul Vallard accused of having stolen a Mulatto Slave from the State of Illinois may be delivered up to the Government of the United States of America, together with the Slave. May it please Your Excellency

The Committee have proceeded to the consideration of the subject matter of this reference with every wish and disposition to aid the Officers of the Government of the United States of America in the execution of the Laws of that Dominion and they regret therefore the more that the present application cannot in their opinion be acceded to.

In the former Cases the Committee have acted upon the Principle which now seems to be generally understood that whenever a

---

11 *Times/Cour du Temps*, Quebec, 20 October 1794

Crime has been committed and the Perpetrator is punishable according to the Lex Loci [law of the land] of the Country in which it is committed, the country in which he is found may rightfully aid the Policy of the Country against which the Crime was committed in bringing the Criminal to justice – and upon this ground have recommended that Fugitives from the United States should be delivered up.

But the Committee conceive that the Crimes for which they are authorized to recommend the arrest of Individuals who have fled from other Countries must be such as are *mala in se* [wrong in themselves] and are universally admitted to be *Crimes* in every Nation, and that the offence of the *Individual* whose person is demanded must be such as to render him liable to arrest by the Law of Canada as well as by the Law of the United States.

The state of slavery is not recognized by the Law of Canada nor does the law admit that any Man can be the proprietor of another.

Every Slave therefore who comes into the Province is immediately free whether he has been brought in by violence or has entered it of his own accord; and his liberty cannot thenceforth be lawfully infringed without some Cause for which the Law of Canada has directed an arrest.

On the other hand, the Individual from whom he has been taken cannot pretend that the Slave has been stolen from him in as much as the Law of Canada does not admit a Slave to be a subject of property.

All of which is respectfully submitted to Your Excellency's Wisdom.

The result was that there was no extradition.[12]

A Trap Set for Osborne Morton

A SLAVE CASE IN CANADA – A fugitive slave named [Osborne] Morton, has been for some months past in the employ of Mr H. Stephens in this city. He was formerly in the possession of a Mr Campbell of the firm of Campbell & Otts, proprietors of a race-

1 2   William R. Riddell, "An International Complication between Illinois and Canada Arising out of Slavery," *Journal of the Illinois State Historical Society* 25 (Apr. 1932–Jan. 1933): 123–6

course at Louisville, Kentucky, and was accounted by them their best horse-trainer. Some time since, these people got wind of Morton's whereabouts, and Otts has recently arrived in this city with the object of getting the man back again if possible. A man was accordingly sent to Mr Stephens, to see him quietly and entice him into the town. This man made a mistake and went to the residence of Mr R.H. Stephens and finding his way to the kitchen was told of his error by the servant boy who accompanied him to Mr H. Stephens. Here the poor fugitive was found. He was asked what wages he got, and told he was a fool to take them, but if he would go back he and his family should be freed, and he would get three or four times as much wages, besides what he could make by betting on the course. The poor fellow was persuaded to consent to go and volunteered to serve his master as long as he should live, if he would give himself wife and child their "liberty papers." Fortunately, Mr R.H. Stephens was informed of what was going on. He was aware that the law of Kentucky prevented the manumission of a slave unless he was sent out of the State, and that the poor fellow's wife and child had been already sold to some man living in one of the back counties of Missouri. The matter therefore assumed the appearance of a plot to entrap the fugitive back into slavery. Mr Otts was accordingly summoned before the Police Magistrate, charged with the offence of enticing a servant away from his master and was in accordance with the provisions of the statute, fined, and subjected to a nominal imprisonment. We are told, however, that he has not given up the hope of getting the man back, and is still staying in town for that purpose. The game, however, is pretty certain in this free country, to be a hopeless one, and we hope Mr Otts may return to his dissolute partner, without the human chattel which he has dared to come upon British ground to seek. Canada is not a place where a slave-catcher's trade is at all likely to prosper. Surely there is no man in Montreal willing to lend such fellows a helping hand.[13]

Attempt to Bribe the Chief of Police

CAN SUCH THINGS BE? – *A proposition for Kidnapping!* – We were yesterday, (the day of its reception), furnished with a copy of the subjoined letter. We lay it before our readers for their enlightenment

13 *Montreal Gazette,* 13 July 1854

with regard to the encroachments of the slave power. Not content with turning the free states of their own union into a hunting ground for fugitive slaves – not content with imposing a law upon the country which makes every freeman in the United States legally bound to be aiding and assisting the slaveholders in recovering their man-chattels, they venture to pursue their game still farther and to attempt to tarnish free and unstained British ground with their damning traffic in men. Our readers were informed last summer of an attempt made in U. Canada similar to that proposed by this ruffian Pope, which was signally discomfitted after it had proceeded as far as to amount to an overt act of kidnapping, as well as of the project to entice away a fugitive slave in the employ of R.H. Stephens, Esq., of this city, which was also promptly met, and defeated. We have now a cool project from a Maryland constable and slave-hunter, to the head of our police force, asking him to break the laws of God and his country, and become a partner in a wholesale scheme to kidnap the poor colored men who have taken refuge among us. We know not whether Mr [Moses Judah] Hays intends answering his most insulting epistle at all; but if he does, we know full well what his answer will be. We know how fiercely he will spurn so outrageous a proposal, as would all others in Canada, save the basest and most abject of God's creatures who dwell among us. And we have one word of advice to give Mr Pope, which is this, that he will do well not to venture one inch beyond the frontier in pursuance of his object. We happen to know that the inhabitants of the frontier, though generally a law-abiding people, have a holy horror of slavery and all its promoters, and clever Mr Pope might come in for some peculiarly disagreeable manifestations of their righteous indignation. He might, indeed, go back a colored man himself. We have no desire to counsel violence towards any man, but such a proposition as that we have just read in this negro-hunter's letter, rouses a spirit of indignation which prevents all calm reflection. If ever the taking of the law into one's own hands were justifiable, it would be in such a case as this. We will not trust ourselves to write more about it to-day, but can only cry shame on the man who would so degrade himself as to make such a proposition! Triple shame on the people whose laws sanction his conduct! And we may thank God once more, and rejoice, that their country is not ours, – that we have no share or participation in their sin: –

Frederick, Maryland,
United States of America
January 1st, 1855

To the Chief of Police, Montreal, Canada:
Dear Sir, – Though the Laws of your Province preclude Slavery,
and you may deem it improper that I should address you relative to
that question, which has created so great sectional animosity at
home, and elicited such disapproval abroad, – still, believing that a
sense of justice influences every right thinking man in the forma-
tion of his judgment, and the mode of his conduct, I have taken
the liberty, which, if it meets not with views alike to mine, will be
pardoned.

Vast numbers of Slaves, escaping from their masters or owners,
succeed in reaching your Provinces, and are, therefore, without
the pale of the "Fugitive Slave Law," and can only be restored by
cunning together with skill.

Large rewards are offered and will be paid for their return, and
could I find an efficient person to act with me, a great deal of
money could be made, as I would equally divide. Many are willing
to come after writing to that effect. The only apprehension we have
in approaching too far into Canada, is the fear of being arrested,
and had I a good assistant in your city who would induce the
negroes to the frontier, I would be there to pay the cash. On your
answer, I can furnish names and descriptions of negroes, which will
fully reward the trouble.

Answer either to accept or decline.

Yours,
John H. Pope,
Police Officer and Constable[14]

---

14 *Montreal Gazette*, 13 January 1855

SOURCES

In these notes, unless some other location is specified, the church and court records and newspapers cited are Montreal ones. From the 1840s on, two basic sources are Montreal's city directories (Lovell's directories, as they are known), which appeared yearly from 1842 on (except in 1851) and are easily accessible on microfilm; and the city tax rolls, starting in 1847, found at the Archives de la ville de Montréal. I used both extensively, so am mentioning them here rather than listing them repeatedly.

ABBREVIATIONS

ANQM   Archives nationales du Québec, Montréal
ANQQ   Archives nationales du Québec, Québec
  DCB   *Dictionary of Canadian Biography*
  JHN   *Journal of Negro History*
   NA   National Archives of Canada, Ottawa

THE TRUTH ABOUT ROSE
Liberator (Boston), 25 March 1859.
"Slavery in Lower Canada," *Lower Canada Jurist* 3 (1860): 257–68.
Judicial Cases concerning American Slavery and the Negro, ed. Helen Tunnicliff Catterall, with additions by James J. Hayden (Washington, D.C.: Carnegie Institution of Washington, 1937), 5:111–13, 162–3, 174, 194–5, 203–5, 216–17, 340–4.

TOUJOURS L'AMOUR
ANQM, notary J.G. Beek, Baux et Protêts, 1:217, 16 November 1787; 218, 3 December 1787; 220, 26 December 1787. The line from Frederick Douglass comes from the first paragraph of his *Narrative of the Life of Frederick Douglass*,

an American Slave (1845; the edition I used was New York: Modern Library, 2000). Catherine died a pauper at the Hôpital Général of the Grey Nuns on 13 August 1811, said to be about 70 years old. Hilaire also died there, on 15 December 1822 (35 years after his first visit to heaven!), age about 89.

MISTER WHISKY HIMSELF
ANQM, notary J.G. Beek, no. 525, 5 May 1789; notary L. Chaboillez, no. 8725, 2 June 1809; notary J.G. Delisle, no. 936, 31 December 1794, no. 2361, 30 January 1797, no. 2493, 7 September 1797; notary A. Foucher, no. 7262, 14 April 1794; notary J.A. Gray, no. 1775, 14 March 1807; notary P. Lukin Sr, no. 1127, 23 January 1798, no. 1166, 26 February 1798, no. 1287, 9 October 1798; notary J. Papineau, no. 2694, 11 January 1798. Court of General Quarter Sessions of the Peace, July term 1815, Gabriel Johonnot deposition 9 June 1815, William Griffin recognizance 10 June. Church registers: Christ Church, Sorel, 9 June 1800; Notre Dame, Montreal, 26 November 1797; St Andrew's Presbyterian, Quebec, 6 December 1814.

J.D. Borthwick, *History of the Montreal Prison from A.D. 1784 to A.D. 1886* (Montreal: A. Periard 1886), 234. A. Johonnot, "The Johonnot Family," *New England Historical and Genealogical Register* 7 (1853): 141. E. Lord, *Memoir of the Rev. Joseph Stibbs Christmas* (Montreal: John Lovell 1868), 152–3. James H. Stark, *The Loyalists of Massachusetts and the Other Side of the American Revolution* (Boston: James H. Stark 1910), 125, 132, 135, 137, 344, 409–11.

IF YOU SAY SO
ANQM, notary J.G. Delisle, 9 August 1790, and no. 872, 4 July 1794; notary P. Lukin Sr, no. 235, 27 July 1793, no. 5298, 25 May 1814; notary F.M. Pétrimoulx, 10 January 1802.

Statutes of the United Kingdom of Great Britain and Ireland, 47 Geo III, 1807, Ch. 36, "An Act for the Abolition of the Slave Trade."

CHARLOTTE, SHE GOT THE BALL ROLLING
See documents "Some Man-Stealing Incidents, 1794–1855," and "First Petition of the Montreal Slave-masters, 1799." See also the story "Trim the Gardener."

ANQM, notary N.B. Doucet, no. 9389, 16 January 1822; notary P. Lukin Sr, nos. 73 and 74, 25 August 1797. Register of Scotch Presbyterian Church in St Gabriel Street, 4 March 1798.

Jacques Viger and Louis Hippolyte LaFontaine, "De l'esclavage en Canada," *Mémoires et documents relatifs à l'histoire du Canada,* Société historique de Montréal, 1–2 (1859): 52–56. Robin Winks, *The Blacks in Canada: A History,* 2nd ed. (Montreal: McGill-Queen's University Press 1997), 99–102.

ONE AMAZING AMAZON
John Durang, *The Memoir of John Durang, American Actor, 1785–1816,* ed. Alan S. Downer (Pittsburgh, Pa.: University of Pittsburgh Press 1966), 83.

CHARITY DIDN'T DO IT
ANQM, notary J.G. Delisle, no. 218, 7 August 1790; notary A. Foucher, no.

5892, 16 November 1785; notary J. Gabrion, no. 10, 14 July 1798; notary J.A. Gray, 22 November 1796, no. 133, 27 November 1797, no. 664, 19 August 1801; notary P. Lukin Sr, no. 1099, 22 November 1797. Church registers: Notre Dame, 8 September 1813; Pointe-aux-Trembles, 8 December 1800. ANQQ, notary P.L. Deschenaux, no. 2830, 18 May 1792. Mount Royal Cemetery, Protestant Old Burial Records, 1:222, 8 November 1800; 1:223, 26 January 1802.

Gazette, 4 March, 8 April, and 5 August 1799.

M. Faribault-Beauregard, *La Population des forts français d'Amérique (XVIIIe siècle)* (Montreal: Editions Bergeron 1982), 1:122, 133, 171.

THE WORLD TURNED UPSIDE DOWN

ANQM, notary J. Papineau, no. 3069, 11 August 1800; notary J.B.H. Deguire, no. 184, 29 November 1799.

Robert Lionel Séguin, "L'esclavage dans la presqu'île," *Bulletin des recherches historiques* 55, nos. 4–6 (1949): 91–4, and nos. 7–9, 168. Marcel Trudel, *Dictionnaire des esclaves et de leurs propriétaires au Canada français*, 2nd ed. (Montreal: Hurtubise HMH 1994), 216.

THE KING OF FRANCE

ANQM, notary J.P. Gauthier, no. 231, 15 September 1792; notary J. Papineau, no. 3069, 11 August 1800. Register of Notre Dame Church, 7 October 1786.

Globe and Mail (Toronto), 14 January 2000, A13, Guy Bouthillier, "Keeping a Bridge to the Past: Rechristening the Papineau-Leblanc Bridge Would Endanger the Memory of a Proud Quebec Name."

For the petitions presented by Joseph Papineau on behalf of the slave owners, see documents "First petition of the Montreal Slavemasters, 1799" and "Second Petition of the Montreal Slavemasters, 1800."

Gérard Parizeau, "Joseph Papineau ou la bourgeoisie montante (1752–1841)," in *La société canadienne française au XIXe siècle* (Montreal: Fides 1975), 382–413. Marcel Trudel, *L'esclavage au Canada français* (Quebec: Presses de l'université Laval 1960), 150–1.

JUST JULIA

ANQM, notary J.A. Gray, no. 2251, 6 February 1809, nos. 1138 and 1139, 11 May 1804.

NA, RG4, B19, "List of persons liable to serve as Jurors residing in the Town and Banlieu of Montreal – June 1811," 1:31.

ISAAC THE IMPOSSIBLE

ANQM, notary J.A. Gray, no. 2437, 3 August 1809; notary H. Griffin, no. 1011, 9 June 1815. Church registers: Christ Church, 3 March 1805; Notre Dame, 30 August 1809.

COLD CASE

ANQM, Court of King's Bench, September term 1815, Rex v. James Douglas and others. Coroner's inquests, 1815, no. 7, "Enqueste on the Body of Joseph

Pearson," 10 March 1815. Register of St Andrew's Presbyterian Church, 11 March 1815.

HOME AT LAST

ANQM, notary A. Jobin, no. 1933, 26 June 1820, no. 1938, 30 June 1820, nos. 1947 and 1949, 4 July 1820. Cour Supérieure, John Trim v. Simon Clark, 1823, no. 162, deposition of Catherine Gayet (Guillet), 23 September 1828; Testaments olographes, 5 September 1815, will of James Dunlop dated 12 July 1811. Register of Scotch Presbyterian Church in St Gabriel Street, 17 December 1799, 26 May 1806 and 12 February 1825.

Claude Perrault, *Montréal en 1825* (Montreal: Groupe d'études Gen-Histo 1977), 315.

A WHOLE NEW LIGHT

ANQM, notary T. Bedouin, nos. 398 to 415, 4 May 1818, no. 421, 9 May 1818, no. 423, 12 May 1818, nos. 533 to 548, 9 December 1818, no. 523, 21 November 1818. Court of King's Bench, August-September 1823, nos. 9, 42, and 43, Rex v. Warren Glossen, Peter Johnson, Jean-Baptiste Bowman, Joseph Yager and Jean-Baptiste Albert. Register of the Court of General Quarter Sessions of the Peace, July term 1819, Rex v. Warren Gaussen alias Glasford Warren, 14, 16, 17, 19 July.

Archives de la ville de Montréal, Fonds des juges de paix de Montréal, 4:1–2, 7–8, 9–10, 95, 110, 117, 141–2.

Newspapers: *Canadian Courant,* 11 and 15 January, 1 February, 1 March, 5 April, 13 September, 25 October and 8 November 1823. *Gazette,* 10 and 17 January, 13 September and 25 October 1823. *Herald,* 25 November 1815; 13 September, 25 October and 8 November 1823.

Statutes of Lower Canada, 58 Geo III, c. 2, "An Act to provide more effectually for the security of the Cities of Quebec and Montreal, by establishing a Watch and Night Lights in the said Cities, etc."

William Henry Atherton, *Montreal 1535–1914,* 3 vols. (Montreal: S.J. Clarke Publishing 1914), 2:403. Camille Bertrand, *Histoire de Montréal,* 2 vols. (Montreal 1935–42), 2:91. Philippe Aubert de Gaspé, *Mémoires* (Montreal: Fides 1971), 258.

TRIM THE GARDENER

ANQM, notary G.D. Arnoldi, no. 623, 7 December 1829; notary T. Barron, no. 1540, 19 April 1809, no. 2438, 30 September 1814, no. 2594, 2 May 1815; notary I. Bourassa, 25 August 1799; notary J.M. Cadieux, no. 58, 2 April 1807, no. 79, 2 May 1807, no. 173, 21 December 1807; notary L. Chaboillez, no. 1366, 27 March 1795, no. 3532, 17 May 1799, no. 7077, 22 August 1805, no. 7586, 2 September 1806, no. 8233, 18 April 1808, no. 8387, 30 September 1808; notary F.M.T. Chevalier de Lorimier, no. 542, 19 September 1832; notary J. Desautels, no. 1570, 21 April 1815; notary N.B. Doucet, no. 5406, 25 July 1818, no. 11617, 10 April 1824; notary J.E. Faribault, 9 February 1803; notary H. Griffin, no. 962, 6 May 1815, no. 6210, 26 January 1826, no. 8420,

14 September 1829; notary L. Huguet-Latour, no. 1280, 13 November 1816; notary P. Lacombe, no. 31, 13 January 1832; notary P. Lukin Jr, no. 2343, 16 November 1831, no. 2759, 8 February 1833, no. 2787, 20 February 1833; notary P. Lukin Sr, no. 747, 21 April 1796, no. 1251, 27 July 1798; notary P. Ritchot, no. 1863, 10 July 1827, no. 2468, 2 September 1829.

Church registers: ANQM, Christ Church, 6 February 1803, 25 September 1808, 23 September 1823, 9 October 1825, 2 April 1826, 28 January 1833, 19 February 1876; Notre Dame, 7 January 1823, 16 October 1826, 9 May 1827, 10 August 1829; St Paul's Presbyterian, 22 June 1833; Scotch Presbyterian Church in St Gabriel Street, 8 August 1815, 4 November 1815, 9 September 1827.

ANQM, Cour Supérieure, John Trim v. Simon Clark, 1823, no. 162; J.D. Lacroix v. Isaac Taylor et al., and Henri Vallotte v. Isaac Taylor et al., 1849, nos. 1910 and 1409, declaration and exhibits of Henri Vallotte; Tutelles et Curatelles, no. 636, 20 December 1825.

Mount Royal Cemetery, Grave G-402; Protestant Old Burial Records, 1:224, 6 February 1803; 2:23, 23 September 1823; 2:115, 17 September 1827; 2:355, 28 January 1833.

NA, RG4, B19, Assessments for the Year 1813, Montreal, 1:48; 1842 census, manuscript returns, Montreal, f. 1350, no. 10; 1861 census, manuscript returns, Montreal, f. 7656; 1871 census, manuscript returns, Montreal, 106/C6:51, no. 10.

Newspapers: *Gazette*, 9 January 1850, 9 July 1853.

Thomas Doige, *The Montreal Directory &c.: An Alphabetical List of the Merchants, Traders and Housekeepers Residing in Montreal*, 2nd ed. (Montreal: James Lane 1820). Claude Perrault, *Montréal en 1825* (Montreal: Groupe d'études Gen-Histo 1977), 199, 377.

AGENT OF THE LIBERATOR

ANQM, register of St. Andrew's Presbyterian Church, 27 October 1832.

Newspapers: *Brockville Gazette*, 19 April, 9 and 23 August, 6 December 1832. *Brockville Recorder*, 31 January 1833. *Canadian Courant*, 8 September, 6 October, 7 and 17 November 1832. *Liberator* (Boston), 12 May, 27 October, 24 November 1832; 23 February 1833. *Montreal Gazette*, 4 October 1832. *Quebec Gazette*, 17 and 21 September 1832.

Paola Brown, *Address Intended to Be Delivered in the City Hall, Hamilton, February 7, 1851, on the Subject of Slavery* (Hamilton: privately printed 1851), Canadian Institute for Historical Microreproductions, no. 49632. Thomas Smallwood, *A Narrative of Thomas Smallwood, (Coloured Man:) Giving an Account of His Birth, etc.*, (Toronto: privately printed 1851), CIHM, no. 64728. David Walker, *David Walker's Appeal, to the Coloured Citizens of the World, but in Particular, and Very Expressly, to Those of the United States of America* (reprint of the third and last edition published by Walker in 1830; Baltimore: Black Classic Press 1993). John C. Weaver, "Paola Brown," *DCB* 8:105–6. Robin Winks, *The Blacks in Canada: A History*, 2nd ed. (Montreal: McGill-Queen's University Press 1997), 254.

THE VALENTINES' DAY

ANQM, notary G.D. Arnoldi, no. 615, 24 November 1829, no. 616, 26 November 1829; notary J.H. Jobin, no. 199, 1 May 1834; notary L. Marteau, no. 951, 4 March 1831; notary J.M. Mondelet, no. 2365, 2 February 1803, no. 2530, 10 October 1803, no. 2707, 15 June 1804, no. 2781, 9 October 1804, no. 2956, 7 October 1805, no. 3099, 17 October 1806. Church registers: Christ Church, 20 November 1829; Notre Dame, 28 January 1843.

MESSING WITH DRAGONS

ANQM, notary I.J. Gibb, no. 924, 9 March 1837 and no. 2130, 10 May 1838; notary E. Guy, no. 1350, 23 March 1837, no. 1496, 19 July 1837; notary W.S. Hunter, no. 17, 10 October 1835; notary J.H. Jobin, no. 756, 10 March 1836. Court of King's Bench, June term 1836, no. 1600, Alexander Grant v. Ann G. Marvin, habeas corpus; August-September term 1836, Rex v. Alexander Grant, George Nixon and Moses Powell Wormley. Court of General Quarter Sessions of the Peace, Ebenezer Marvin v. Betsy Freeman, complaint of desertion by Ann G. Marvin, 13 June 1836; July term 1836, Rex v. Daniel Arnoldi. Cour Supérieure, Tutelles et Curatelles, 11 July 1834, no. 513B. Church registers: Christ Church, 30 July, 2 August 1834, 22 August 1838; Notre Dame, 8, 31 July 1834.

Mount Royal Cemetery, Protestant Old Burial Records, 2:418, 2 August 1834; 3:110, 22 August 1838; 3:181, 6 April 1841.

NA, 1831 census, manuscript returns, Montreal, v. 13, part 2, f. 80.

Newspapers: L'Ami du Peuple, 22 August 1838. Canadian Courant, 21 July 1830. Gazette, 25 July 1833; 2 and 19 August, 23 October 1834; 16 June, 15 September 1836; 21 August 1838. Herald, 27 December 1836. Liberator (Boston), 11 October 1839. Minerve, 23 and 25 October 1834; 16 June, 25 July, 8 and 19 September, 3 November 1836. Transcript, 13 February, 21 August 1838. Vindicator, 6 August 1833; 16 May, 29 July, 24 October 1834; 14, 17 June, 15, 19 July, 4 November 1836.

Statutes of the United Kingdom of Great Britain and Ireland, 3 & 4 William IV, 1833, Ch. 73, "An Act for the Abolition of Slavery throughout the British Colonies; for Promoting the Industry of the manumitted Slaves; and for compensating the Persons hitherto entitled to the Services of such Slaves."

Henry Clay, The Papers of Henry Clay, ed. Robert Seager (Lexington, Ky.: University Press of Kentucky 1988), 9:332–3, and (1991), 10: 176–7. Fred Landon, "Social Conditions among the Negroes in Upper Canada before 1865," Ontario Historical Society Papers and Records 22 (1925): 153. Robert V. Remini, Henry Clay: Statesman for the Union (New York: W.W. Norton 1991), 532–7. Robert-Lionel Séguin, Le Mouvement insurrectionnel dans la Presqu'île de Vaudreuil 1837–1838 (Montreal: Librairie Ducharme 1955), 135.

THINGS YOU'VE GOT TO WONDER ABOUT

ANQM, Régistre de Prison – Montréal: box 50, no. 173, 30 June 1828; no. 203, 11 July 1828; nos. 501–601, 30 April 1829; nos. 3557–64, 6 August 1833; box 56, no. 355, 21 April 1837; no. 82, 7 November 1839; no. 262, 24 February 1841; box 54, no. 3, 2 January 1839; no. 281, 4 April 1839; no. 874, 6 June

1839; no. 1380, 2 October 1839; no. 1527, 7 November 1839; no. 189, 19
February 1840; no. 300, 22 March 1840; no. 518, 22 May 1840; no. 710, 7
July 1840; no. 655, 7 August 1840; no. 782, 14 September 1840; no. 1412, 22
December 1840; no. 274, 24 February 1841; no. 458, 26 April 1841; no. 521,
19 May 1841; no. 809, 27 July 1841; no. 963, 9 October 1841; no. 1034, 23
October 1841. Coroner's inquests, 1841, no. 421, Martha Hyers, report of
prison doctor Daniel Arnoldi. Church registers: Scotch Presbyterian Church
in St Gabriel Street, 1 April 1819, 28 February 1820; First Baptist, 5 August
1835; Notre Dame, 26 November 1841; St Andrew's Presbyterian, 11 August
1822, 1 June 1823.
    Mount Royal Cemetery, Protestant Old Burial Records, 2:31, 2 June 1823.

GABRIEL, BE AN ANGEL AND BLOW THAT HORN
ANQM, notary J. Blackwood, no. 906, 8 September 1845; notary J. Desautels,
no. 1334, 16 January 1815; notary J.A. Gray, Engagements, 24 April 1804, 22
March 1809; notary L. Hughet-Latour, no. 922, 30 May 1814; notary P. Lukin
Sr, no. 4942, 5 May 1812, no. 5001, 21 May 1812, no. 5063, 28 December
1812, no. 5075, 10 December 1812, nos. 5126 and 5127, 16 February 1813.
Church registers: Christ Church, 4 August 1816, 21 November 1846; Notre
Dame, 8 May 1797, 27 July 1821; Quebec Anglican Church, 30 September
1804; St Andrew's Presbyterian, Quebec, 6 December 1814; Scotch Presbyterian Church in St Gabriel Street, 23 February 1807, 22 July 1812, 4 September
1814, 26 November 1815, 11 March 1816, 26 October 1816, 5 January 1819,
5 March 1819, 23 October 1819, 26 October 1820, 3 September 1821, 5
August 1821, 14 July 1828. Régistre de Prison – Montréal, box 50, no. 1939,
27 July 1832; no. 3195, 24 January 1833; no. 3331, 1 May 1833; nos. 3557–64
(and no. 3559 in descriptions of prisoners at end of volume), no. 3578, 10
August 1833; no. 3874, 22 January 1834; no. 4052, 29 May 1834; no. 5038,
28 July 1834; box 55, no. 51, 5 September 1834.
    ANQQ, E21, s64, ss4, Ministère des terres et forêts, Lower Canada Militia
Claims, no. 10038–9.
    Mount Royal Cemetery, Protestant Old Burial Records, 4:67, 21 November
1846.
    NA, RG9, IA7, Militia and Defence Pre-Confederation Records, Adjutant
General's Office, Lower Canada, militia muster rolls and pay lists, v. 1–7.
    Camille Bertrand, *Histoire de Montréal*, 2 vols. (Montreal 1935–1942),
2:275–87. Thomas Doige, *The Montreal Directory &c.: An Alphabetical List of the
Merchants, Traders and Housekeepers Residing in Montreal*, 1st and 2nd eds. (Montreal: James Lane, 1819–20).

BAD NEWS LEWIS
ANQM, notary J.H. Isaacson, 30 May 1847. Church registers: East End
Lagauchetière Street Methodist, 7 June 1847; St James Methodist, 1 August
1847.
    Mount Royal Cemetery, Protestant Old Burial Records, 4:89, 7 June 1847;
4:115, 31 July 1847.
    Newspapers: *Daily Albany Argus* (Albany, N.Y.), 12 February 1834. *Liberator*

(Boston), 9 April 1831; 14 January 1832; 9, 23 February, 9 March 1833; 2 May 1835; 2, 16 July 1836.
  Marilyn Baily, "From Cincinnati, Ohio, to Wilberforce, Canada: A Note on Antebellum Colonization," *JNH* 58, no. 4 (October 1973): 427–40. Benjamin Drew, *A North-Side View of Slavery – The Refugee: Or the Narratives of Fugitive Slaves in Canada* (Boston: John P. Jewett 1856); there have been several modern reprints of this work. Israel Lewis, *Crisis in North America: Slavery, War, Balance of Power and Oregon* (Montreal: Harrison Printer 1846) Canadian Institute for Historical Microreproductions, no. 22016. W.H. Pease and J. Pease, *Black Utopia: Negro Communal Experiments in America* (Madison, Wisc.: State Historical Society of Wisconsin 1963), 46–62. Emmett D. Preston, "The Fugitive Slave Acts in Ohio," *JNH* 28, no. 4 (October 1943), 422-477. Austin Steward, *Twenty-Two Years a Slave and Forty Years a Freeman* (Rochester, N.Y.: William Alling 1857), reprinted in *Four Fugitive Slave Narratives* (Reading, Mass.: Addison-Wesley Publishing 1969). Richard C. Wade, "The Negro in Cincinnati, 1800–1830," *JNH* 39, no. 1 (January 1954): 43–57. Robin Winks, *The Blacks in Canada: A History,* 2nd ed. (Montreal: McGill-Queen's University Press, 1997), 153–62.

TAKING CARE OF ROBERT
ANQM, notary L. Huguet-Latour, no. 1062, 24 June 1815; notary J.A. Labadie, no. 2311, 13 June 1832, with addendum 9 January 1847, no. 10080, 9 January 1847, no. 11360, 5 December 1848, no. 11362, 7 December 1848, no. 14278, 13 May 1856, no. 14855, 26 September 1859, no. 14959, 6 October 1860. Cour Supérieure, Tutelles et Curatelles, 200, 21 April 1818. Register of Notre Dame Church, 13 April 1861.
  NA, 1851 census, manuscript returns, Montreal, Hôpital Général; 1861 census, manuscript returns, Montreal, Hôpital Général, f. 15722.
  Pilot, 19 December 1848.

PHILOMÈNE'S THIRD BIRTHDAY
ANQM, notary J. Belle, no. 10676, 5 December 1848; notary J. Blackwood, no. 968, 15 May 1846, no. 972, 22 May 1846, no. 990, 12 August 1846; notary A. Brogan, nos. 4 and 5, 28 February 1867; notary G.H.Z. Cadieux, no. 1992, 4 May 1847; notary J.H. Isaacson, no. 345, 17 April 1847, no. 365, 22 April 1847, no. 1183, 19 October 1849, no. 1186, 19 October 1849, no. 2307, 29 June 1852, no. 3126, 12 May 1854, no. 4901, 30 September 1857, no. 4906, 2 October 1857; notary J.H. Jobin, no. 5295, 4 February 1846; notary J.A. Labadie, no. 9677, 9 May 1846; notary A.N. Mathon, no. 1, 6 February 1847; notary W.A. Phillips, no. 250, 15 December 1853. Church registers: Église Évangélique Française, 7 August 1865; Notre Dame, 16 August 1843, 23 October 1849, 18 September 1851, 22 May 1856, 13 May 1862, 17 August 1866, 18 August 1868; St James Methodist, 13 May 1866; St Paul's Presbyterian, 10 April 1841. Cour Supérieure, 1849, nos. 1910 and 1409, J.D. Lacroix v. Isaac Taylor et al., and Henri Vallotte v. Isaac Taylor et al.; Tutelles et Curatelles, no. 400, 3 November 1866. Régistre de prison – Montréal, box 54, no. 886, 24 September 1840.

NA, 1861 census, manuscript returns, Montreal, ff. 2674, 4931, 7284.

JERICHO!
ANQM, notary C.E. Belle, no. 2127, 27 July 1857; notary J.C. Griffin, no. 14347, 3 March 1857, no. 15691, 8 April 1858, no. 15739, 20 April 1858. Newspapers: *Gazette*, 11 December 1856. *Pilot*, 5 May, 20 July 1857.

THE CENTAUR
ANQM, notary R. Beaufield, no. 5162, 1 April 1870; notary H. Brodie, no. 1222, 31 December 1868; notary J.H. Isaacson, 10688, 19 February 1862, no. 19702, 16 April 1869; notary J.H. Jobin, no. 11509, 21 February 1867, no. 11526, 5 March 1867, no. 11591, 13 April 1867; notary W.F. Lighthall, no. 4742, 29 September 1869. Cour Supérieure, 1869, no. 2426, Wilson v. Morton. Register of the Anglican chapel, Montreal General Hospital, 6 August 1887. Mount Royal Cemetery, Grave M-266m.

NA, 1861 census, manuscript returns, Montreal, f. 4960; 1871 census, manuscript returns, Jacques Cartier district, Parish of Lachine, 108/A:15, nos. 8–9. Newspapers: *Commercial Advertiser*, 16 August 1862. *Daily Star*, 5, 6 August 1887. *Gazette*, 13 July 1854; 10 September 1859; 3, 16 August 1860; 16 August 1861. *Pilot*, 29 and 30 April, 1858; 7 September, 17 October 1859; 3, 16 August 1860; 17 August 1861.

R.P. Zirblis, *Friends of Freedom: The Vermont Underground Railroad Survey Report*, compiled for the Vermont Department of State Buildings and Vermont Division for Historical Preservation, December 1996, 35.

TRIAL OF THE CENTURY
ANQM, notary J. Belle, no. 14770, 28 February 1855; notary J. Smith, no. 3219, 18 March 1857, no. 3866, 20 February 1858, no. 5131, 17 April 1859, no. 6259, 21 February 1860; no. 7442, 22 February 1861. Court of General Quarter Sessions of the Peace, August term 1859, The Queen v. Elizabeth Malloy, indictment 4 August, depositions of Margaret Scott and John Abbott 1 August, voluntary statement of Eliza Molloy 1 August, Precept: Schedule A – list of petty jurors, "List of Prisoners and of Their Ages," "Calendar of Convictions," "List of Convictions"; court register, 6–14 August 1858, 4, 5 and 13 August 1859.

NA, 1861 census, manuscript returns, Montreal, f. 9684; 1871 census, manuscript returns, Montreal, 106/C3:46, nos. 16–20, and 47, no. 1. Newspapers: *Pilot*, 29 April 1858; 5 and 15 August 1859. *Transcript*, 2 August 1859.

Gary Collison, *Shadrach Minkins: From Fugitive Slave to Citizen* (Cambridge, Mass.: Harvard University Press 1997), 189–90.

MR WOOD AS A MATTER OF FACT
City Archives of Kingston-upon-Hull, CQB 244/494-503, Court of Quarter Sessions, Kingston County, Hull, England, December 1853. Newspapers: *Pilot*, 25 December 1852; 26 November, 2, 5, 10, and

17 December 1859; 5 January 1860. *Transcript,* 11 June, 23 July 1859; 1 March 1860. *Witness,* 15 June 1859.

COOK'S PLACE
ANQM, notary J. Belle, no. 17676, 18 February 1859; notary J.E.O. Labadie, no. 2341, 25 February 1856, no. 2865, 21 February 1857, no. 3570, 15 February 1858. Register of First Baptist Church, 6 April 1863.
Mount Royal Cemetery, Grave H-17.
NA, 1861 census, manuscript returns, Montreal, f. 9558; 1871 census, manuscript returns, Montreal, 106/C3:73, nos. 1–5.
Newspapers: *Argus,* 28 December 1857; 27 May, 21 June 1858. *Daily Star,* 5 June 1876. *Gazette,* 16 November 1860; 31 January 1861. *Pilot,* 10 and 28 September 1858; 26 and 30 April 1859; 16 and 17 August 1861. *Transcript,* 29 February 1860.

SAME OLD SONG
ANQM, notary T.B. Doucet, no. 15848, 19 February 1861; notary J.B. Houlé, no. 7682, 15 May 1860; notary J.H. Jobin, no. 10813, 13 April 1865; notary E. McIntosh, no. 1821, 23 February 1860, no. 2855, 30 April 1861; notary J. Simard, no. 594, 9 February 1853. Raisons sociales (registry of company names): Jones & Watkins, no. 1894, 30 April 1861. Church registers: First Baptist, 6 December 1859; Mountain Street Methodist, 3 October 1867.
NA , 1861 census, manuscript returns, Montreal, ff. 4494, 6448, 15385; 1871 census, manuscript returns, Montreal, 107/A1:54, nos. 17–18, and 106/A10:64, nos. 8–10.
Gazette, 24 February 1862; 18 March 1863. *Pilot,* 9 April 1850; 1, 4, 6, 8, 11, 13, 15 June 1855; 21 August, 3 September 1856; 5, 20, 28, 30, 31 March, 1, 2, 6, 8 April, 9, 19, 24, 25 September 1857; 12, 22, 24, 25, 26, 27 February, 1 March 1862. *Transcript,* 19, 25, 29, 30 September, 2 October 1857; 14 April 1860.
Quebec City directories, 1862–63 to 1868–69.

THE PERFECT CRIME
ANQM, Court of Queen's Bench, March term 1882, The Queen v. Charles Albert Smith.
Newspapers: *Daily Star,* 25, 27 and 28 February, 1, 3, 6, 7, 8, 9, 10 March 1882. *Gazette,* 27, 28 February, 1, 4, 8, 9, 10 March 1882. *Herald,* 27, 28 February, 1, 3, 4, 8, 9 March 1882.

FURTHER READING

If you are interested in finding out more about the history of black people in Canada, particularly in Montreal or Quebec, here are some publications you may want to look at.

Dorothy Williams has devoted two books to the Montreal scene: *Blacks in Montreal 1628–1986: An Urban Demography* (Cowansville, Que.: Éditions Yvon Blais 1989) and, more recently, *The Road to Now: A History of Blacks in Montreal* (Montreal: Véhicule Press 1997). Both focus mainly on twentieth-century developments and deal summarily with the decades after slavery was ended.

One work that attempts to dispel some of the obscurity surrounding nineteenth-century blacks in Quebec is Daniel Gay's mimeographed *Des empreintes noires sur la neige blanche: les Noirs au Québec (1750–1900)* (Projet de recherche RS-1033, Département de sociologie, Université Laval, Rapport final soumis au Conseil québécois de la recherche sociale, novembre 1988).

More narrowly focused is Gary Collison's very readable *Shadrach Minkins: From Fugitive Slave to Citizen* (Cambridge, Mass.: Harvard University Press, 1997). This book traces the life of a fugitive Virginia slave who, captured in Boston in 1851 and on the point of being returned to slavery, was spirited away to Montreal, where he settled. Written by an American, it offers a rare glimpse into the lives of flesh-and-blood black Montrealers of the 1850s–60s. So does Collinson's article "Loyal and Dutiful Subjects of Her Gracious Majesty, Queen Victoria: Fugitive Slaves in Montreal, 1850–1866" *Quebec Studies* 19 (fall 1994–winter 1995): 59–70.

Of course, where the subject of Canadian slavery is concerned, the indispensable work is Marcel Trudel's *L'esclavage au Canada français* (Quebec: Presses Universitaires Laval 1960) and its companion, *Dictionnaire des esclaves et de leurs propriétaires au Canada français* (Montreal: Hurtubise HMH, 1990; 2nd revised edition, 1994). Trudel summarized his findings in "Quand les Québécois pratiquaient l'esclavage," chapter 9 of his *Mythes et réalités dans l'histoire du Québec* (Montreal: Hurtubise HMH 2001), 175–92.

Earlier works on slavery, available in their original format or in microform, and well worth a look, include the seminal work on the subject, begun by Jacques Viger, Montreal's first mayor, and completed after his death by Louis Hippolyte LaFontaine: "De l'esclavage en Canada," *Mémoires et documents relatifs à l'histoire du Canada* 1–2, Société historique de Montréal (1859); William R. Riddell's "Notes on Slavery in Canada," *Journal of Negro History* 4, no. 4 (October 1919): 396–411; and his "The Slave in Canada," *Journal of Negro History* 5, no. 3 (July 1920): 261–377; and T. Watson-Smith's "The Slave in Canada," *Collections of the Nova Scotia Historical Society* 10 (1896–98): 1–161.

For the broader picture of blacks across Canada from the earliest times to the modern day, the standard reference work is Robin W. Winks's information-packed book, *The Blacks in Canada: A History* (Montreal and Kingston: McGill-Queen's University Press, 1971; 2nd edition, 1997).

Other easily accessible works that range broadly in time or space, each with something different to offer, include the following:

Alexander, Ken, and Avis Glaze. *Towards Freedom: The African-Canadian Experience*. Toronto: Umbrella Press 1996

Bertley, Leo W. *Canada and Its People of African Descent*. Pierrefonds, Que.: Bilongo Publishers 1977

Hill, Daniel G. *The Freedom Seekers: Blacks in Early Canada*. Agincourt, Ont.: Book Society of Canada, 1981.

Walker, James W.St.G. *A History of Blacks in Canada: A Study Guide*. Hull, Que.: Canadian Government Publishing Centre 1980.

Some Missing Pages: The Black Community in the History of Quebec and Canada. Produced by the Provincial Association of Social Studies Teachers, the Quebec Board of Black Educators, and the Quebec Ministry of Education, 1995; revised 1996

These are a few of the works available, but if you are seriously interested in exploring the history of blacks in Canada, go fishing. There are suggested reading lists and bibliographies that will point you toward what others have found; but since so much remains to be discovered, read those books and then look beyond. The little detail turned up by chance can sometimes complete a picture, solve a riddle, or open doors to further research. Who, for instance, would think to find anything of interest to blacks in Montreal in the life story of the romantic Irish rebel Lord Edward Fitzgerald? Yet if you read Stella Tillyard's *Citizen Lord: Edward Fitzgerald, 1763–1798* (London: Chatto & Windus, 1997), you will find Tony Small, a former South Carolina slave, devoted to Fitzgerald, who accompanied him on a journey in 1788–89 from the Maritimes to Quebec, then on to Montreal, Lake Ontario and beyond.

So cast a wide net and keep your eyes open.

If your interest is such that you are eager to move beyond published works and go rooting through old papers, you can explore some of the main archival sources used for this book (see pp. 211–20).

ILLUSTRATIONS